POSTCARD HISTORY SERIES

The Citrus Industry in the Sunshine State

POSTCARD HISTORY SERIES

The Citrus Industry in the Sunshine State

Brian Weaver and Richard Weaver

ARCADIA PUBLISHING

ISBN 978-0-7385-0302-8

Published by Arcadia Publishing
Charleston, South Carolina

Printed in the United States of America

Library of Congress Catalog Card Number: 99-067077

For all general information contact Arcadia Publishing at:
Telephone 843-853-2070
Fax 843-853-0044
E-Mail sales@arcadiapublishing.com
For customer service and orders:
Toll-Free 1-888-313-2556

Visit us on the Internet at www.arcadiapublishing.com

We dedicate this book, with love, to Pam Weaver, wife and mother.
Thank you for everything.

Contents

Acknowledgments		6
Introduction		7
1.	Oranges and Grapefruit	9
2.	The Groves	19
3.	"Come Down and Pick Oranges"	47
4.	Packing the Fruit	81
5.	Touring the Groves	97
6.	"How's This for a Peach among the Oranges?"	103
7.	"Down South We Roam"	117

Acknowledgments

We wish to thank our friend Barbara Eggleson, a Port St. Lucie, Florida postcard dealer, for her kindness and generosity in allowing us to use the postcard featured on the cover of our book, as well as several other cards displayed in this citrus postcard history.

Thank you to our editor, Christine Riley!

Special Recognition

Professor Thomas B. Mack used to be a "bird dog." That's someone who would travel across the state "sniffing" out citrus crops to buy. Since those days, Professor Mack has sniffed out all there is to know about citrus, and he shares his knowledge in an unparalleled storytelling style. We thank him for the advice and memories that have been invaluable to this project. Professor Mack has spent more than 50 years spreading his enthusiasm and interest in the Florida citrus industry to his students. He has been associated with Florida Southern College for the past 47 years, teaching citrus and horticulture, and currently, he directs his energy into the Thomas B. Mack Citrus Archives there. In 1981, he earned the distinction of professor emeritus, and in 1997, he was inducted into the Florida Citrus Hall of Fame. If you have any memorabilia, records, or photographs of the Florida citrus industry that you are interested in preserving for history, we urge you to contact him at the Thomas B. Mack Citrus Archives at Florida Southern College in Lakeland, Florida, 33801.

INTRODUCTION

Good morning! Chances are you've begun your day with a glass of Florida orange juice or half of a Florida grapefruit. An industry employing tens of thousands of people in Florida works to satisfy the demand for citrus fruit. "The Sunshine State" produces millions of boxes of fruit each year for domestic and international consumption, far outdistancing other regions of the United States with citrus industries. Citrus is second only to tourism as Florida's most important industry.

Oranges and grapefruit are the two most popular citrus varieties in Florida, and there are whole laboratories, schools, and institutes devoted to the citrus industry. This book is designed for people who just enjoy citrus; it is an overview of the industry from a grower's perspective. We've paired facts and anecdotes with old postcards of fruit, fruit pickers, fruit packing, fruit transportation, and finally, enjoyment of that fruit.

In some instances, we have used some of the writings on the back of the postcards as captions. Quotation marks have been placed around anything originating on the postcards, including the printed text on the back. Wherever possible, we have also indicated the postmarks; however, not all of these postcards were mailed. Listed postmarks mention cities located in Florida, unless another state is noted. The postmark is denoted exactly as it is printed on the card; that is why it may say "St. Petersburg" in some places and "Saint Petersburg" in others.

There are many growers' terms we have sprinkled throughout the book. Our vocabulary comes from firsthand knowledge, as citrus has been in the family since 1951, when Montie Weaver (our father and grandfather) bought his first citrus grove in Ft. Pierce.

Finally, when you see a caption or comment in the first person, it's Brian Weaver who is speaking in his own voice.

—Brian Weaver and Richard Weaver
August 1999

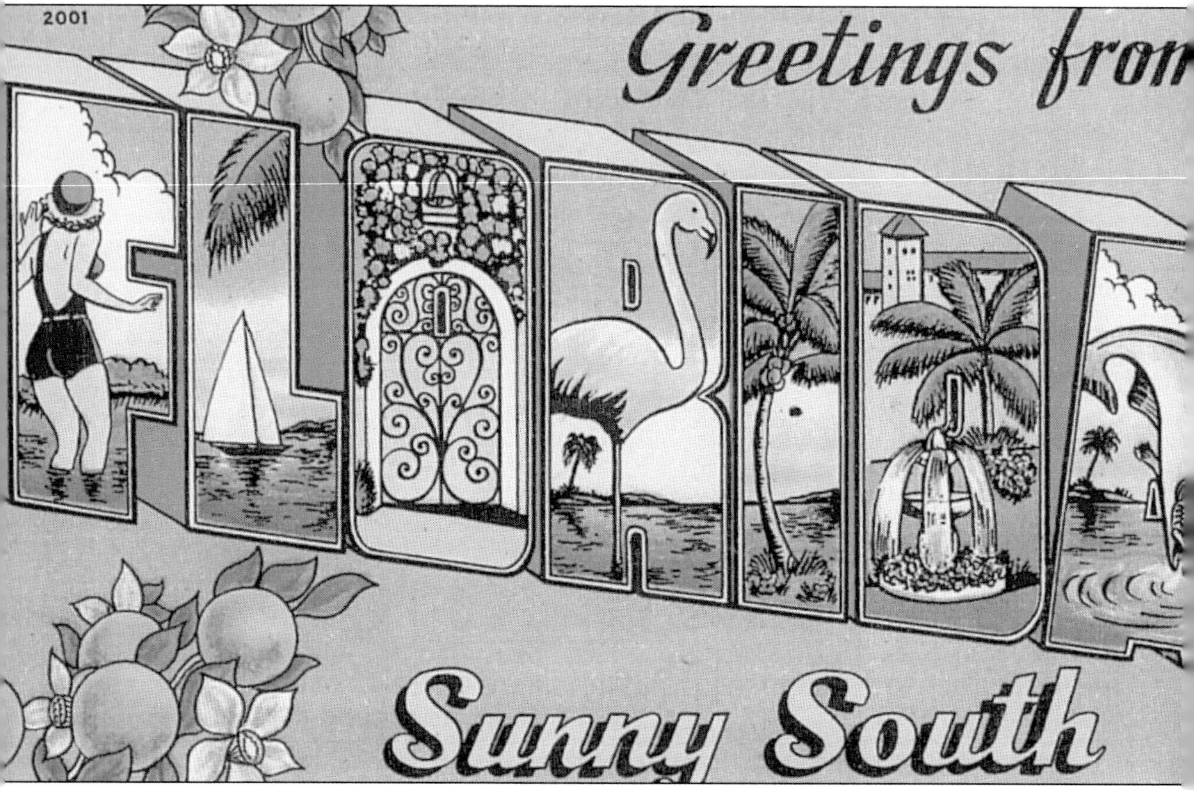
2001
Greetings from
Sunny South

One

Oranges and Grapefruit

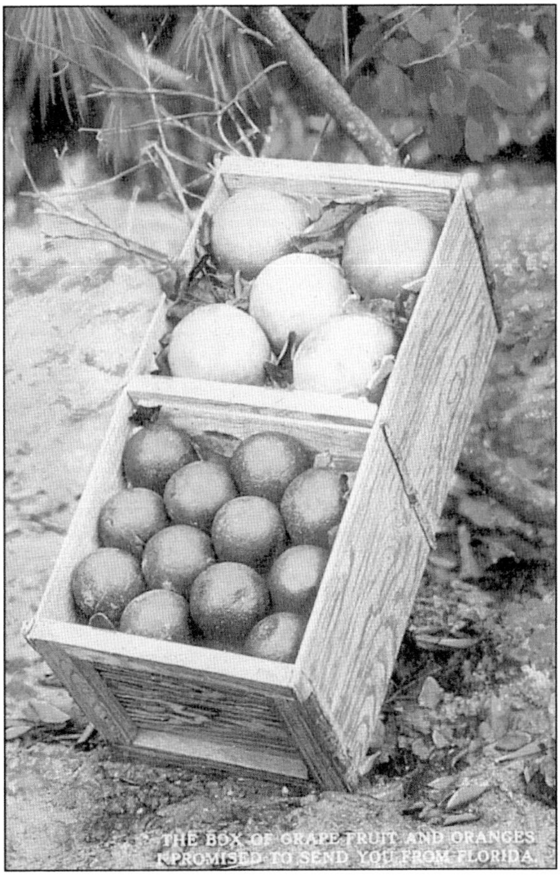

Citrus is not native to the Americas; it originated in China several thousand years ago. Christopher Columbus brought oranges to the New World in 1493 on his second voyage. Spanish law required each sailor to carry 100 seeds with him. It is said that the Spanish explorer Ponce de Leon introduced oranges to North America in 1513 when he discovered Florida. Grapefruit was relatively late in coming to the New World. It is generally thought that grapefruit originated in the islands of the West Indies. It was found in Barbados around 1750 and was called "the forbidden fruit." The seeds were carried to the west coast of Florida around 1830. At this time, the fruit was called "pomelo."

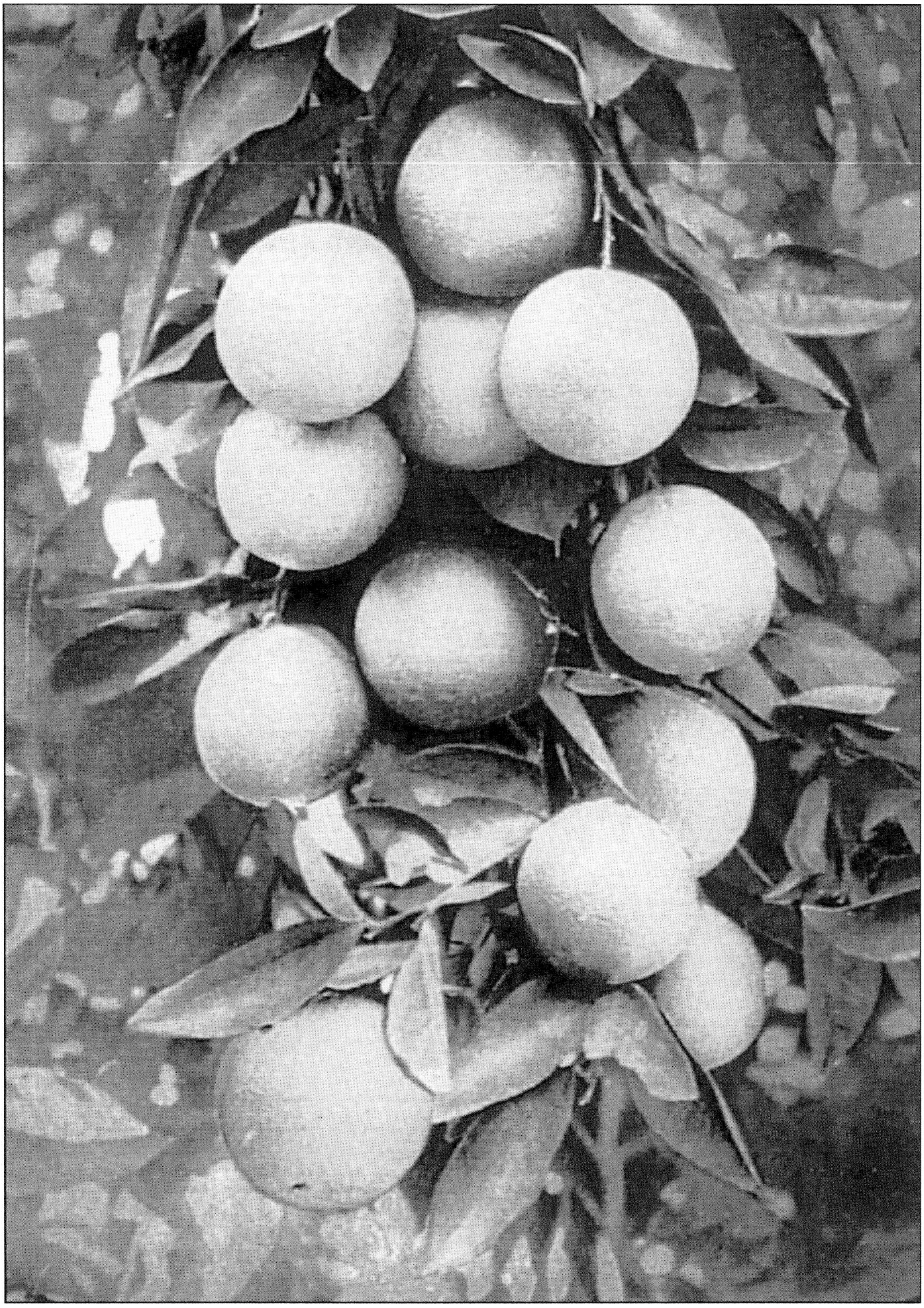

When we were growing up, our breakfast fruit juice came from our own backyard. Hamlin and Temple oranges and pink grapefruit provided plenty of Vitamin C, or "liquid sunshine," for our family. (Courtesy of Barbara Eggleson.)

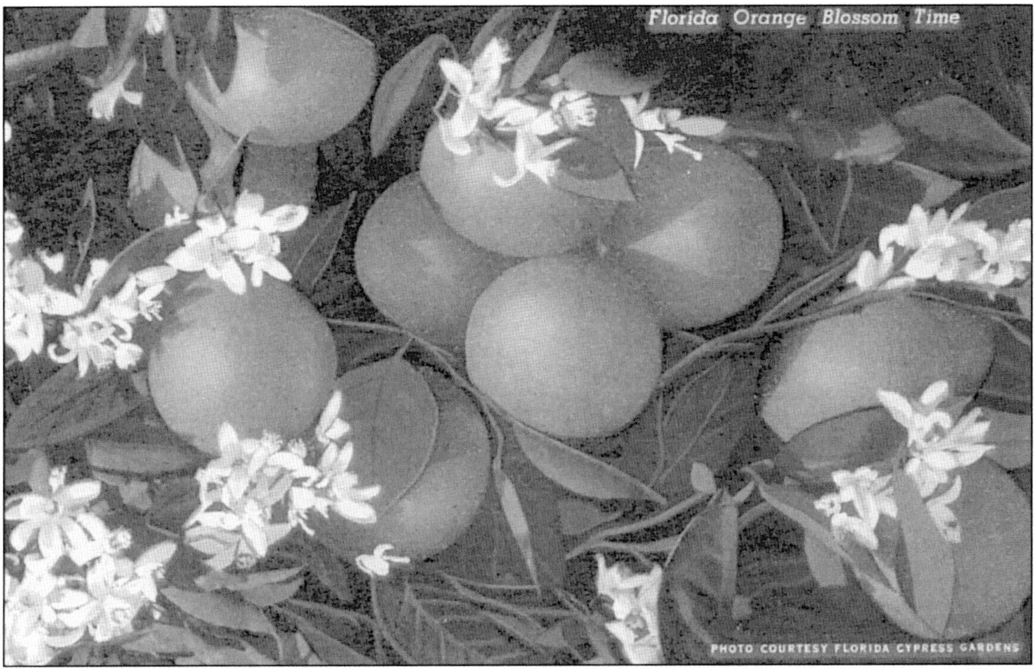

It takes four years for a citrus tree to bear fruit profitably. There are approximately 107 million citrus trees in Florida. Hamlin, Navel, Pineapple, and Valencia are the most popular kinds of oranges; White Marsh and Ruby are the most popular kinds of grapefruit. The bottom image is postmarked St. Petersburg, March 11, 1935.

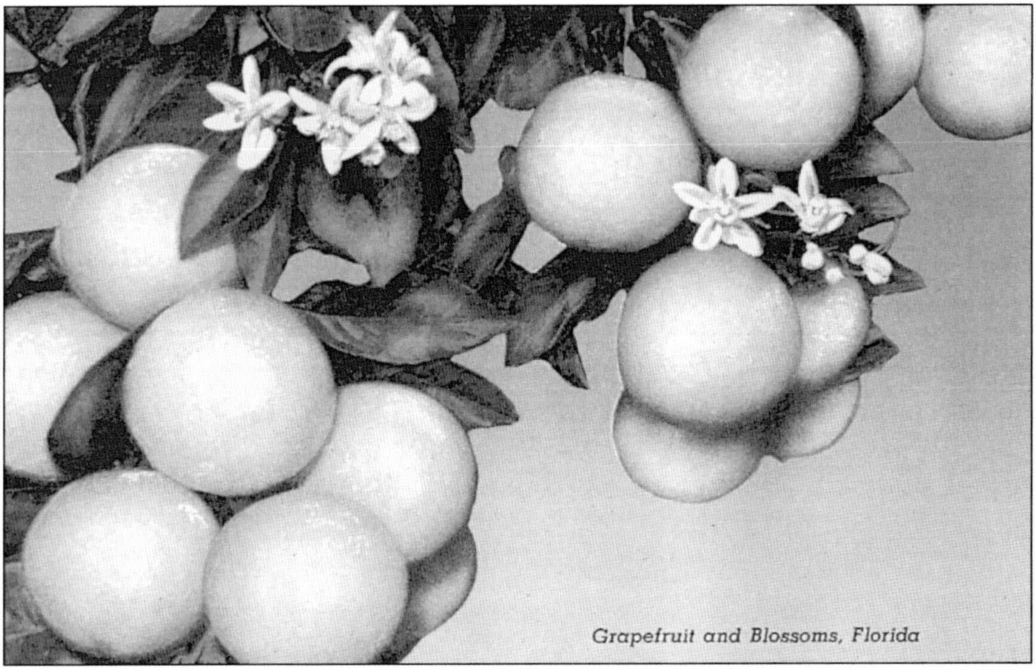

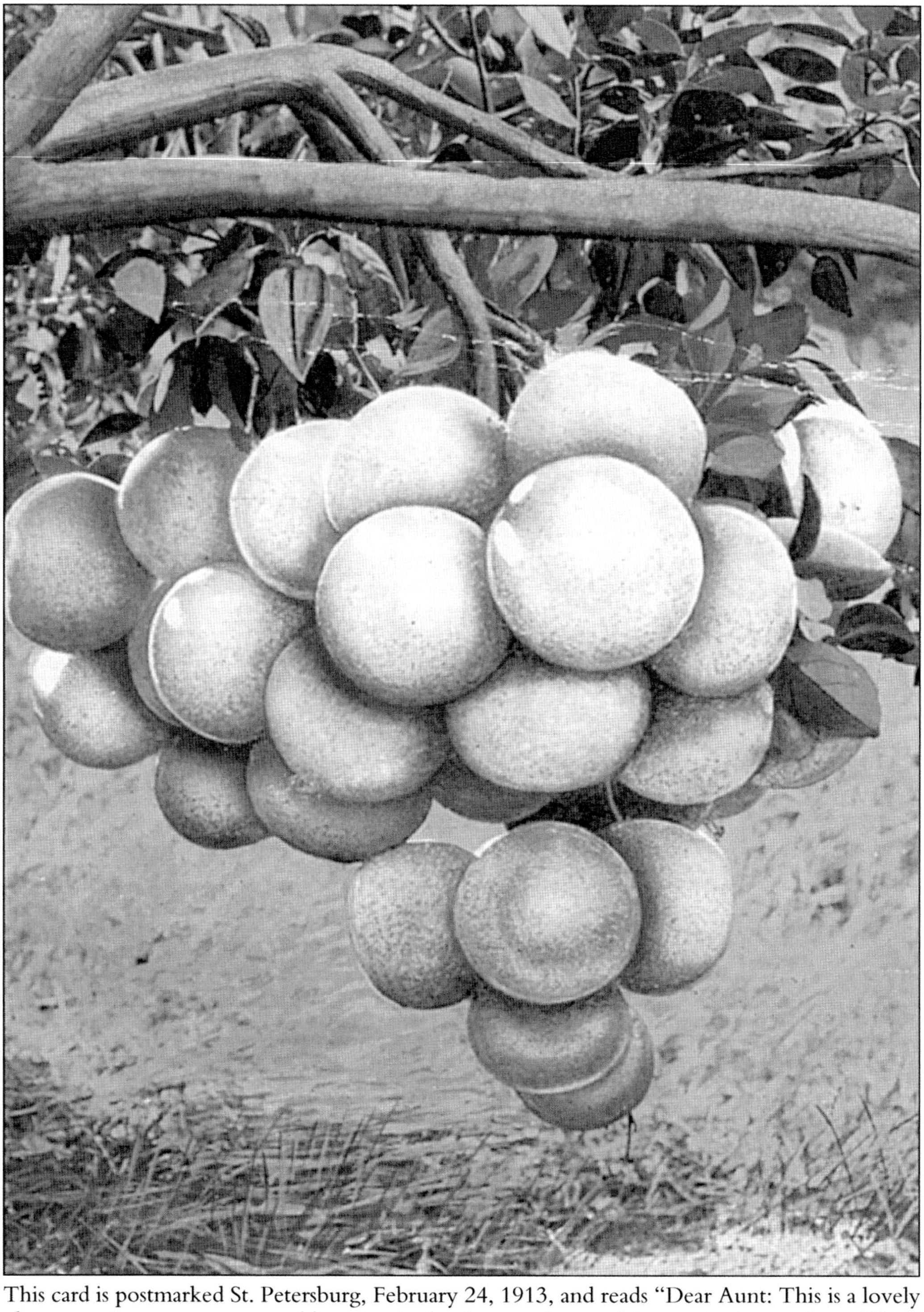

This card is postmarked St. Petersburg, February 24, 1913, and reads "Dear Aunt: This is a lovely place . . . it is so warm . . . roses blooming in the door yards . . . robins are singing . . . lots of black birds . . . doors and windows all open . . . children bare footed . . . we rent rooms and take our meals at a hotel . . . we will stay 2 weeks . . . Maxine."

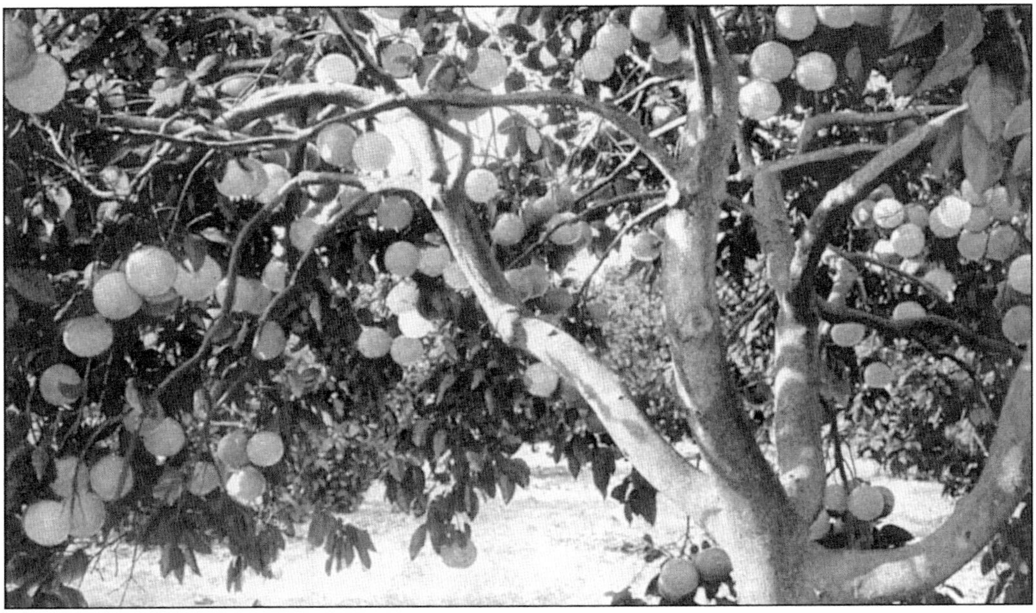

Grapefruit such as these are grown primarily for the fresh fruit market. They must meet high standards of both external and internal quality. Grapefruit that does not meet the fresh grade standards are sent to juice plants.

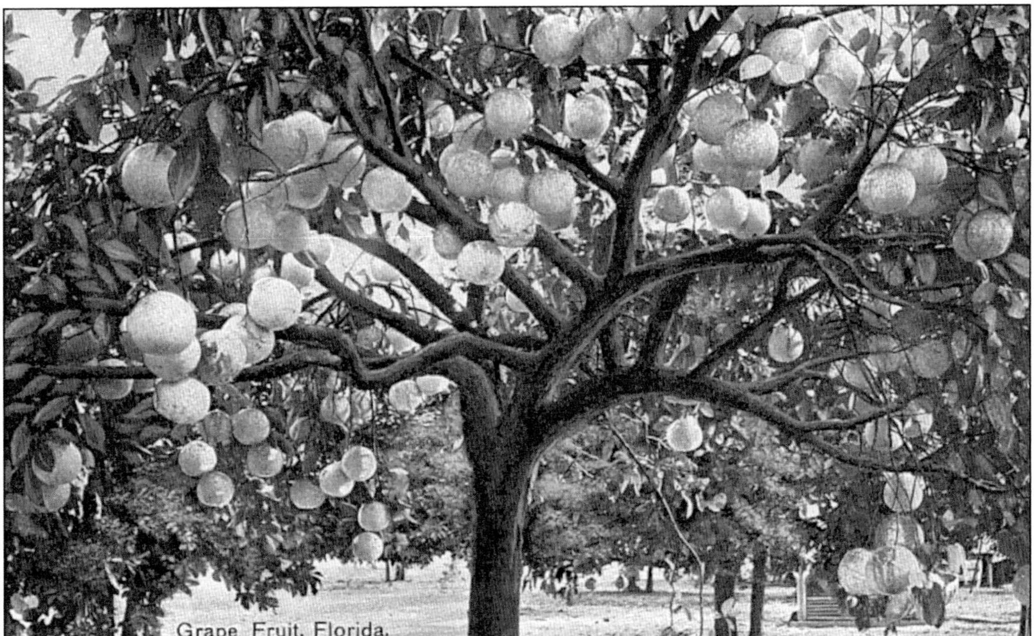

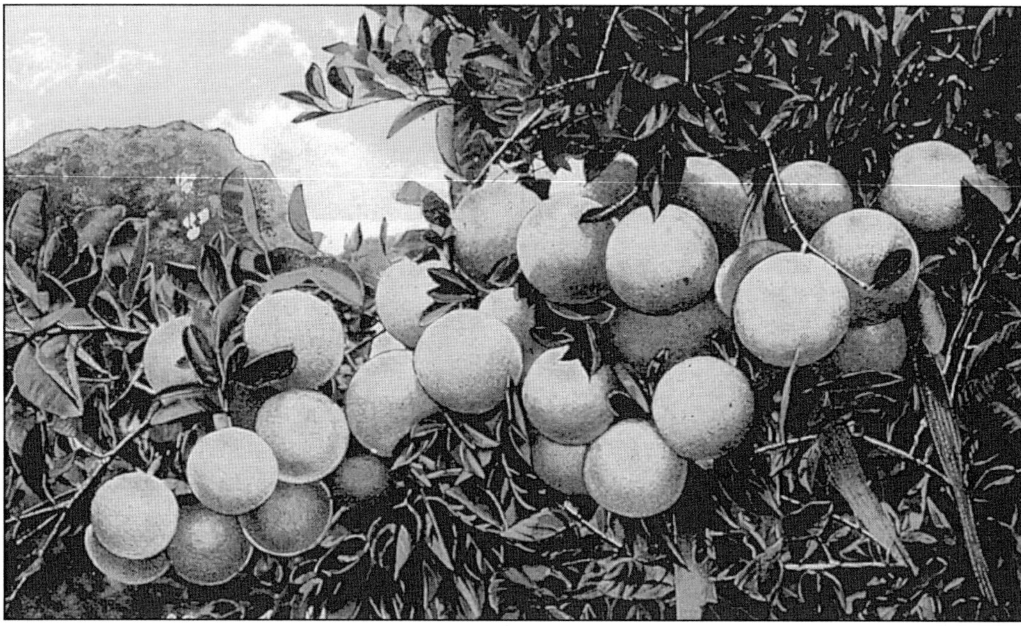

This postcard is titled "Fifty-two Grape Fruit on one Limb, Florida." Grapefruit tree limbs could have supported as many as 52 grapefruit and maybe a few more. Individual stems would hold 10 to 12 grapefruit, and there would be four of five stems per limb. Because the bunched fruit looked like a bunch of grapes, Florida growers in the late 1800s decided to call the fruit "grapefruit," rather than "pomelo."

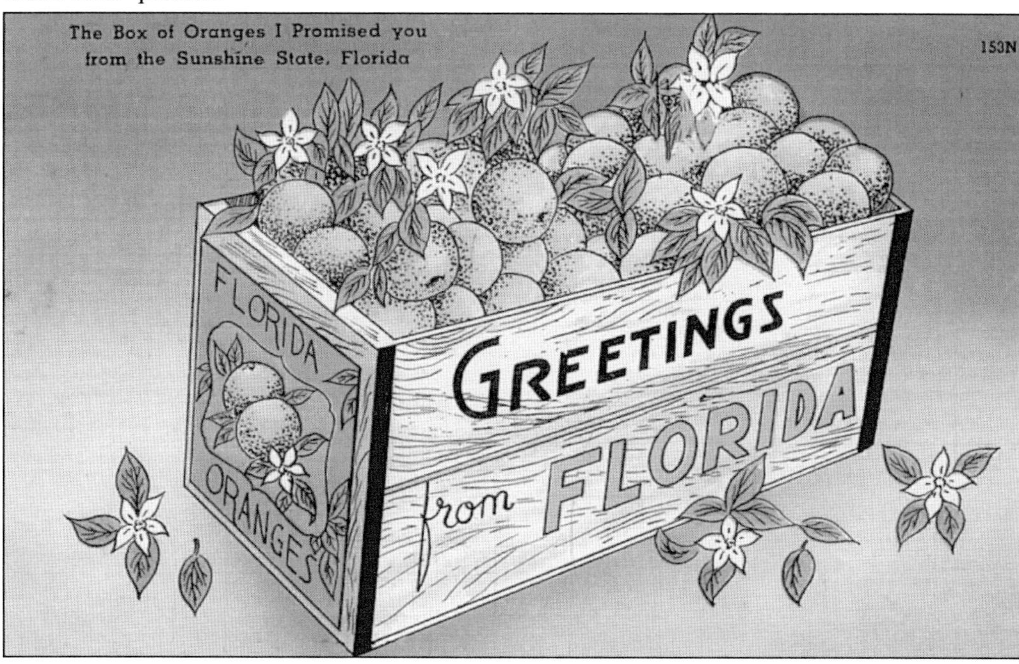

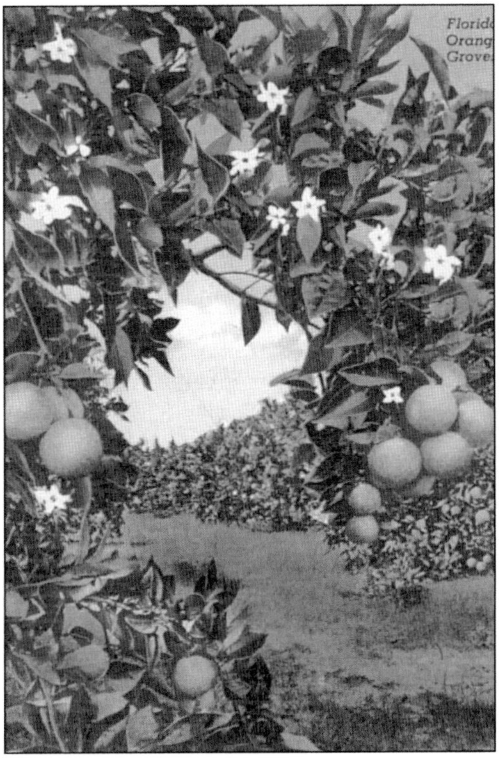

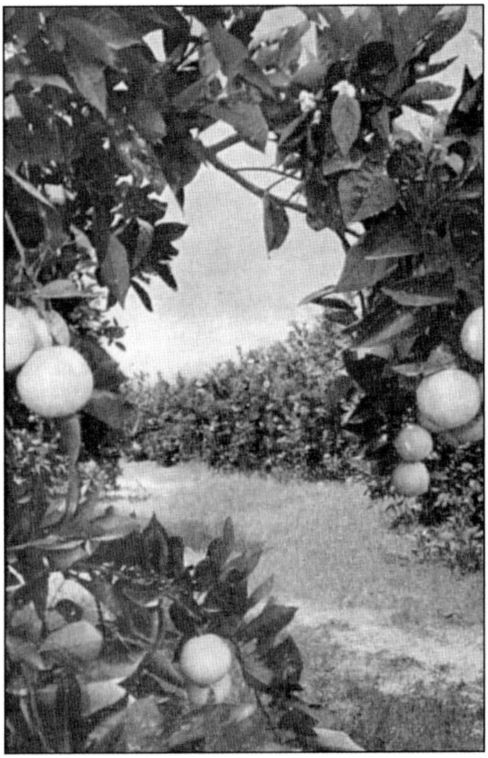

"The swimming is wonderful and not cold. Sunday we went to St. Augustine and drank from the fountain of youth. See you soon, Marian." Not even the fountain of youth could work the magic needed to add blossoms to these orange trees. Postcard companies' artists would often embellish images by adding things or changing colors, with many purchasers none the wiser. The postcard below is postmarked Miami, February 11, 1941, and the card at top right is postmarked Ormond Beach, April 2, 1946.

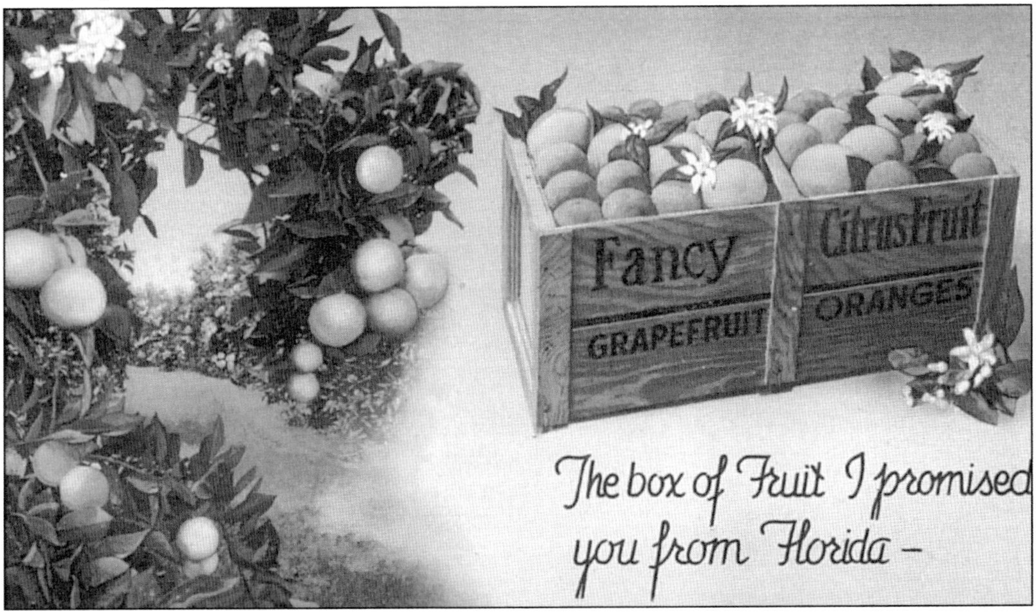

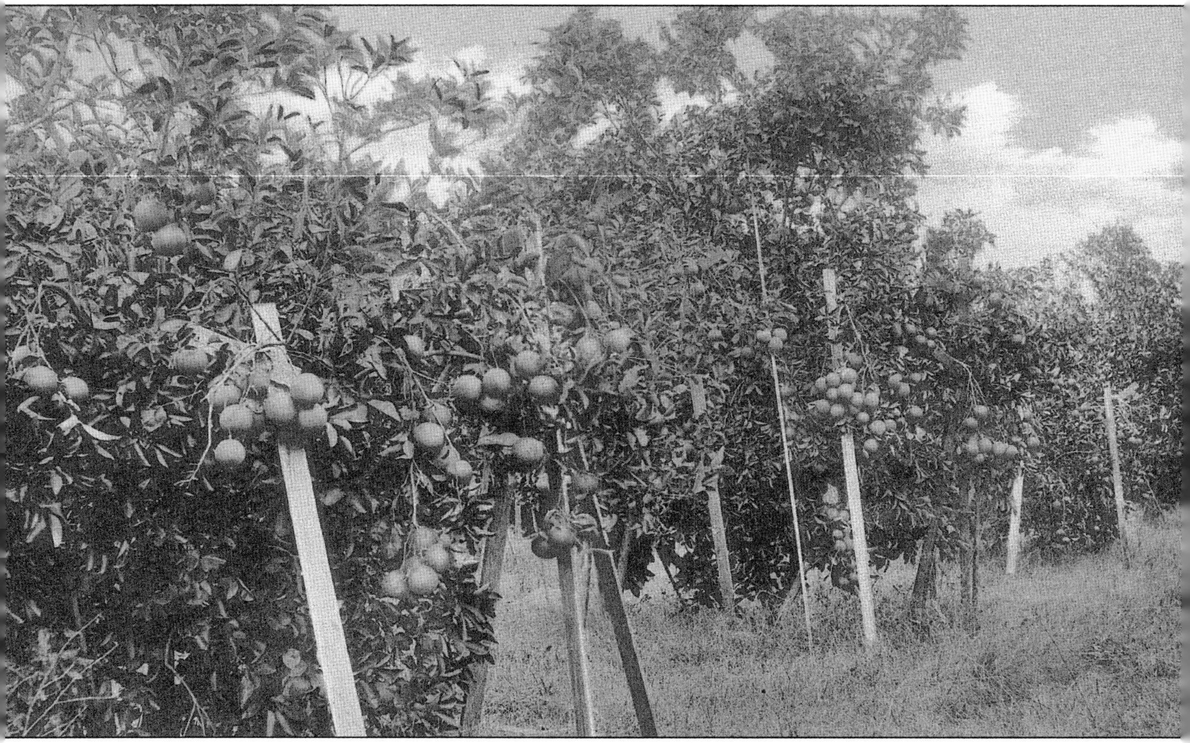

Tree branches sometimes sag with the weight of the fruit, if the limbs have not been properly pruned to promote strength. Boards are sometimes strategically placed to support these limbs and to prevent them from breaking and damaging the tree. This is generally not done on a commercial basis, however. Growers sometimes refer to a particularly heavy crop as a "limb-breaker."

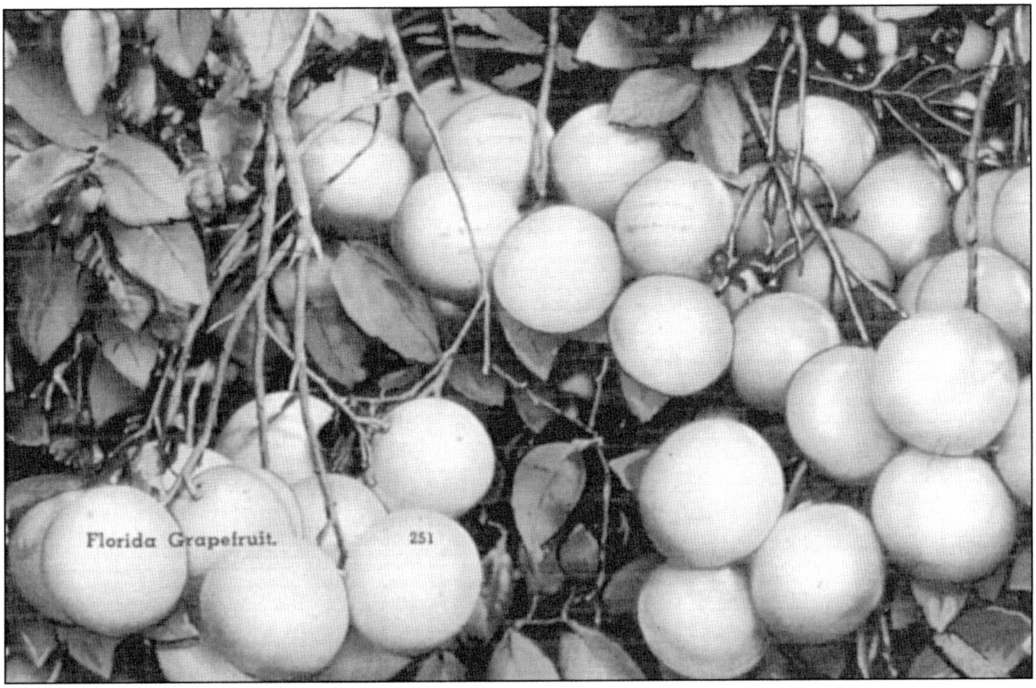

The above postcard is postmarked Bartow, January 27, 1948. Its message reads, "Luxuriant flowers, palms and trees grow in Florida. There are miles and miles of orange and grapefruit groves, a busy and thriving industry here. Florida's smiling skies invite you to visit and play in the sun."

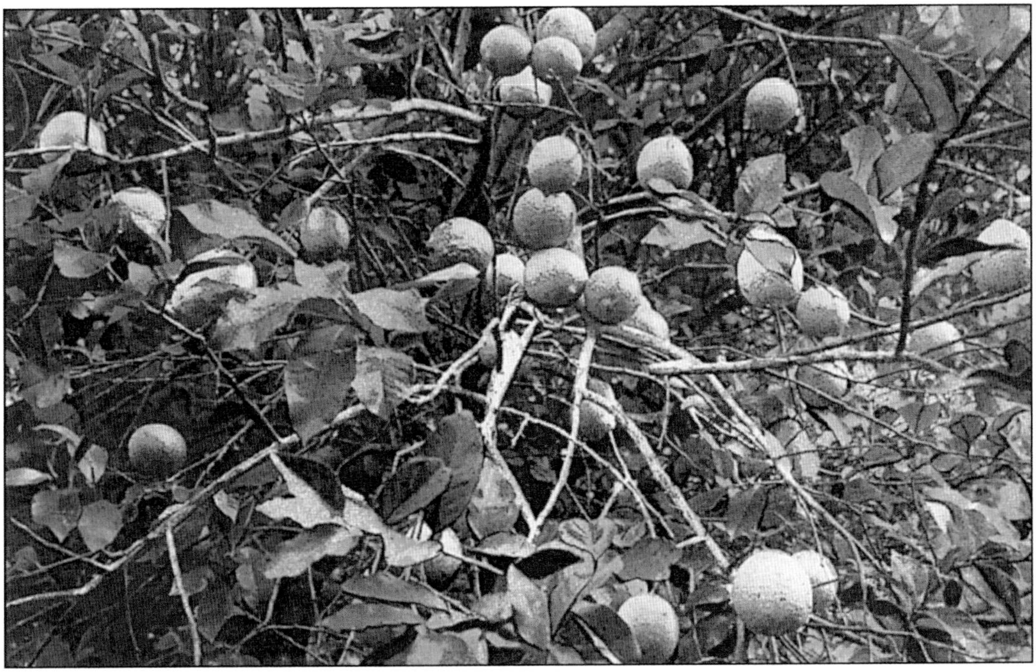

This postcard is postmarked St. Petersburg, March 11, 1935.

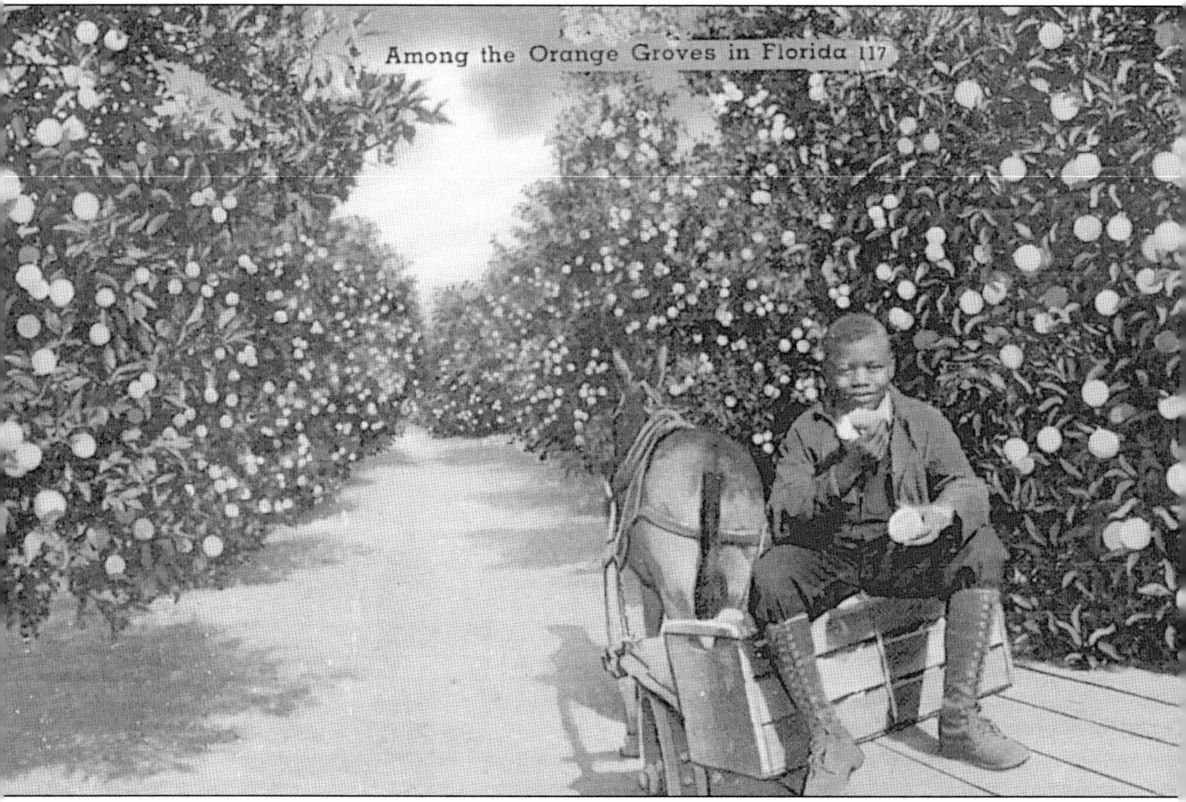

Occasionally, oddly shaped fruit known as a "chimera" will grow on a citrus tree. This is a genetic variation that causes an extra ridge to jut out from the side of the fruit. Otherwise, chimeras are no different from regular fruit.

Two

THE GROVES

The most famous early grove in Florida belonged to Captain D.D. Dummitt and was located on Merritt Island. It became the oldest grove in the nation when it survived the hard freezes of 1894 and 1895. Captain Dummitt settled in the Merritt Island area after he fought in the second Seminole Indian War. He started his grove with the sour orange trees he found growing wild there. These same trees could be traced back to the original orange seeds brought to Florida by Spanish explorers. The trees thrived in the soil and climate for centuries.

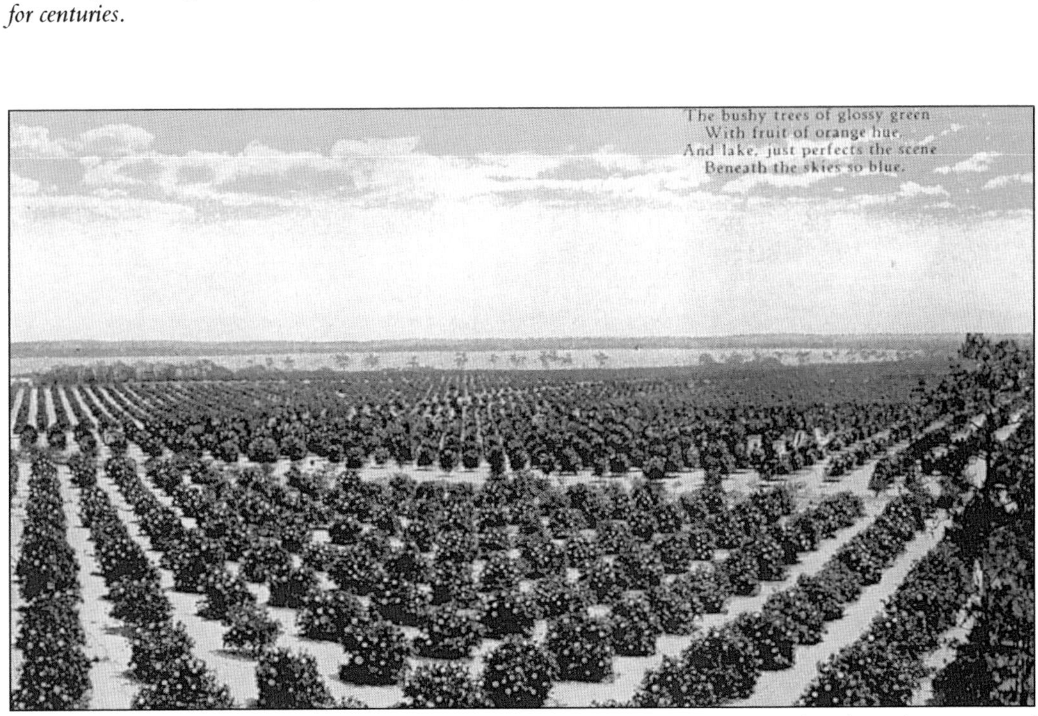

Cold winters have pushed the Florida citrus industry to the warmer central and southern parts of the state. Today, more than 800,000 acres are planted in citrus.

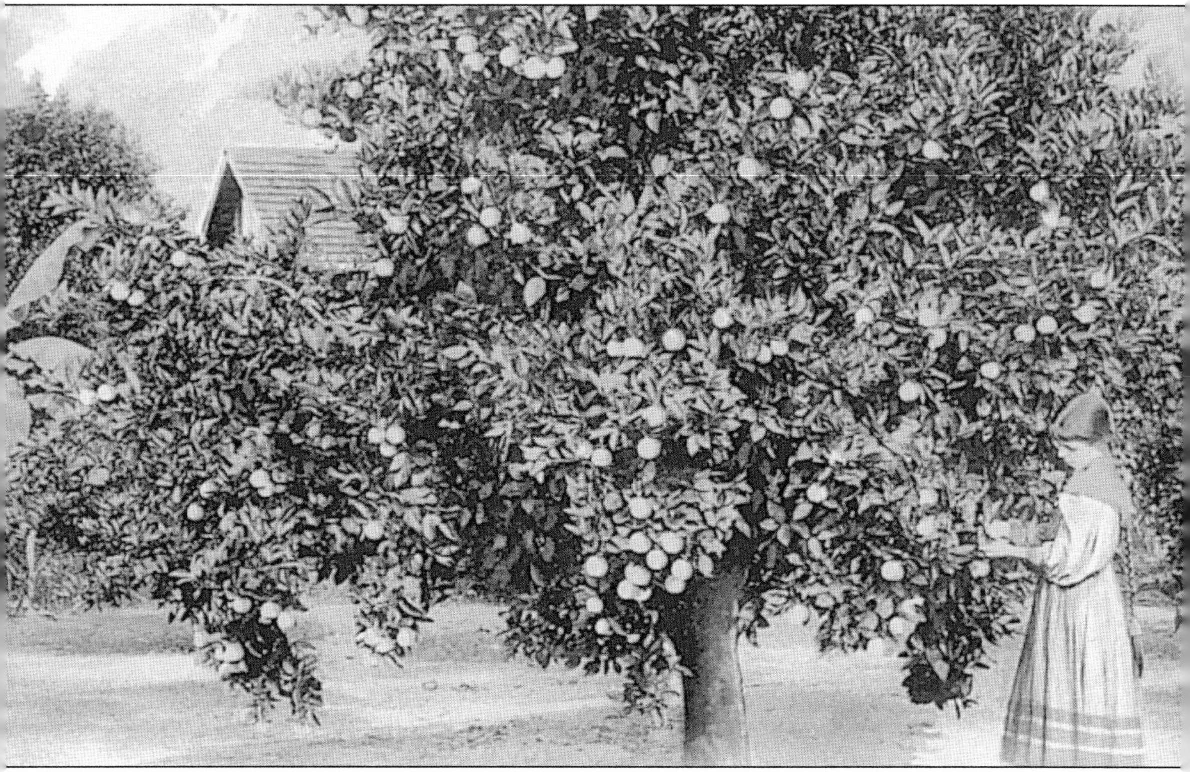

Legend has it that Native Americans in Florida helped orange trees proliferate across the state after the Spanish introduced them into the hemisphere. Trees grew where the Native Americans dropped citrus seeds after eating the fruit.

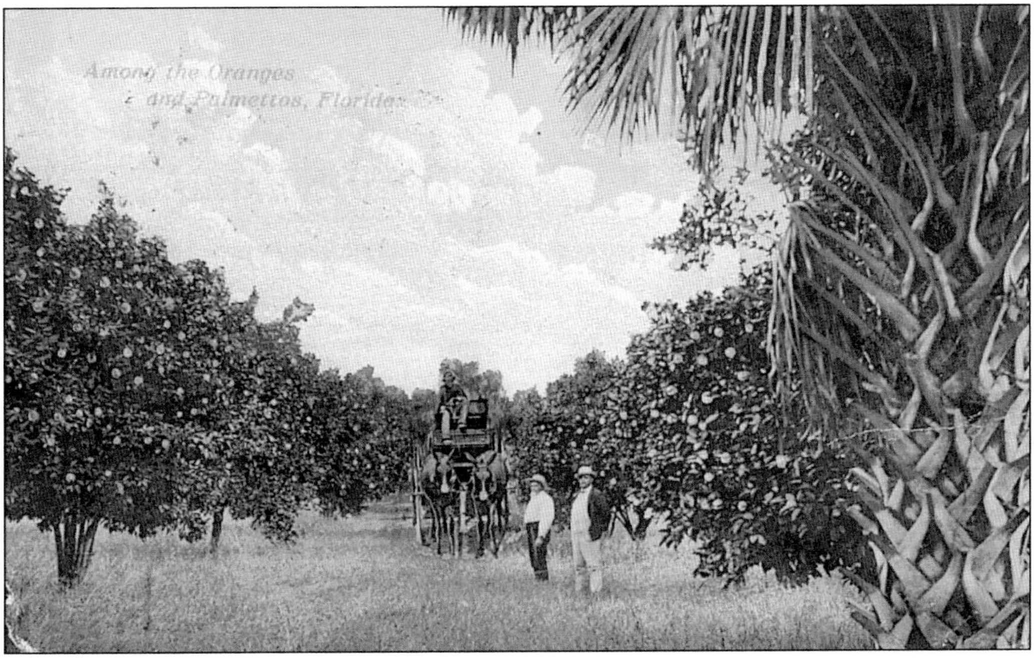

Pioneer citrus growers in Florida had the Herculean task of first clearing the land and "grubbing palmettos" before setting out their grove. It would take about a week for four men to clear 1 acre of land using cross-cut saws, grub hoes, double-edge axes, and a quick hand for slapping the mosquitoes that infested the land.

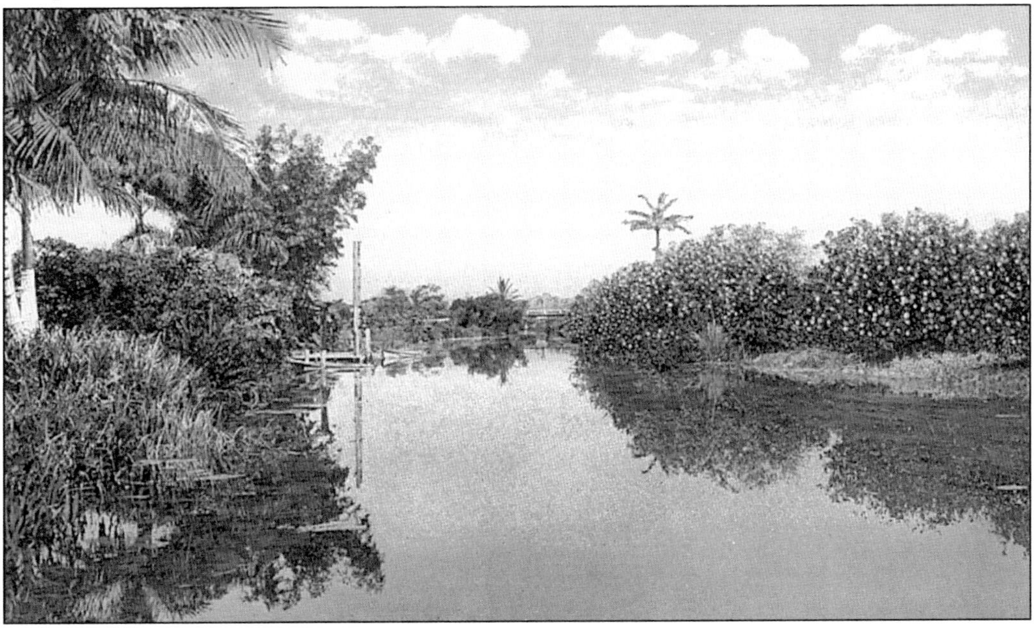

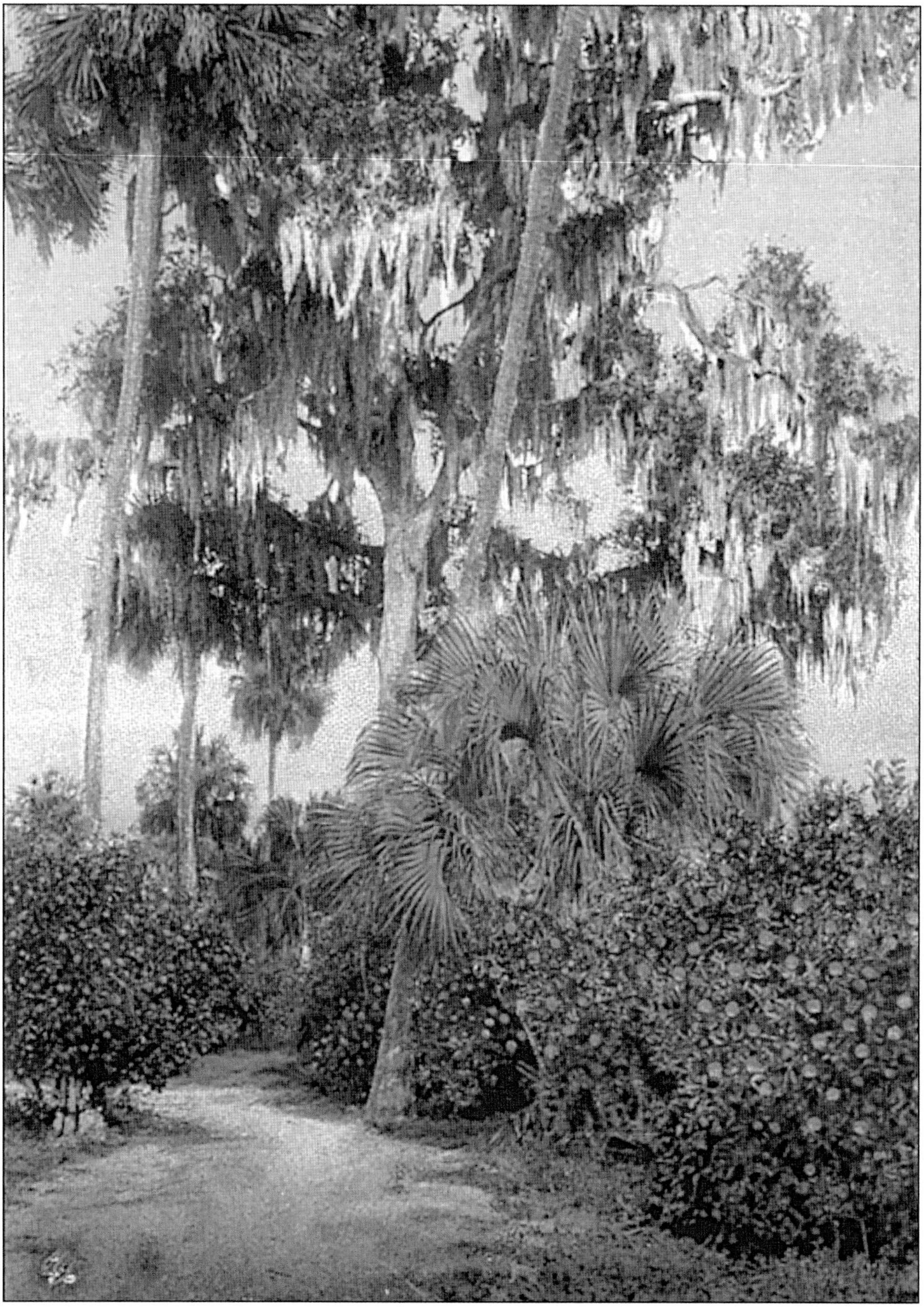

Hammocks are areas in citrus groves where the land is of a slightly higher elevation than the rest of the grove. The soil composition on these raised areas is richer than the typically sandy soil surrounding it, and it can support trees and other vegetation that require more nutrients.

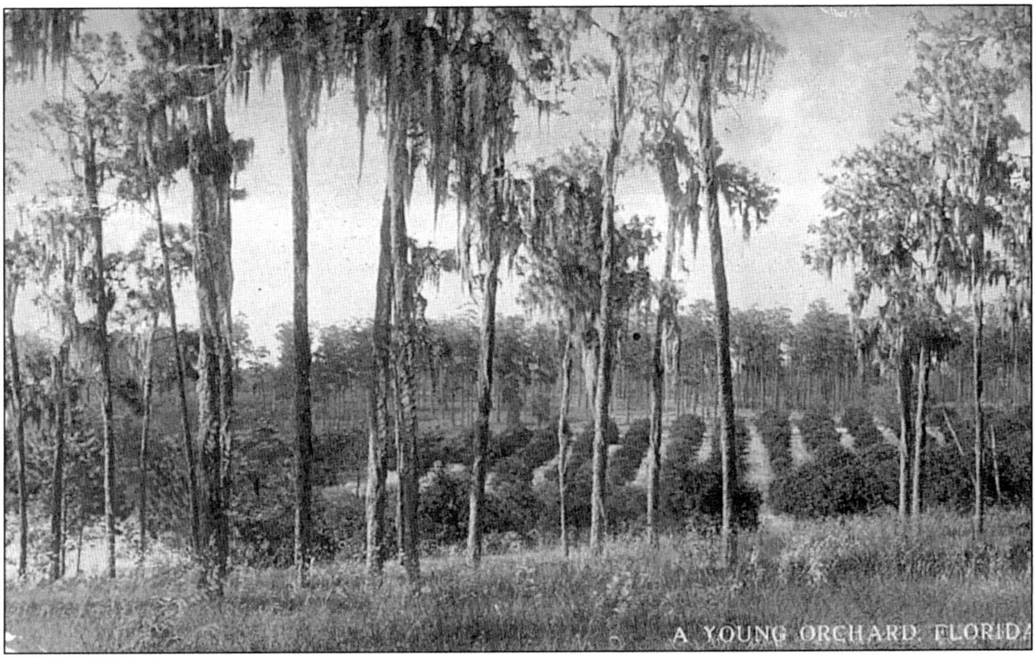

Many people unfamiliar with the citrus industry refer to citrus plantings as "orchards" rather than "groves." A grove is a natural grouping of trees; explorers found citrus trees growing together where seeds from a piece of fruit had been dropped. When citrus growers began arranging trees in an ordered fashion, the term "grove" stuck, even though tree crops are commonly referred to as "orchards."

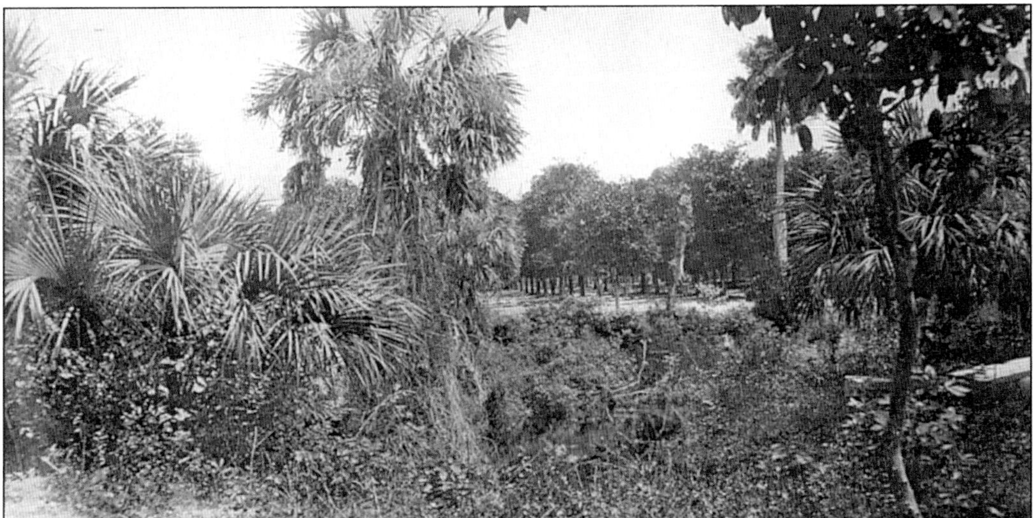

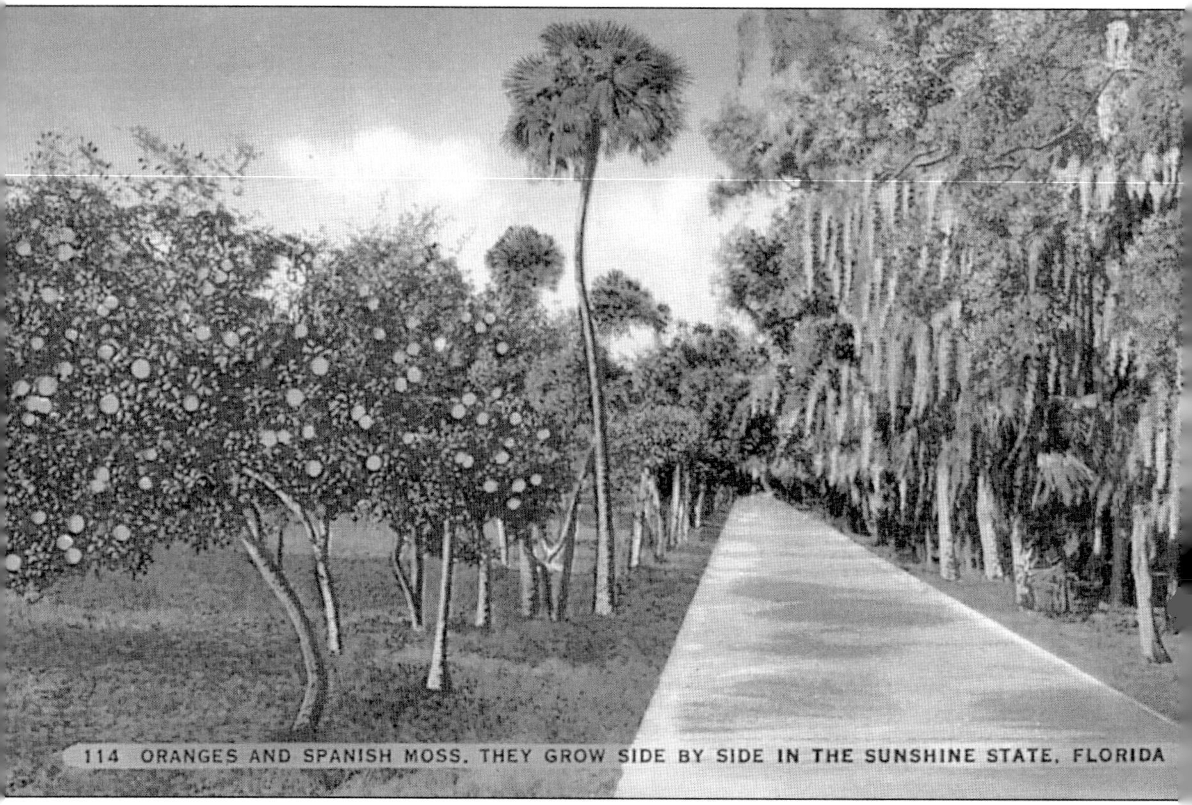

Young trees that growers purchase already have a great deal of work in them. Nurseries grow the "rootstocks" (or host) from seed and then "bud" (attach) a particular variety of orange or grapefruit onto the trunk of a rootstock. Purchasers make their decision based on the soil and other conditions of the area where they will plant the tree. Some rootstocks work best in sandy soil, while others need more heavy land. The budded trees cost $3.50 to $4 each. This card is postmarked Bradenton, November 26, 1951.

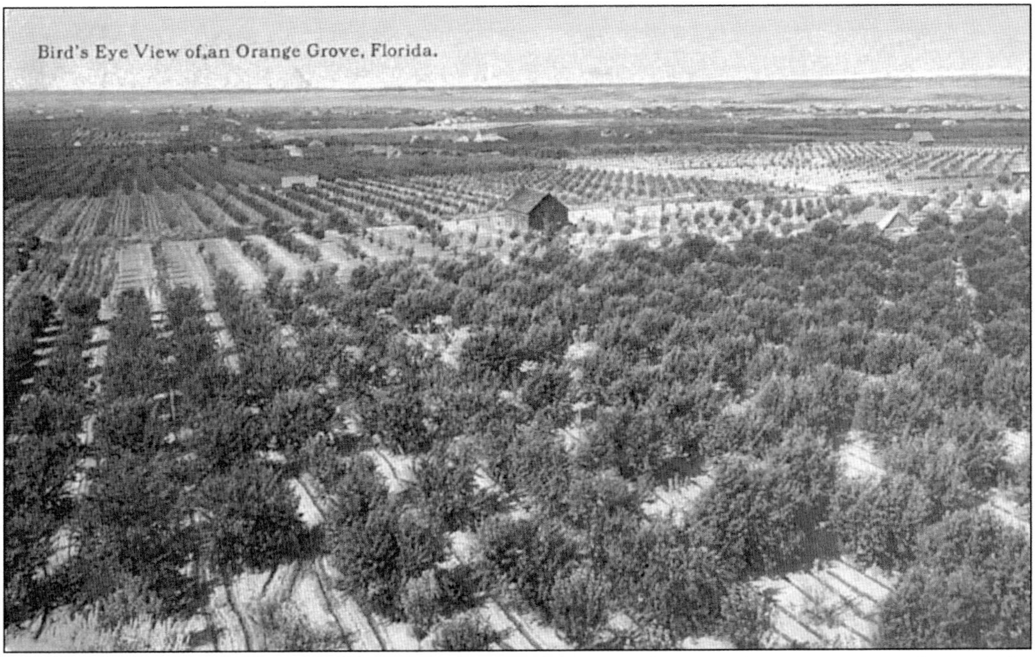

Citrus trees require a large amount of water; each day the tree loses moisture through its leaves in a process known as evapotranspiration. The tree's roots must take up water to replace what has been lost. Growers use canals, wells, and pumping from lakes to irrigate groves. Florida's generous rainfall is the main source of water. The top image is postmarked Clearwater, February 17, 1914.

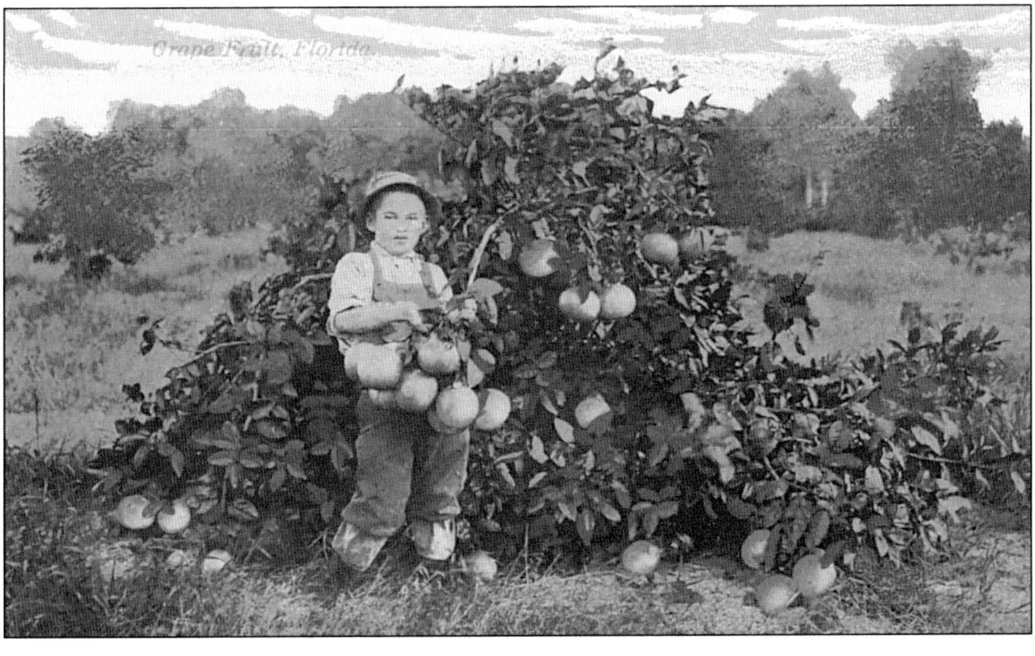

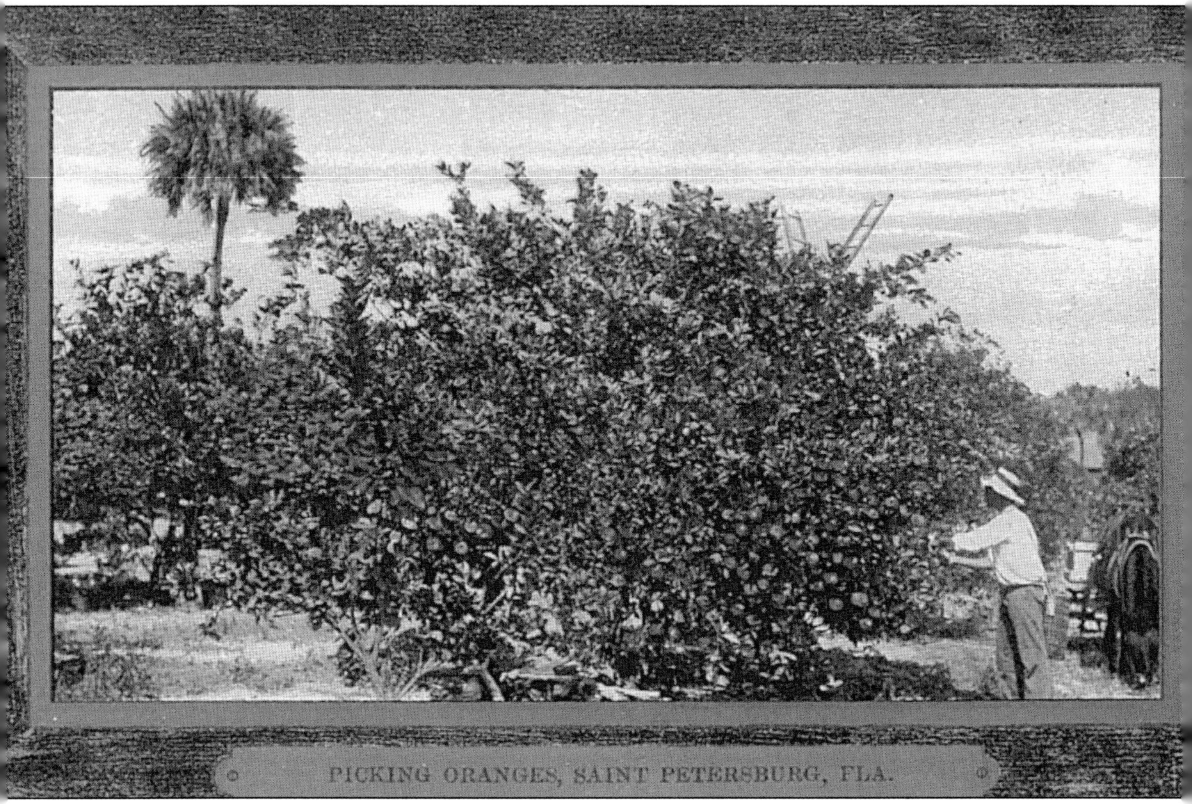

All citrus needs regular applications of fertilizer, because Florida soil does not naturally contain all the nutrients a tree needs. The amount of fertilizer varies based on considerations including the size of the trees, the variety, and the type of soil.

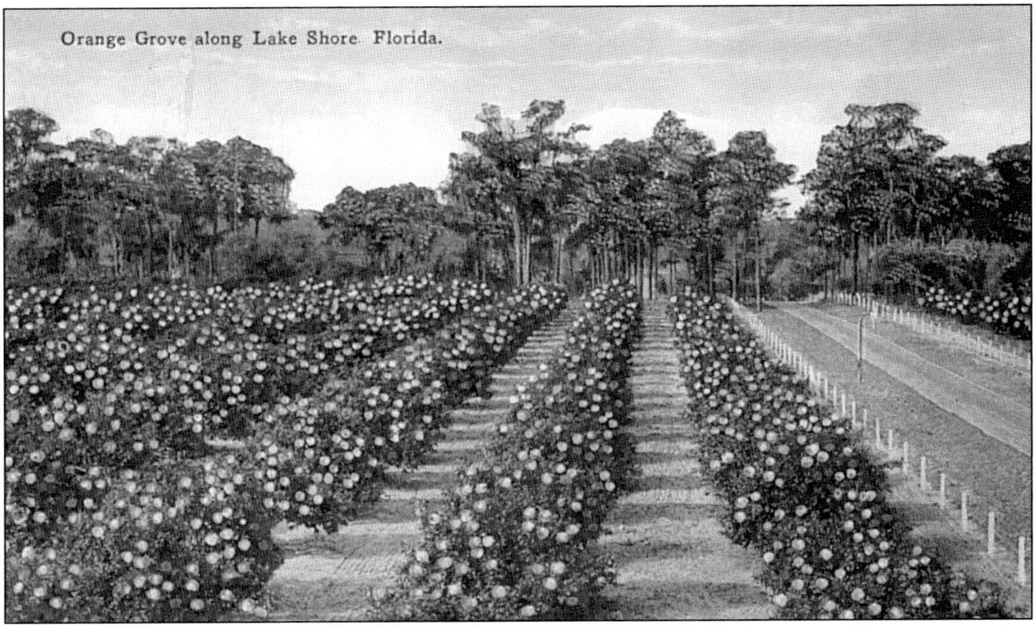

Citrus trees are now planted approximately 10 to 12 feet apart, far closer than the 20 to 30 feet of spacing growers initially used. These wide spaces between the trees were disced (the soil was turned up) to keep weeds and other vegetation under control. The ridges created by the discing resembled thumbprints. The card below is postmarked Arcadia, February 23, 1937.

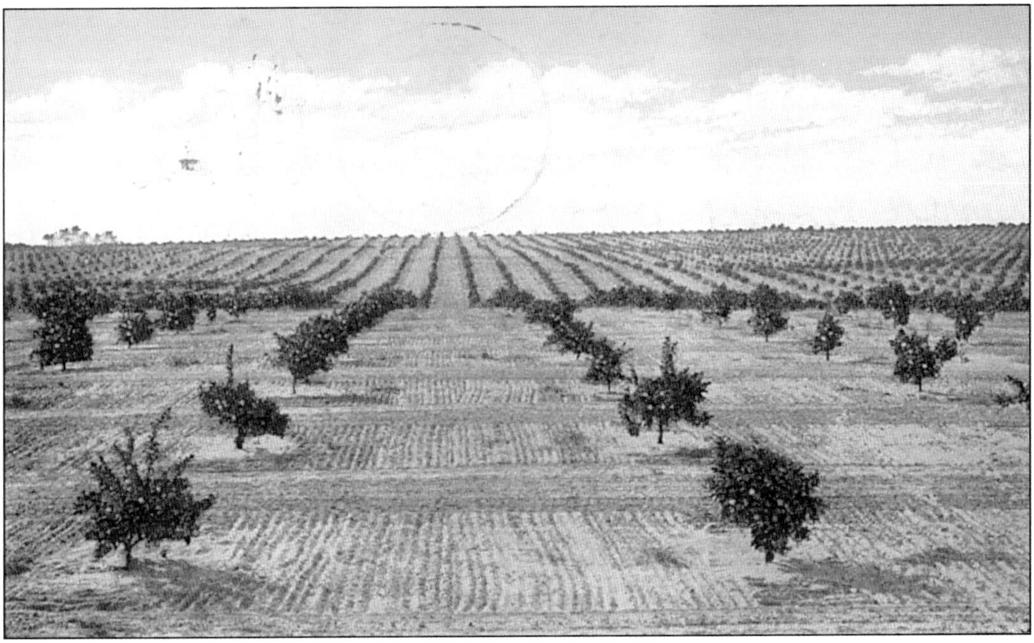

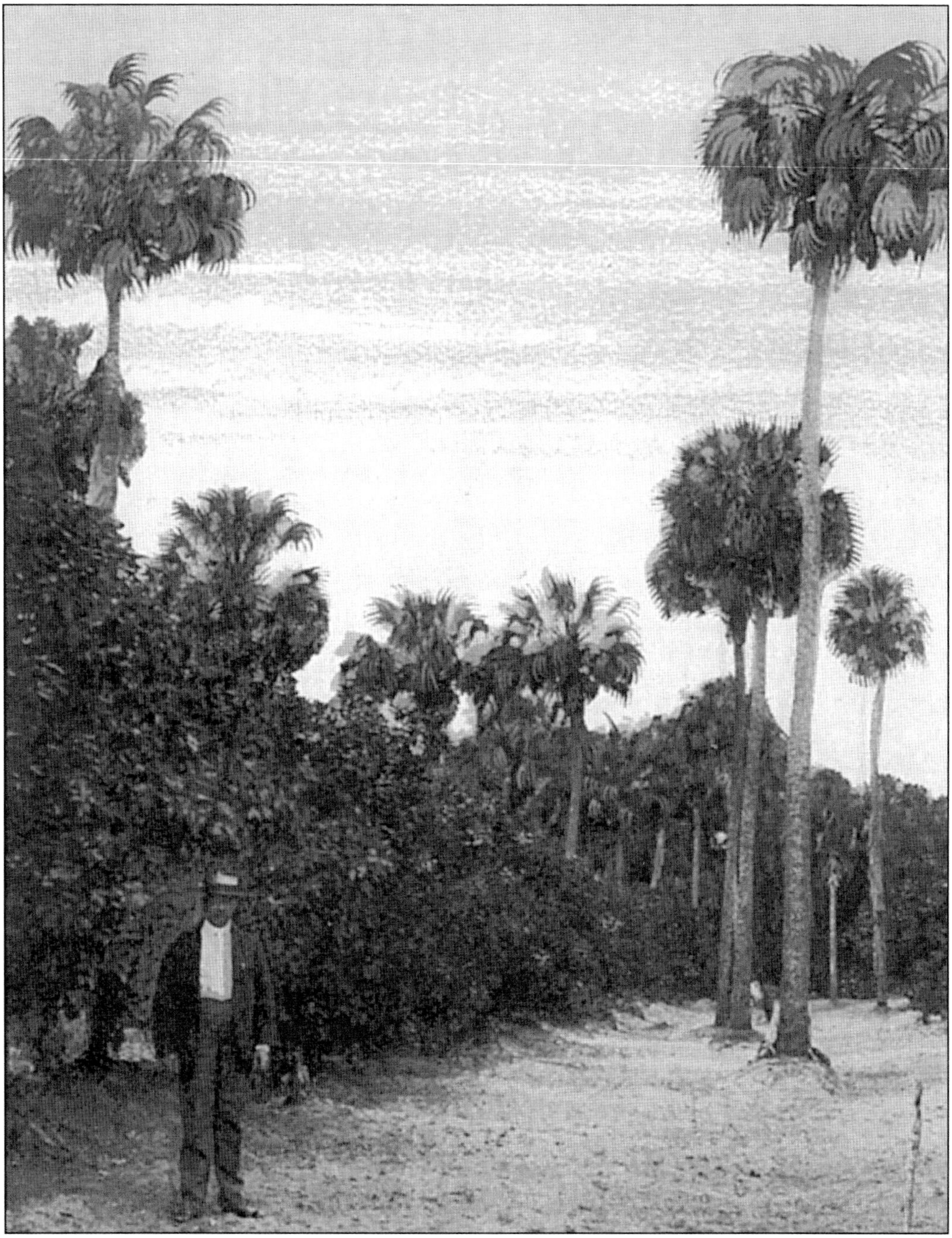

Palm trees commonly grow alongside citrus trees in southern Florida, and they are a typical sight in the tropical landscape. Late summer and fall is hurricane season in Florida, and unfortunately, the Florida citrus belt sometimes lies in the pathway of these tropical storms. Citrus is quite vulnerable to the severe winds and heavy rainfall of hurricanes. In 1960, Hurricane Donna passed through our family grove in Groveland, Florida, blowing 9 acres of orange trees on their sides. We used a tractor to pull the trees upright and covered the roots with dirt. Most of the trees recovered.

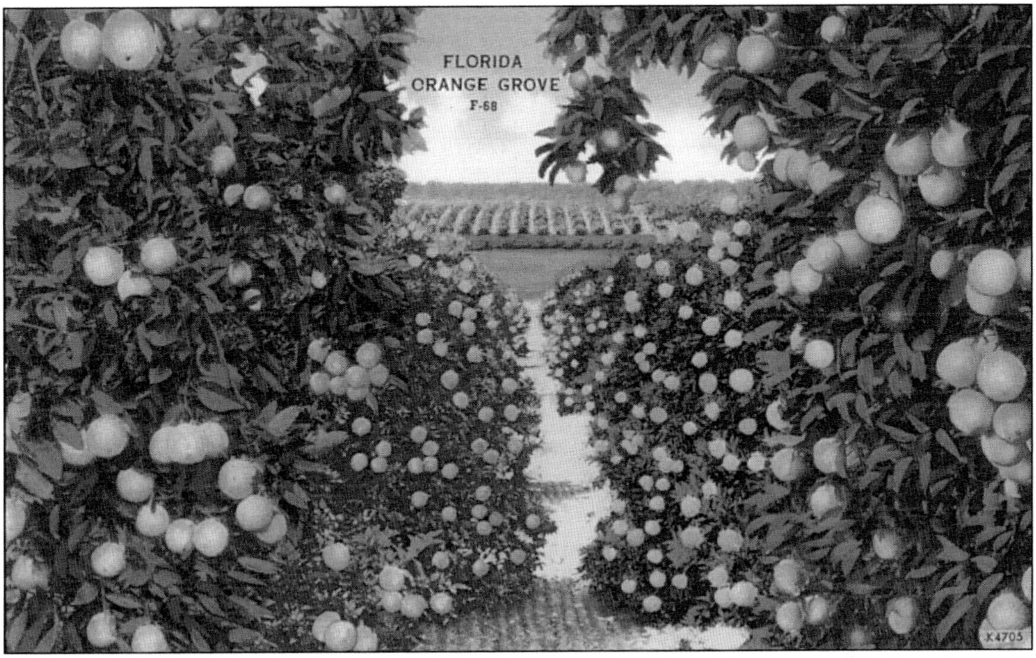

The lake depicted here has likely since disappeared. As Florida's water table has dropped, many "sand bottom" lakes have dried up. The bottom image is the reverse of the postcard pictured above.

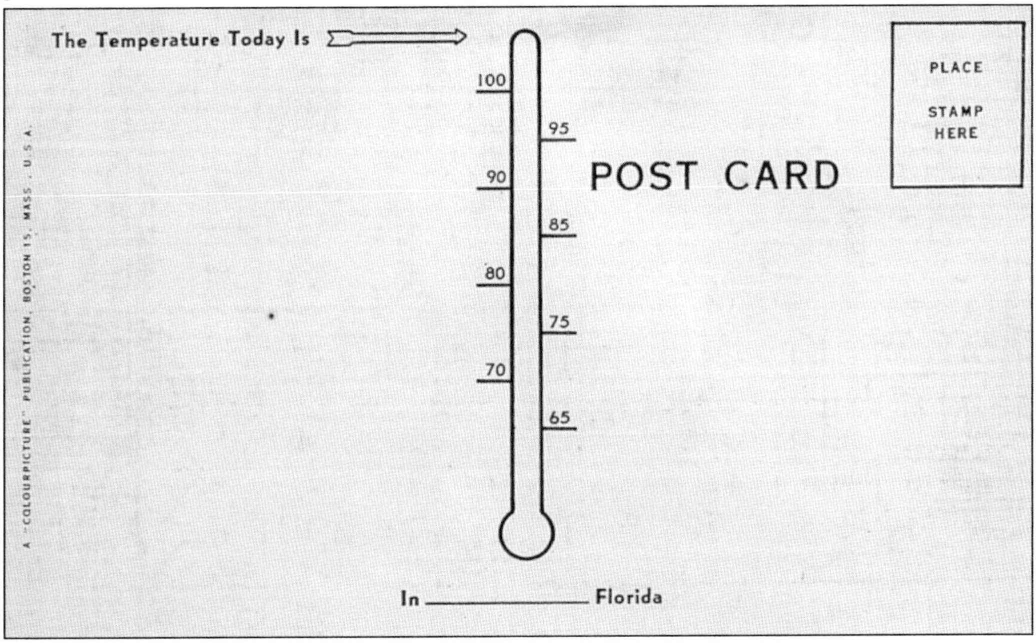

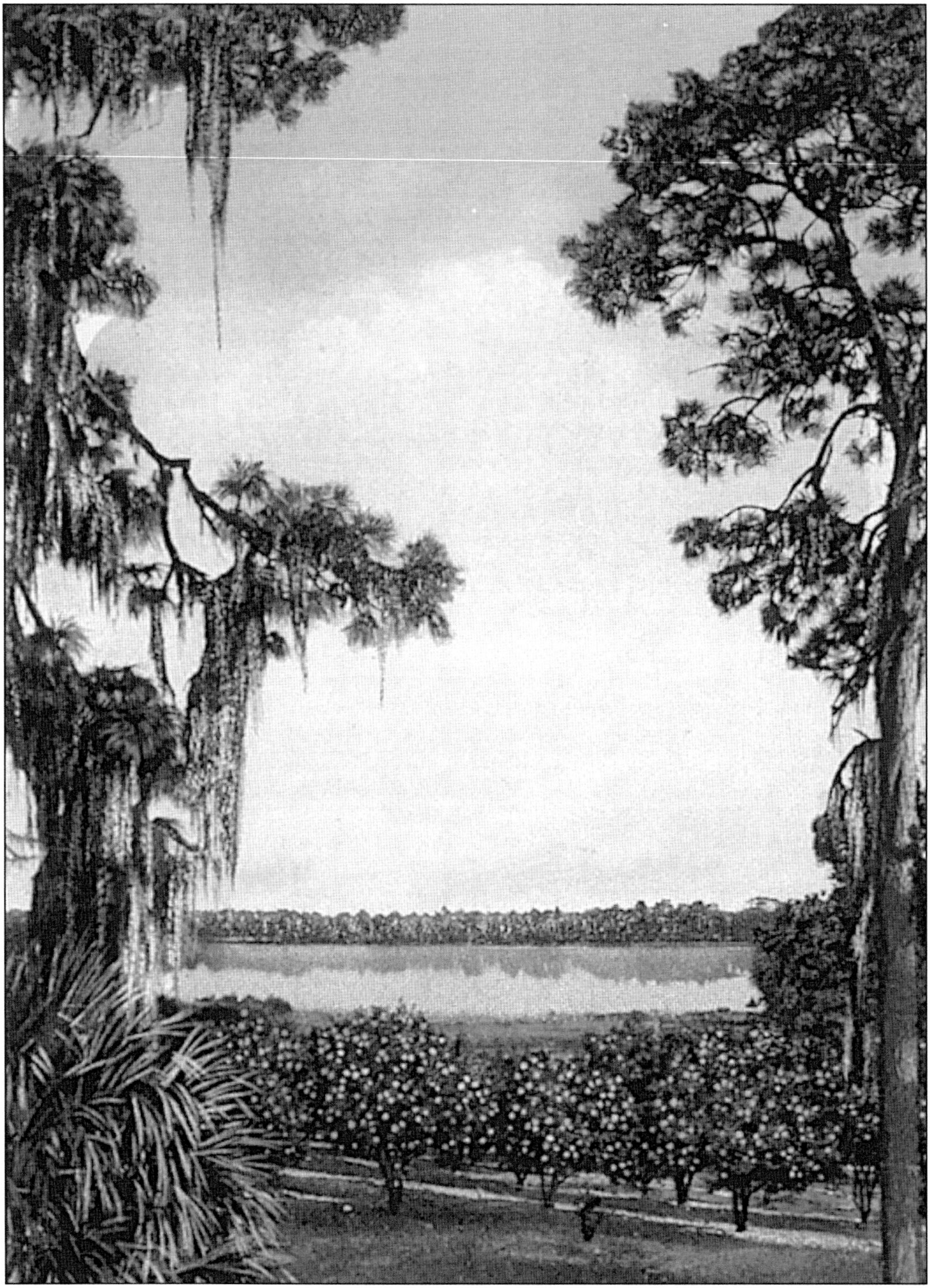

Until recent freezes, there were many groves nestled beside the lakes of central Florida. The lakes' water was used for irrigation, and it also was a source of warmth. Growers know that the south side of a large lake is relatively warmer than all other sides because the water buffers the cold winds.

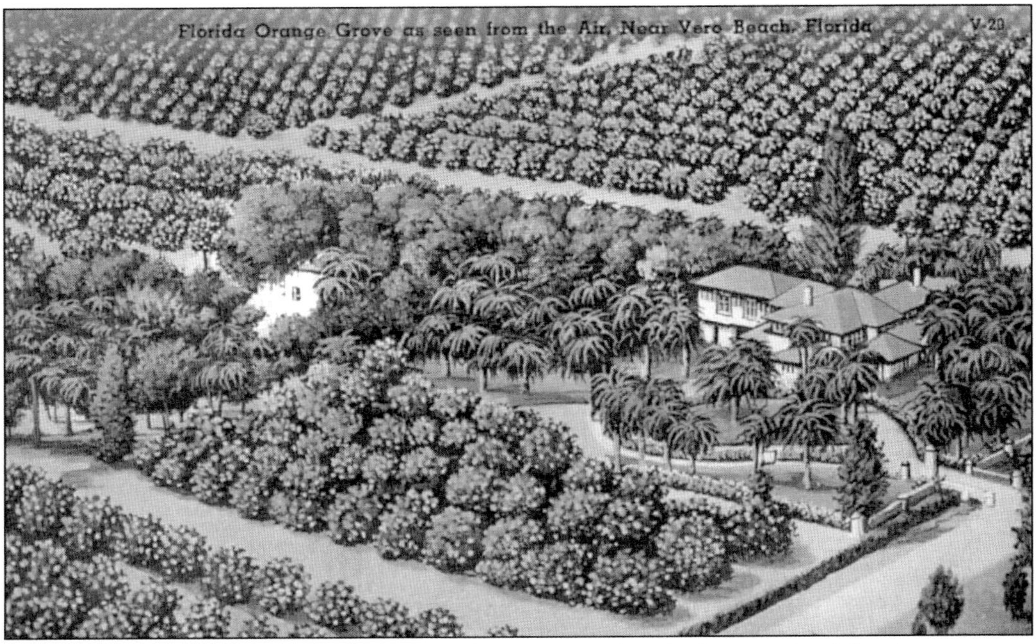

Printed on the back of the above postcard, from Hays and Malcolm, was the following:

From our groves direct to you by prepaid express.

	Crate	Bushel	1/2 Bu.
Oranges $	7.50	$5.50	$3.50
Grapefruit	6.00	4.50	3.00
Assorted	7.00	5.00	3.25

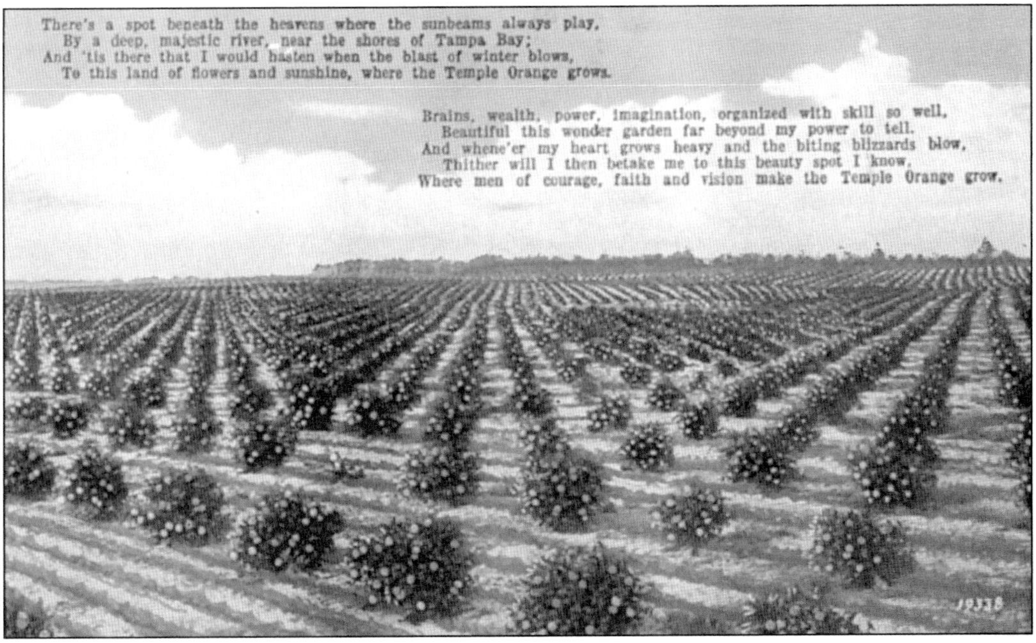

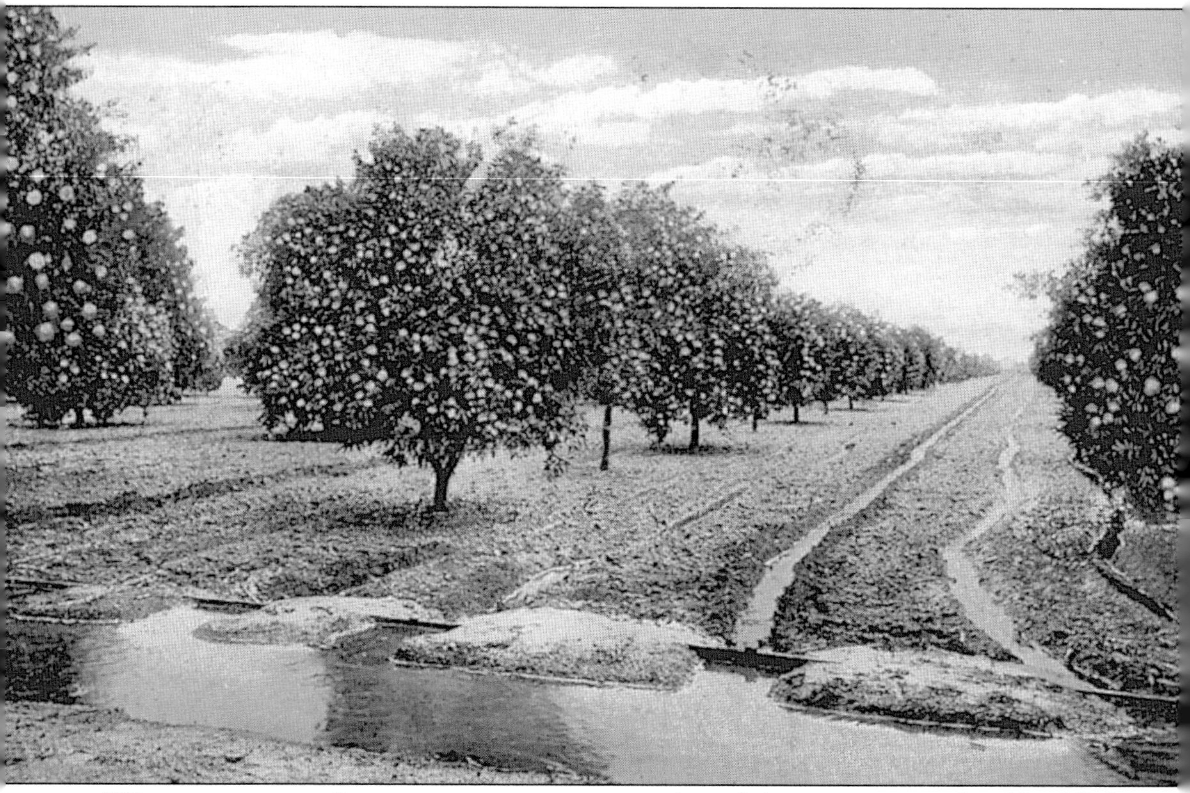

When temperatures dip, some growers pump water into their groves. Water that "floods" the grove is warmer than the outside air, and this can raise the temperature of the tree as a whole by several degrees. Growers no longer use heaters nor burn tires or logs, a practice that raised the temperature of the air around the trees. The high cost of fuel and environmental concerns were behind the change. This card is postmarked Tampa, March 4, 1919.

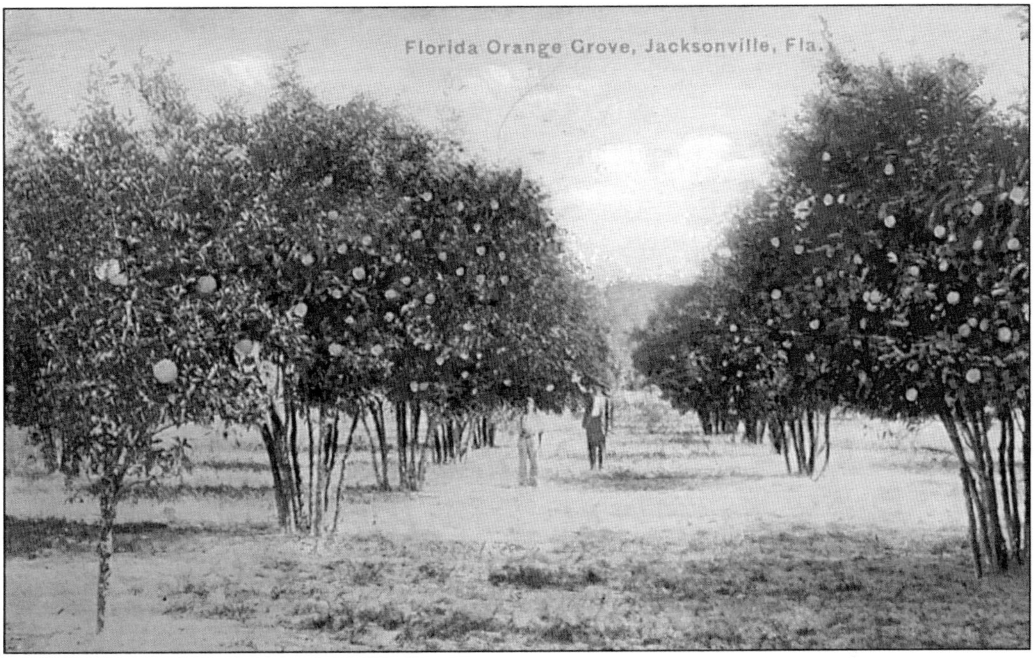

The splintered appearance of the trees in the above postcard may be due to a winter freeze. In cold enough weather, the trunk of the tree will die; the trees will push up smaller sprouts, which, if allowed to grow, will create many smaller trunks. The heartiness of the tree itself is not affected and the taste of the fruit is the same.

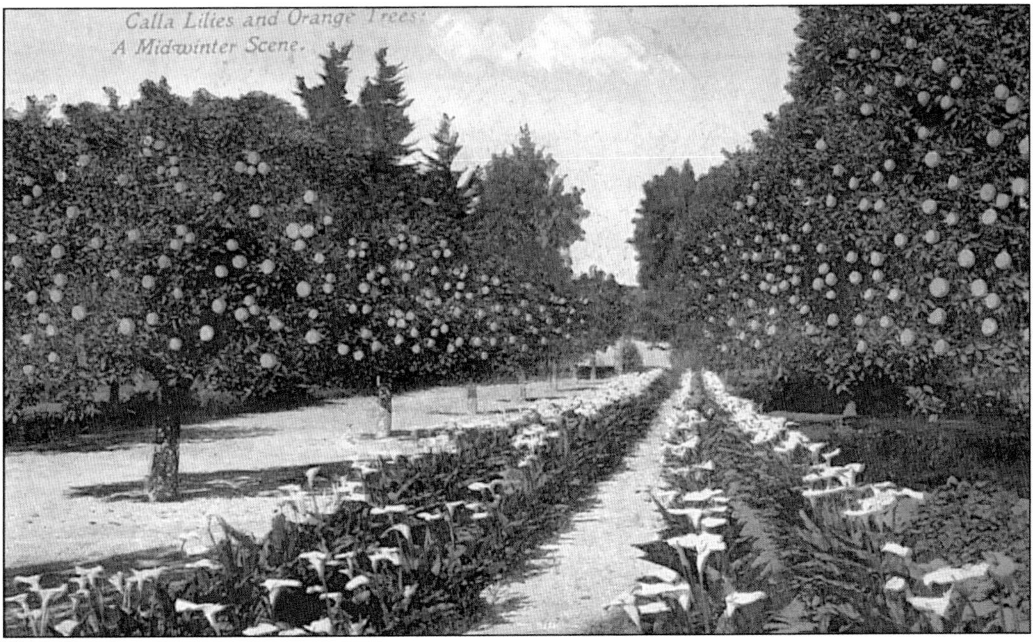

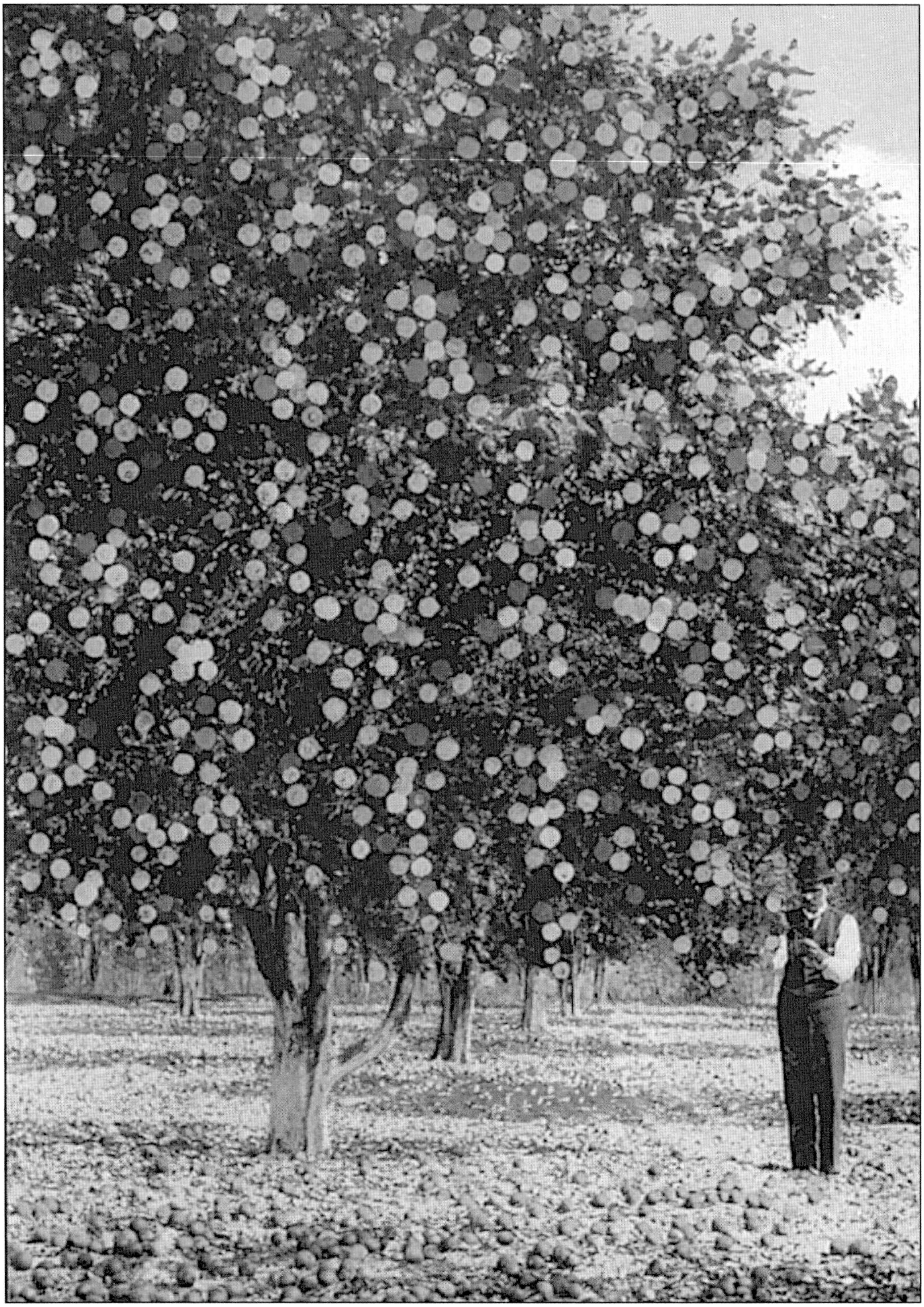

These trees may have topped out at 40 feet; their growth upward, instead of outward (as budded trees will grow) may indicate that they were grown from seedlings. Horticulturists later determined that pruning the trees to half that size resulted in more fruit on the tree.

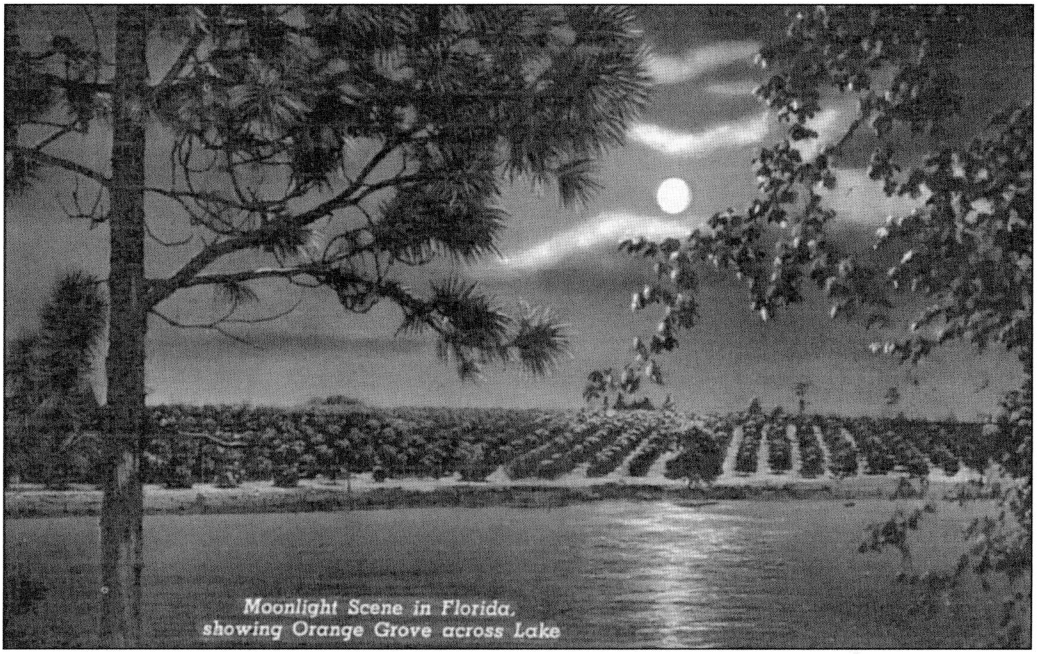

"Having a nice winter without snow. Hear you have plenty snow. Keep shoveling . . . As ever, Fannie." This was written on the image above that is postmarked St. Petersburg, January 12, 1957.

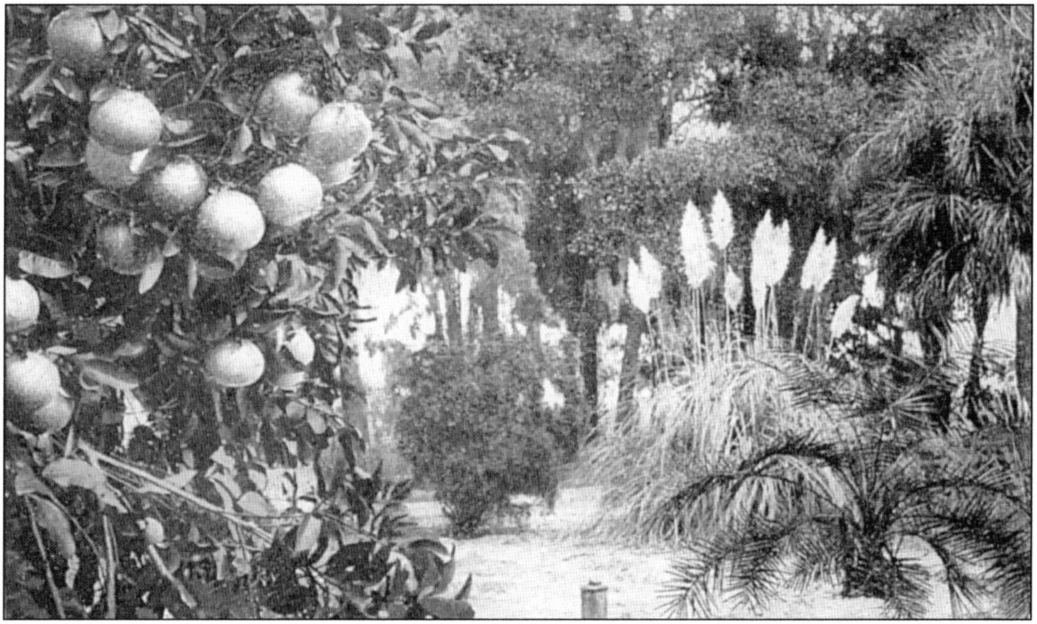

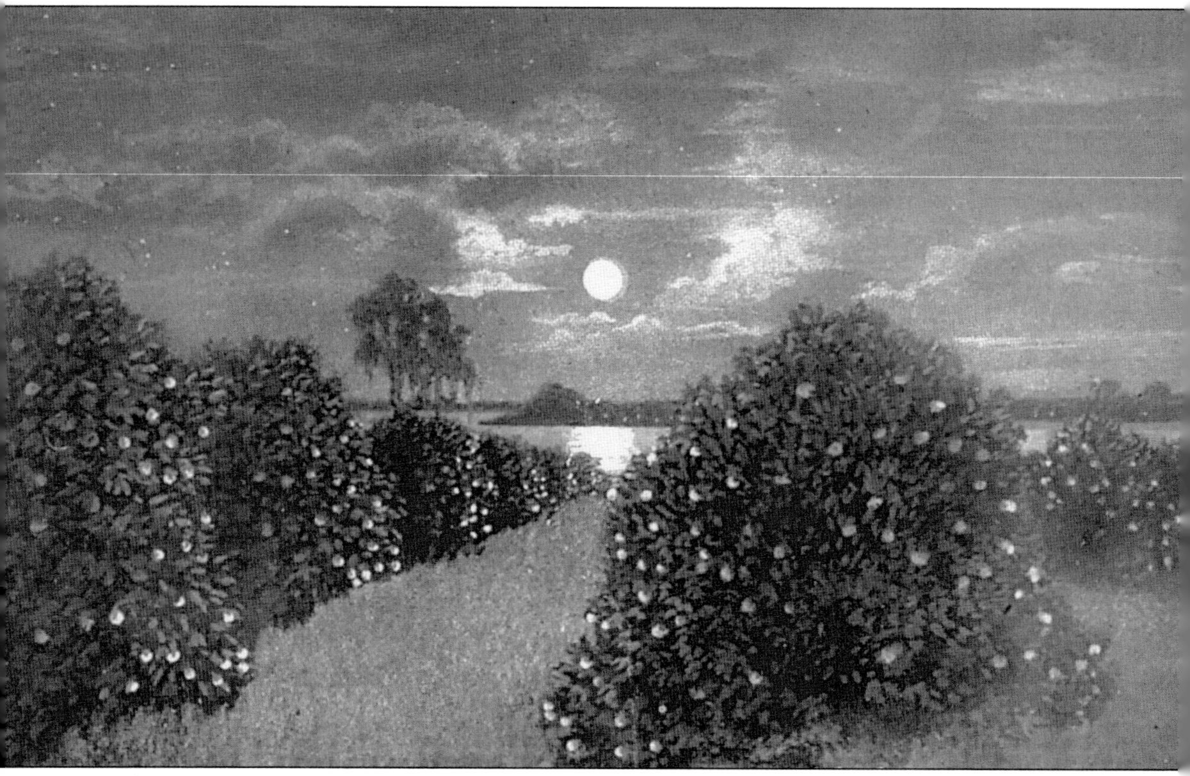

When I was a freshman at Florida Southern College in the winter of 1966, my fraternity brothers and I spent a freezing night in groves around Lakeland belonging to the Minute-Maid Corporation. We were paid $15 each to spend the entire night lighting fuel oil in grove heaters and firing "smudge-pots" in an effort to warm the groves. We returned to campus after sunrise, tired and covered with soot. We had just a short time to clean up and get to our first class. This card is postmarked Titusville, April 6, 1936.

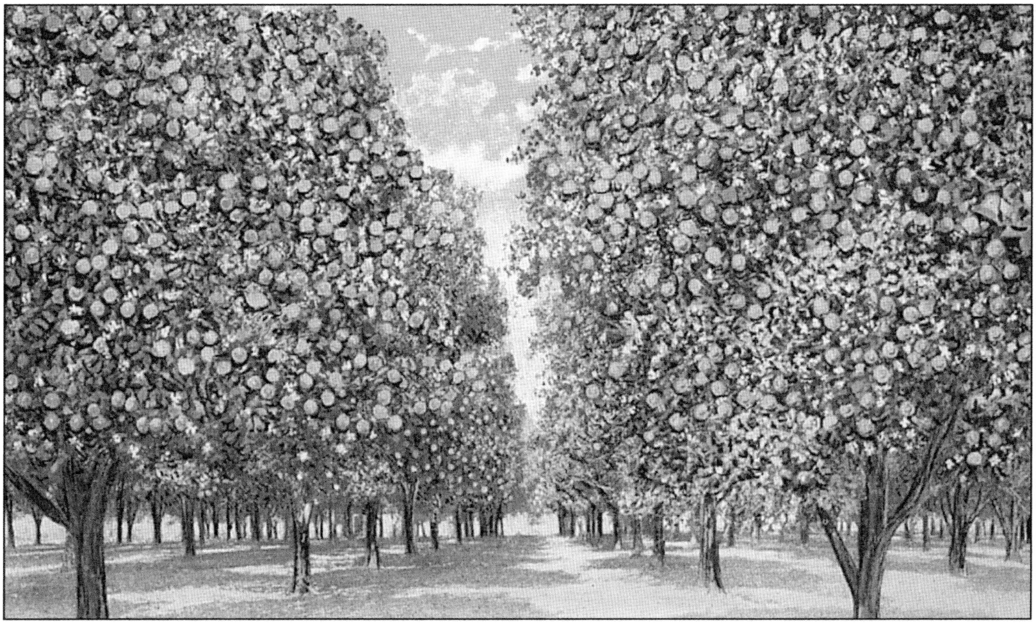

Blossoms appear on a citrus tree sometime between late February and mid-April, depending on the weather. Only one or two percent of all blossoms will actually become fruit. It takes several months for old blossoms and small fruit to fall off, leaving behind the viable fruit that will fully develop. Growers know irrigation is crucial at blossom time to keep the trees from dropping the new bloom.

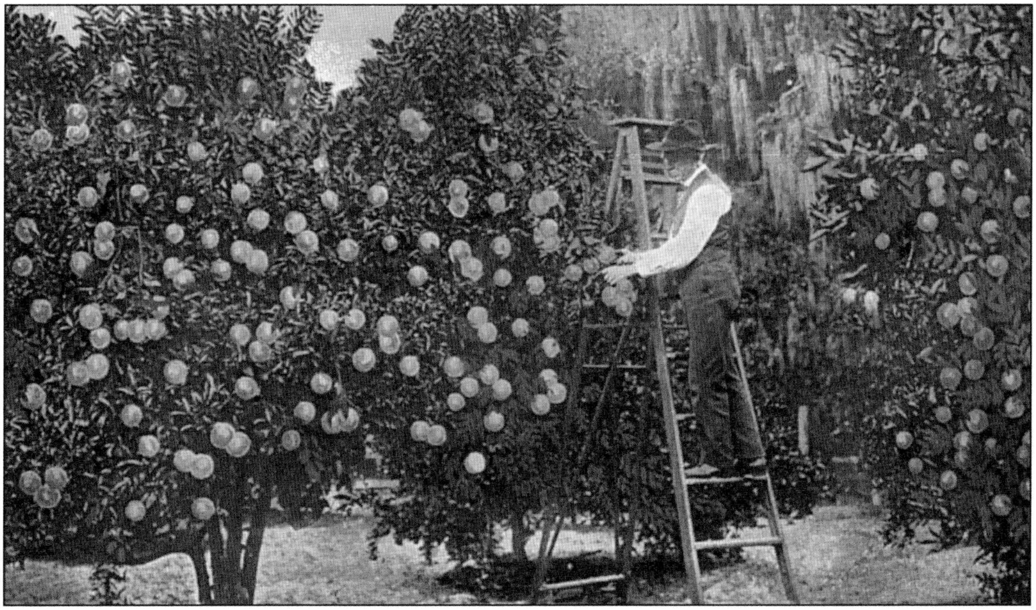

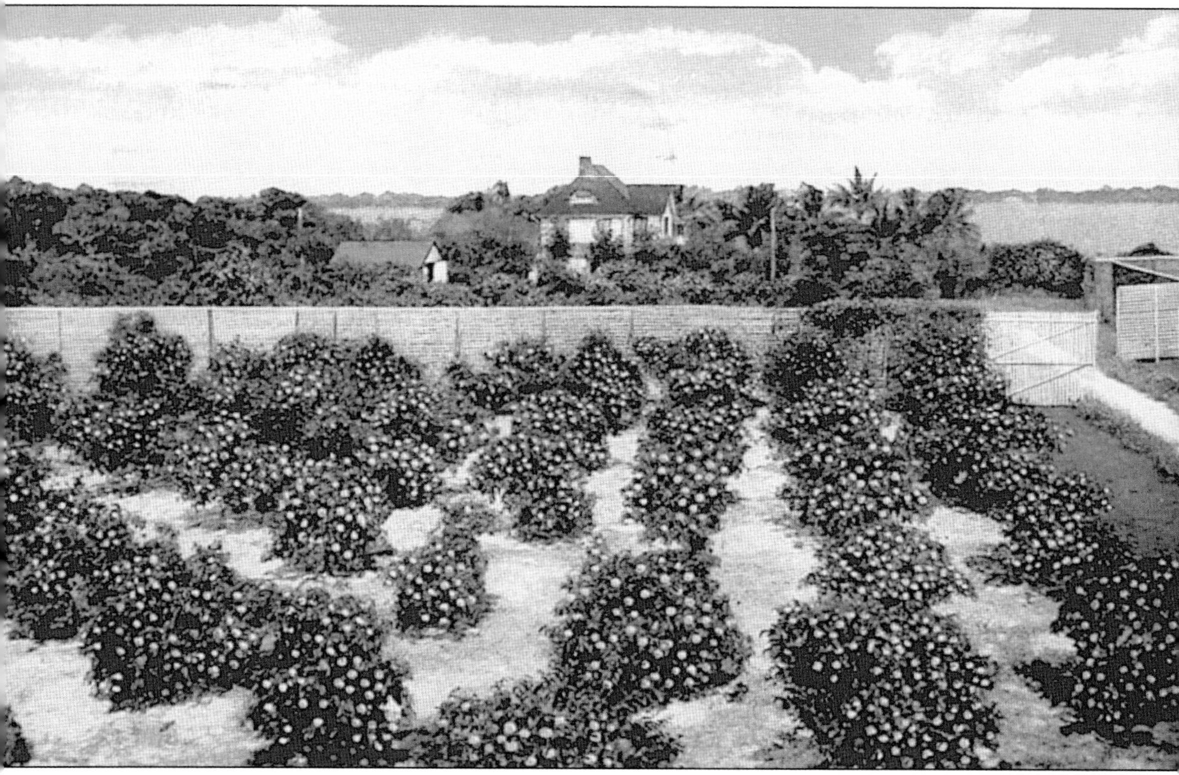

Around bloom time, beekeepers fan out and approach grove owners about a trade. The beekeepers will set their hives of bees in the groves, where the bees will pollinate the varieties of trees that are not self-pollinating. In turn, the bees will create "orange blossom honey," which the beekeepers can sell. The honey is mild and has a light, golden color. This card is postmarked St. Petersburg, January 12, 1957.

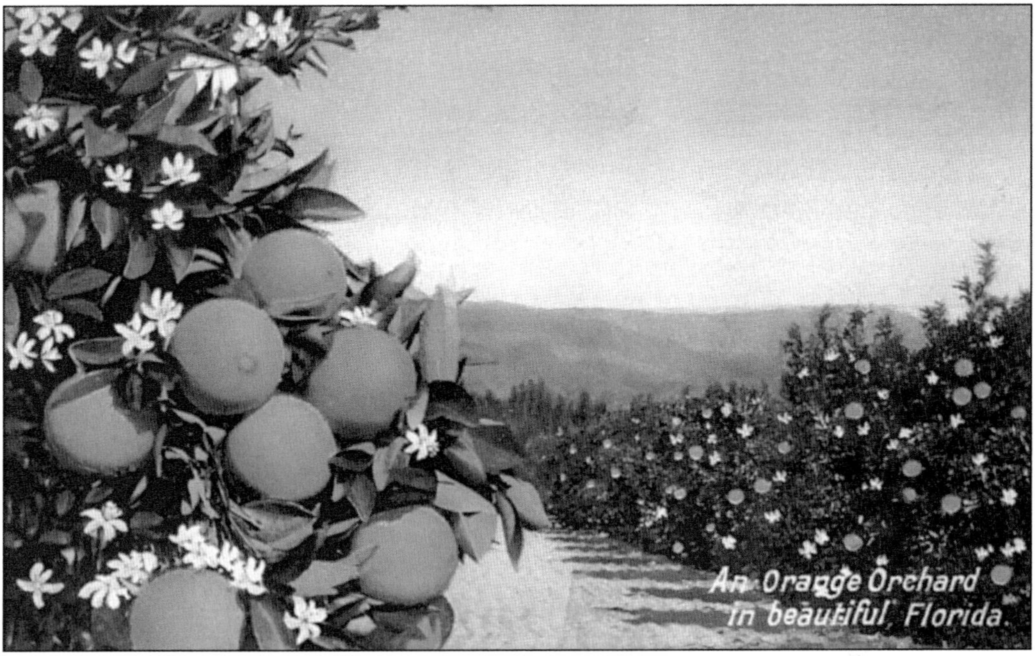

There are no mountains in Florida like the ones pictured here; perhaps a designer got carried away, forgetting to remove the mountains when he changed the color of the fruit and added clouds and a poem. The above postcard is postmarked St. Cloud, December 27, 1909, while the one below is marked Ontario, California, December 21, 1912.

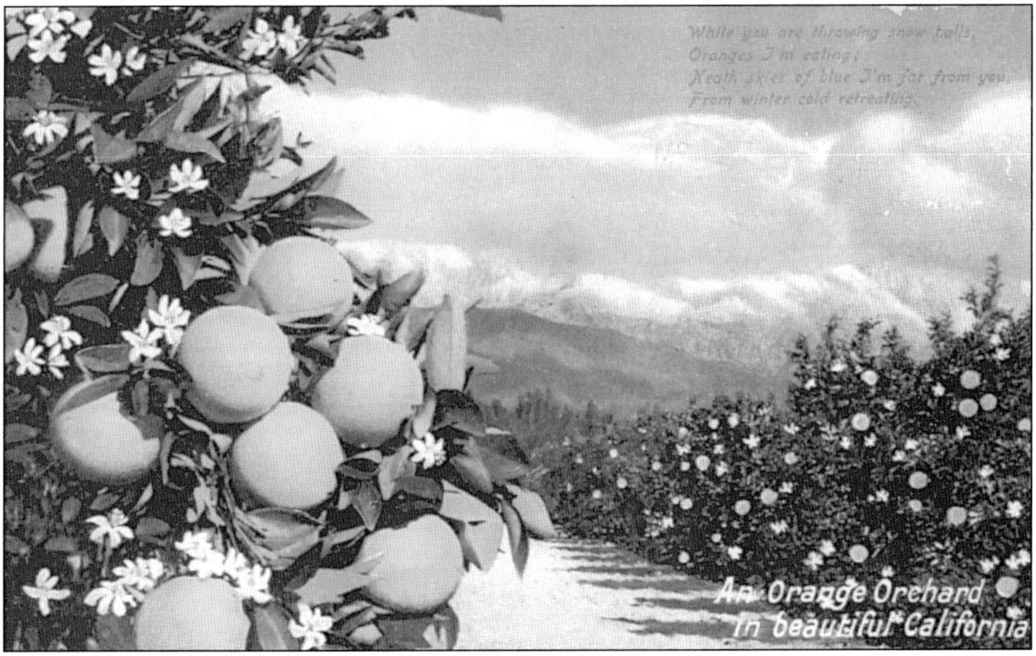

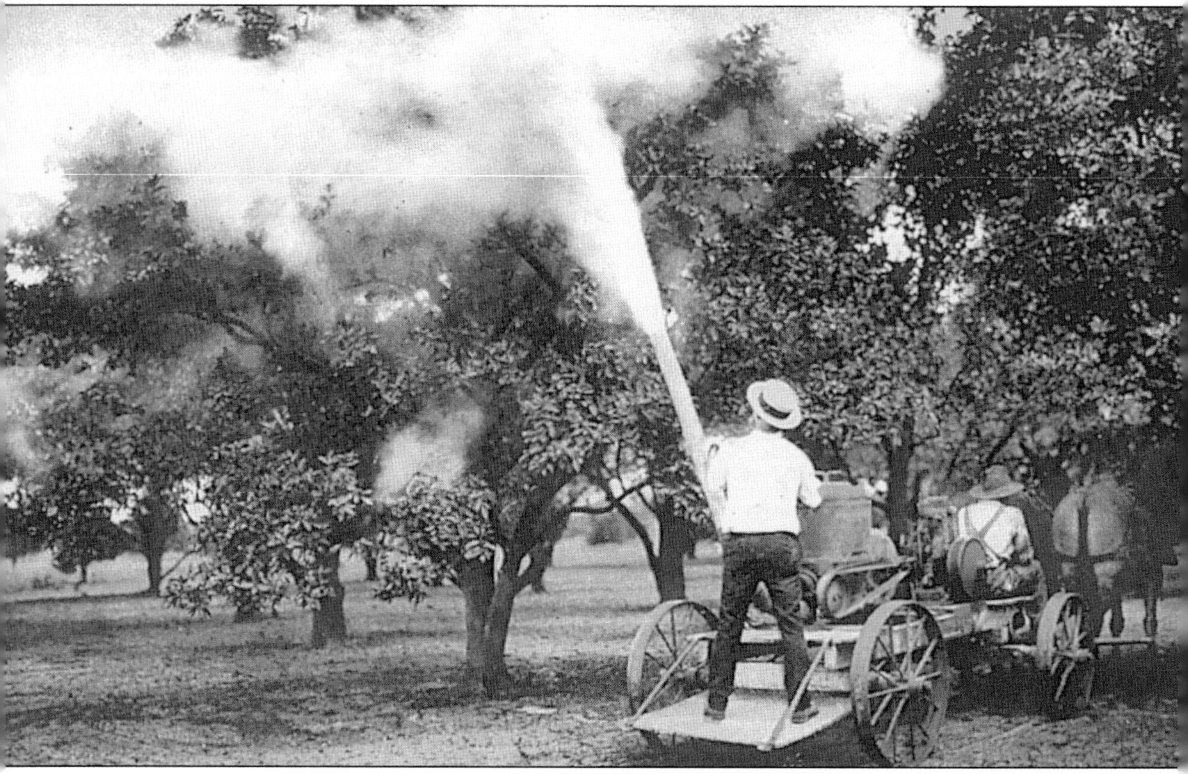

In the early years, spraying was done by hand instead of by tractor-drawn machinery. Growers use insecticides to prevent the advance of mites in the groves. Rust mites cause blemishes on the surface of citrus fruit. The mites do not harm the taste of the fruit but do make unsightly marks that prevent the fruit from being packed for the fresh market. Rust mite-marked fruit is made into juice. Melanose is a fungal disease that causes small specks and also mars the appearance of the fruit.

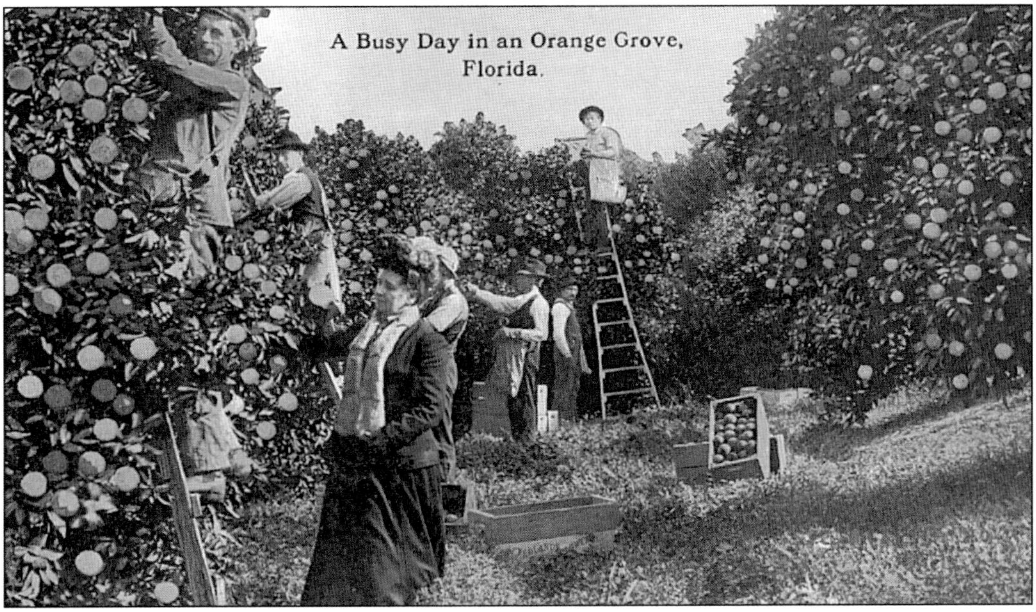

The Mediterranean fruit fly attacks more than 250 kinds of vegetables and fruit, including citrus. The fly burrows into fruit and lays its eggs inside, ruining the fruit. The Florida Department of Agriculture uses an aerial spray to kill the flies, or it releases sterile flies to mate with the female fruit flies, who die after mating and produce no offspring.

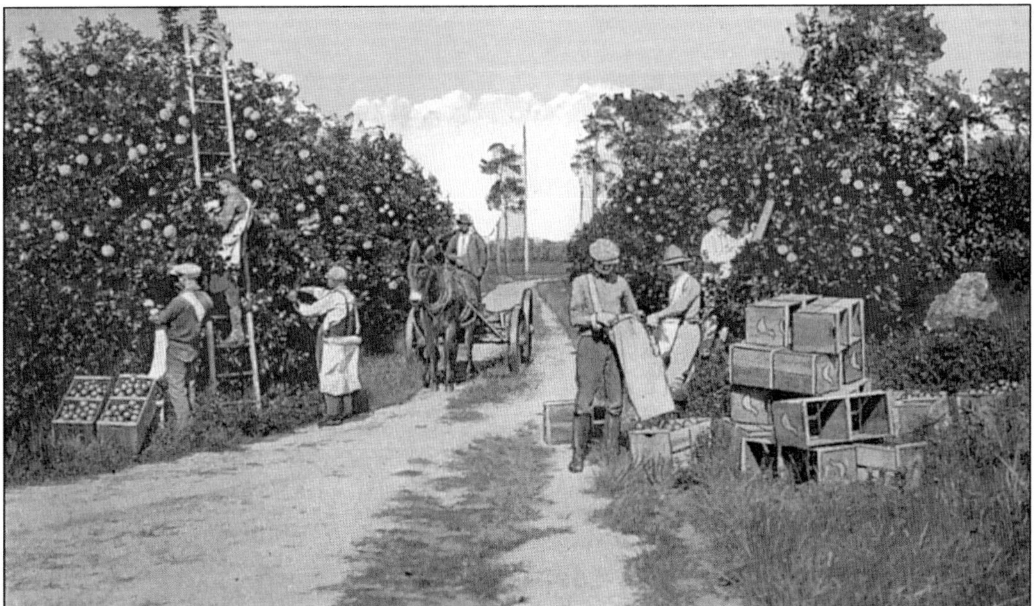

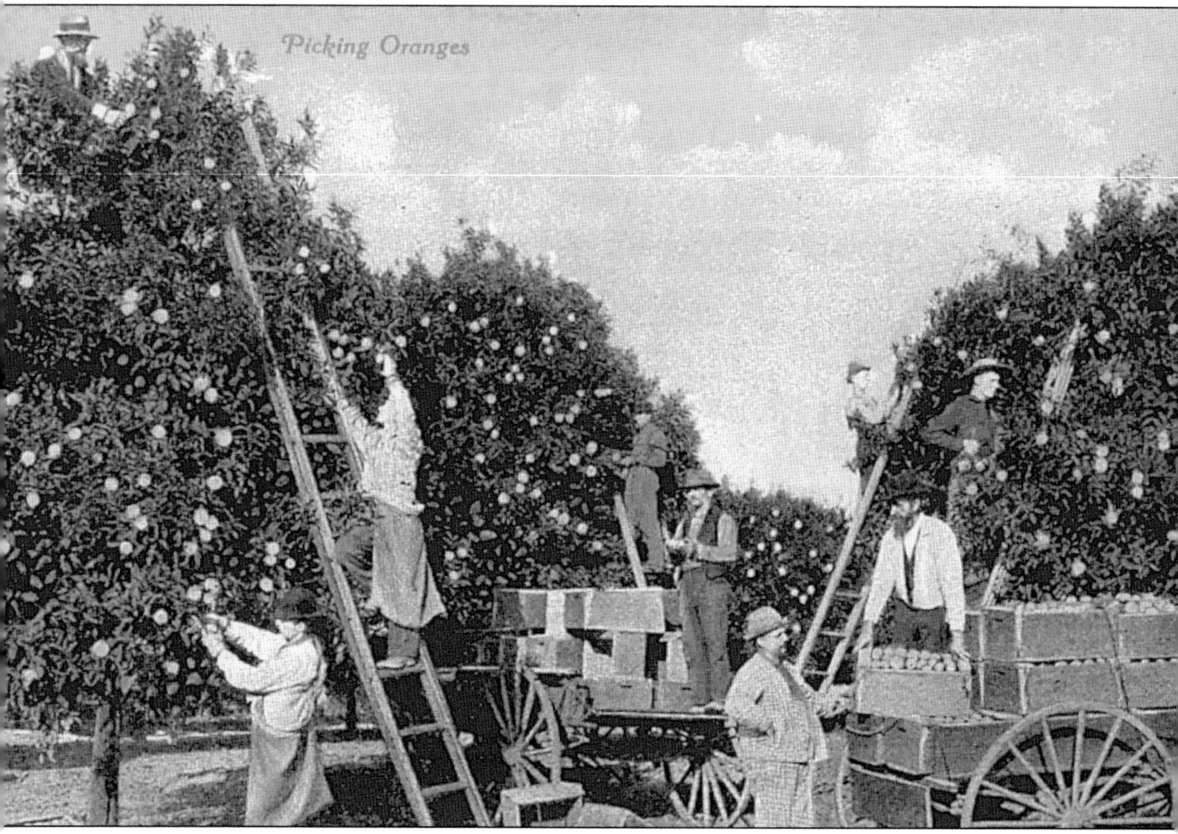

Growers have always faced the threat of "citrus canker," a bacterial disease that attacks trees, lessens their productivity, and damages fruit. The only known way to prevent the spread of canker is to uproot the tree and burn it. The disease is spread by wind, rain, human contact, and machinery.

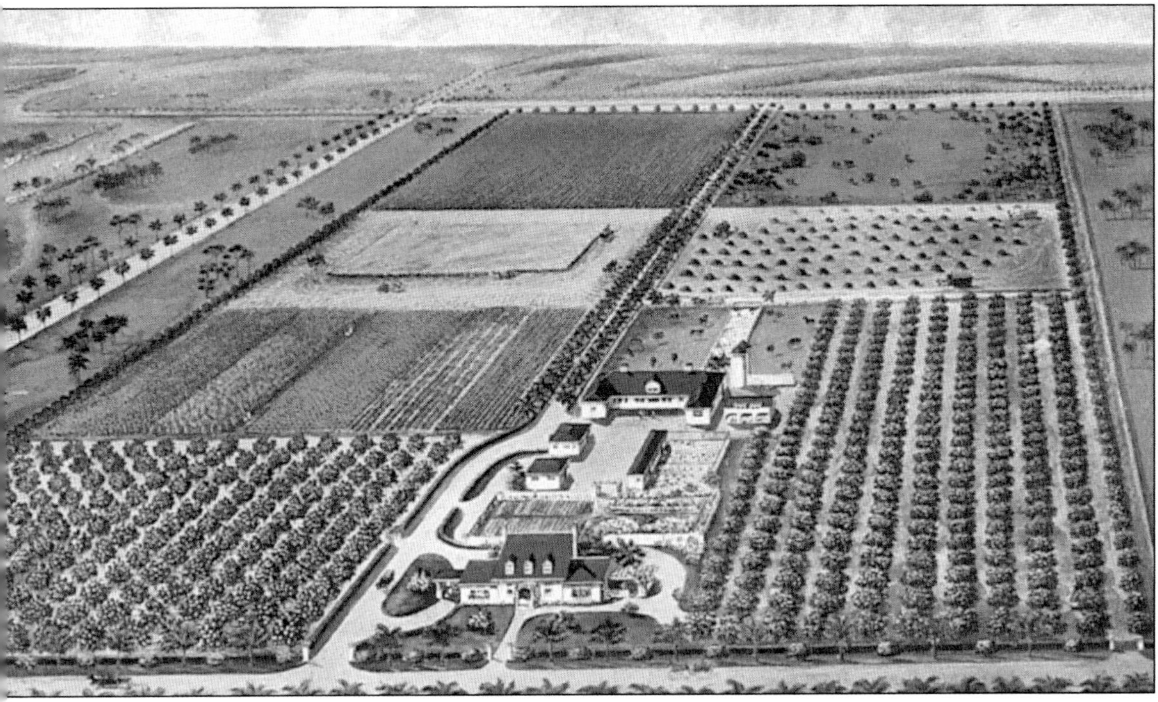

"This sub-division of a forty-acre farm and home arrangement comprising attractiveness and horticultural beautification with a variety of crops for profit. Dividing the tract thru the center with a roadway from either side of which are fields: five acres for pasture, five acres for Hog and Forage Crops, five acres for Corn, Sugar Cane or Grain, five acres for Potatoes, five acres for Winter Truck Crops such as Tomatoes, Eggplant, Peppers, Beans, Strawberries, etc; the balance for Citrus Fruits, such as Oranges, Grapefruit, Tangerines, Avocado Pears, Mangoes, Pineapples, etc. together with Farm Buildings, Barns, and Corrals, Chicken Houses and Runs and no forgetting the Home Garden for Table Delicacies and Flowers. A proportionately larger acreage could be divided into larger fields.
Indian River Farms Company
Developing Indian River Farms and the Town of Vero, Fla.
Northern Office Southern Office
Davenport, Iowa Vero, Florida
Information Free"

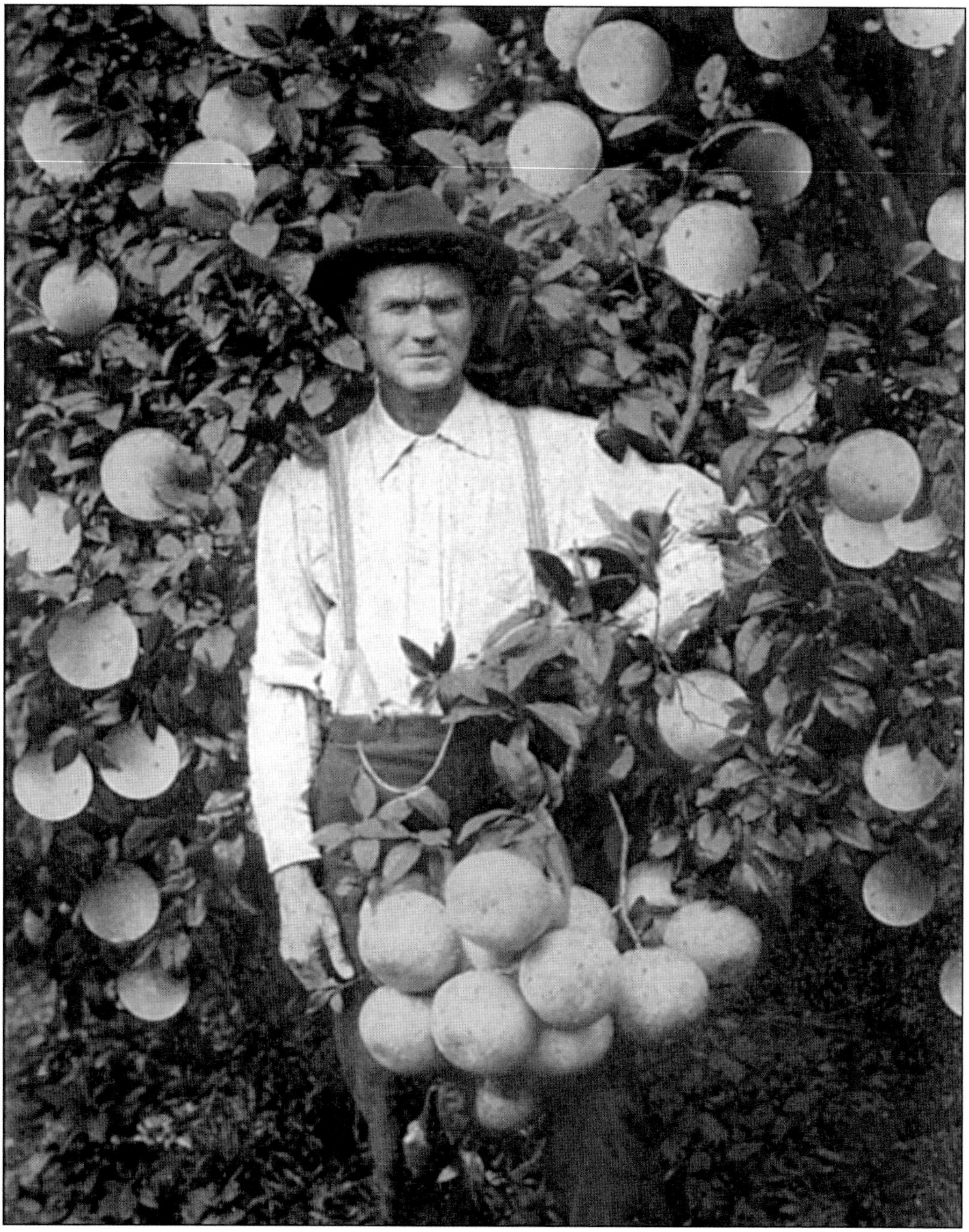

"The E.C. Walker orange and grapefruit grove in the center of Indian River Farms at Vero, Florida, is for its size and age, one of the most famous in Florida. This fine grove is a good example of what can be done in Indian River Farms by men or women of energy and determination. Visiting this grove, for visitors are always welcome at the Walker Grove, and hearing from Mr. Walker the story of his success, is one of the most enjoyable parts of a trip to Vero and groves, more vividly than words can tell, an appreciation of this Opportunity-laden section which awaits only the attention of man to become 'The Garden Spot of America.' The Fruit from ten acres in the Walker Grove sold on the trees for $7700.00."

Growers often let other plants, including flowers, grow amidst the trees. However, it is unlikely that rose bushes of this size grew in the groves. It is possible that this postcard is a result of the printer's creative license.

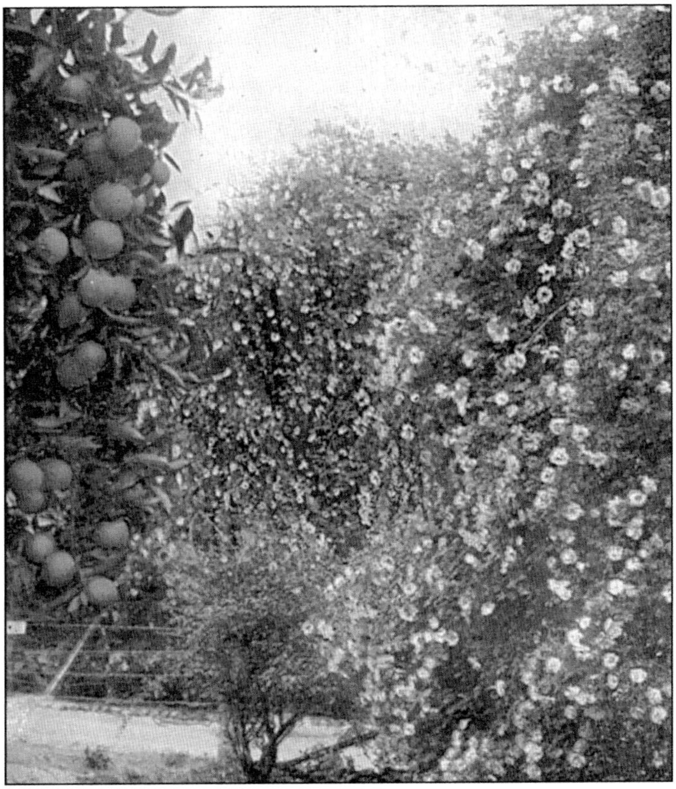

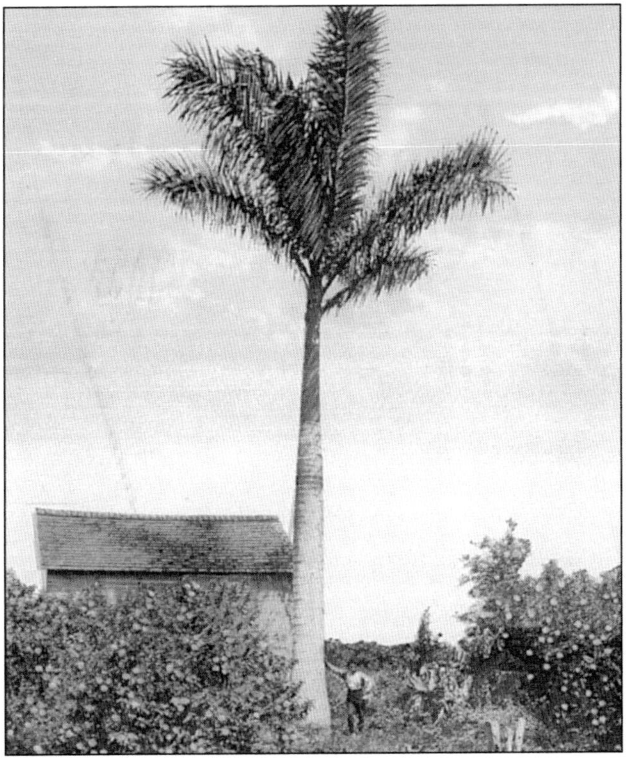

Postmarked Fort Myers, December 9, 1918, this card has a message that reads, "Gene is going to bring home some of these trees for his back yard - want some?- M."

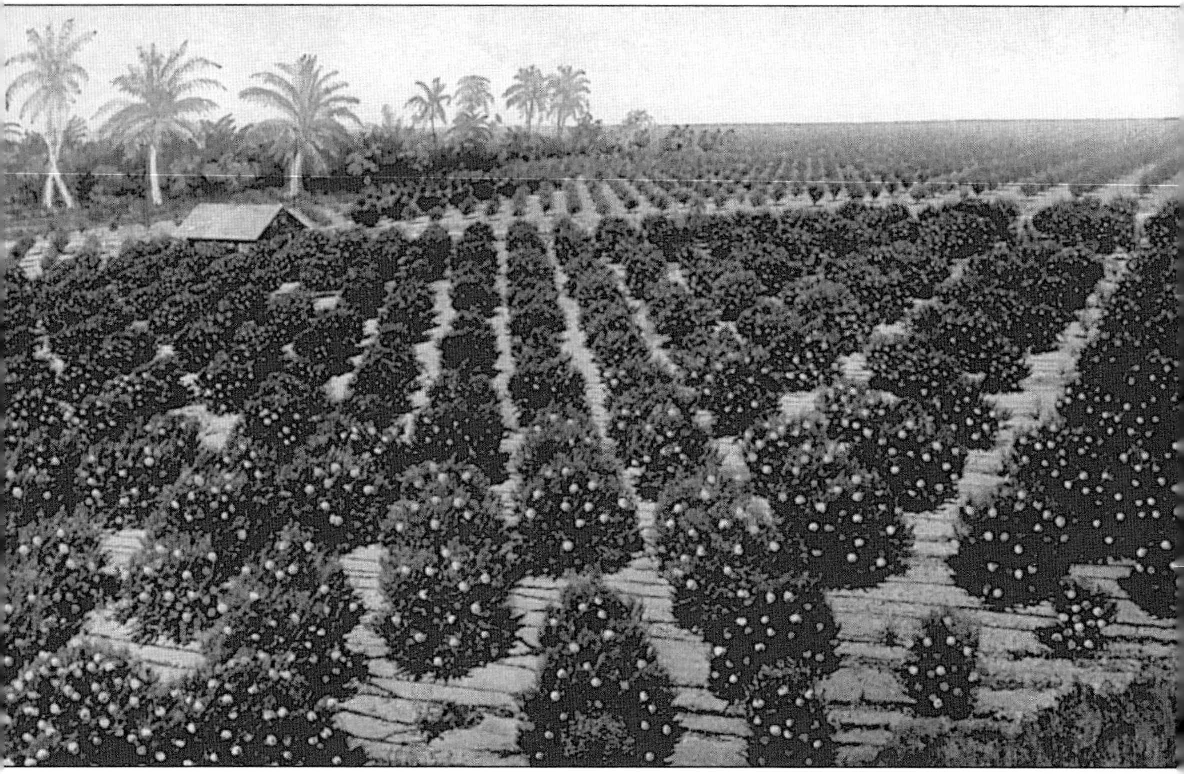

Most growers view citrus as more than a source of income; there is a simple pleasure in having a grove and working in the open air. We often say owning groves is like having a company with a lot of employees who stand in neat rows and don't say anything. If you take good care of them, they will reward you for your efforts.

Three

"Come Down and Pick Oranges"

The citrus industry is big business, and it all begins with the workers who pick the fruit from the tree, one piece at a time. This hard work, under all types of conditions, is the start of a long process that brings the product to the consumer.

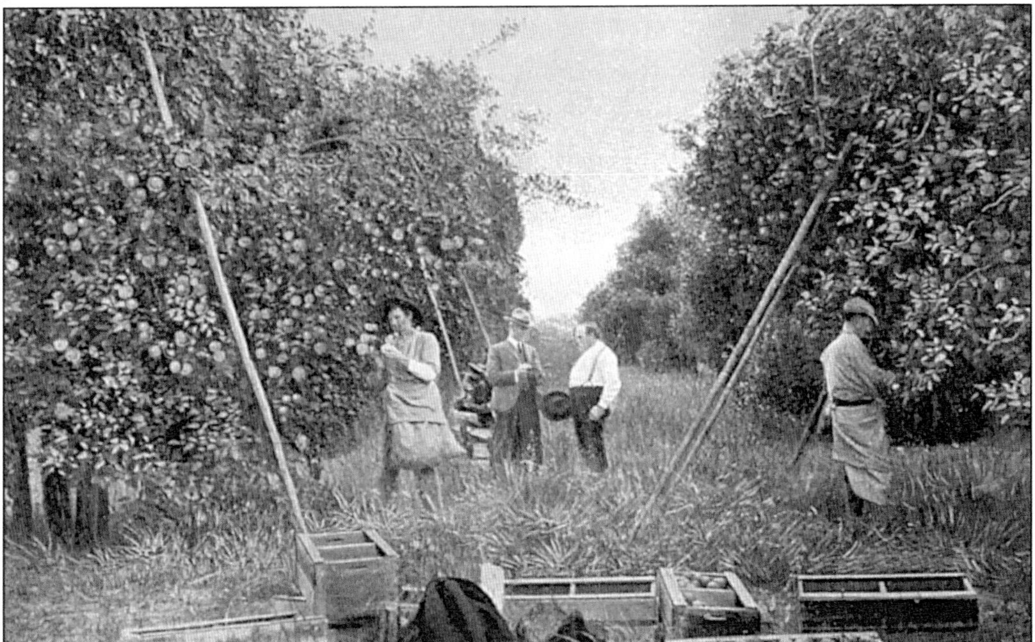

"Purchasing Crop. One of the leading crops of Florida is the orange, although it has been subject to great changes. In 1894, 1895, and 1899 many millions of trees were frozen, and the crop diminished from 5,000,000 boxes a year to 75,000, but it is now well on the increase. Merchants usually buy fruit in bulk, or by the thousand, while it is still on the tree."

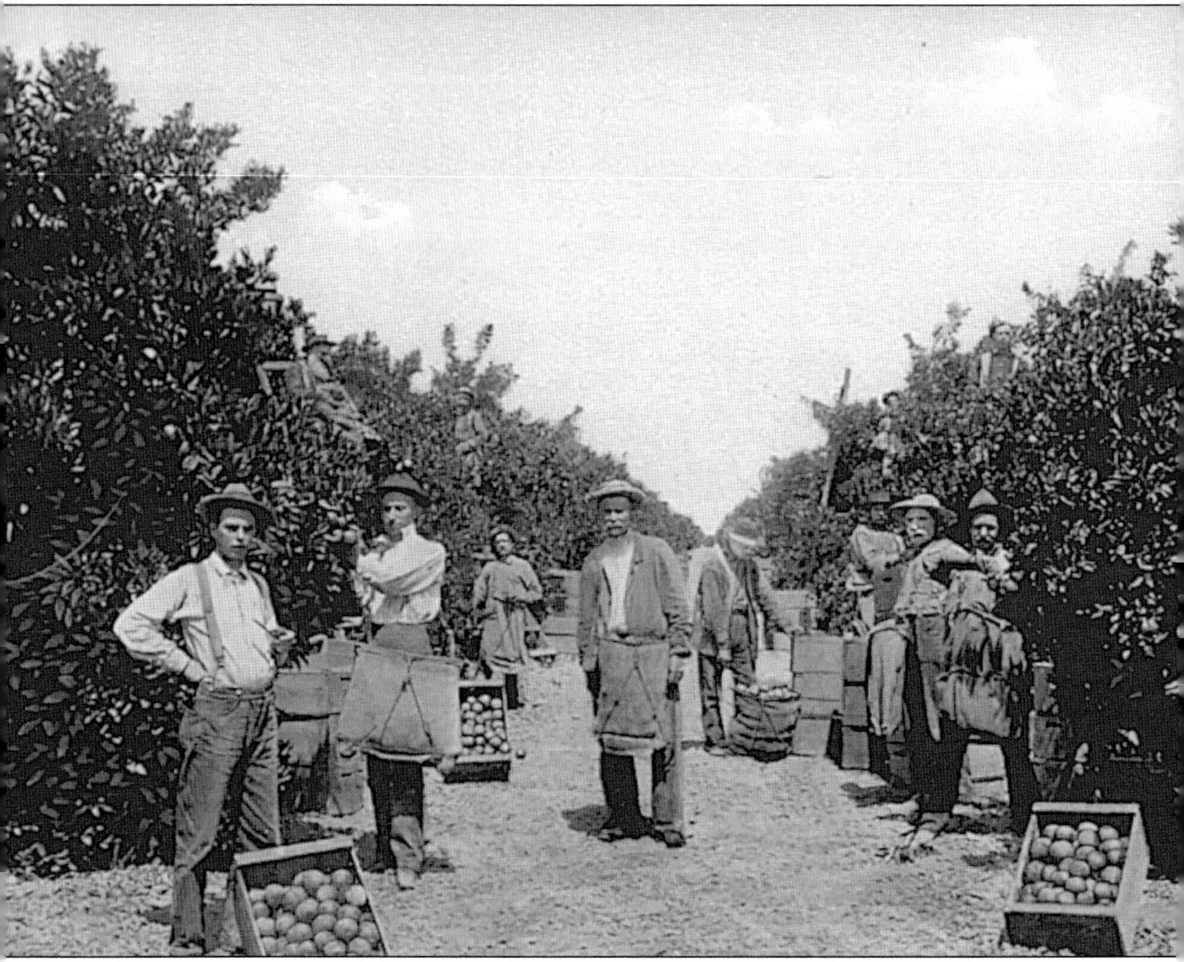

Picking season varies depending on the variety of citrus being picked. Citrus blooms in March and April, and the trees bear fruit beginning in October. The variety of the orange determines when that fruit is harvested. Grapefruit is sometimes ready in October and is good through May. The fruit is generally better when picked later in the season.

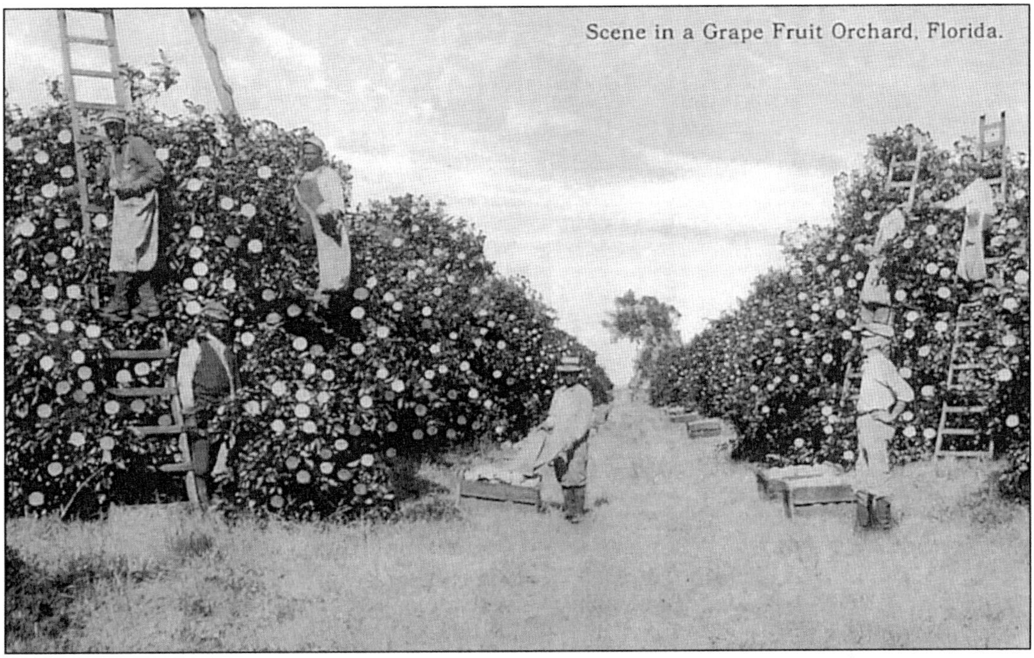

When is fruit ready to be picked? Growers use a test extractor rented from the state of Florida. The device applies pressure on test fruit and squeezes them. They are then tested for acid and brix (the percentage of sugar by weight). This test measures whether the crop meets the state standards for maturity and is ready to be taken from the tree and sent to the packing house or juice plant. The bottom card is postmarked Miami, April 2, 1943.

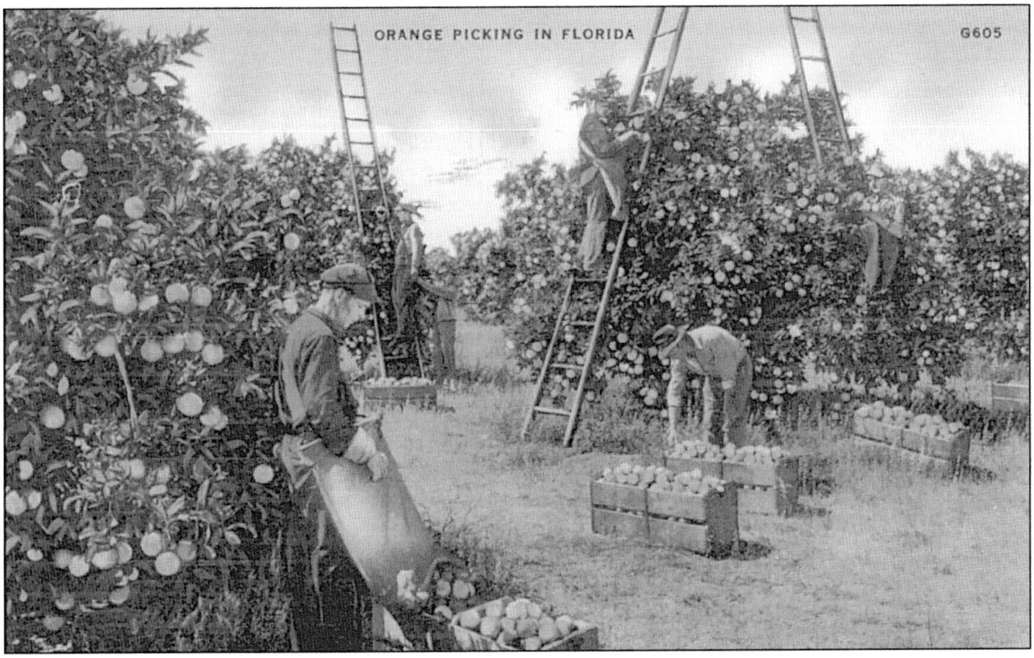

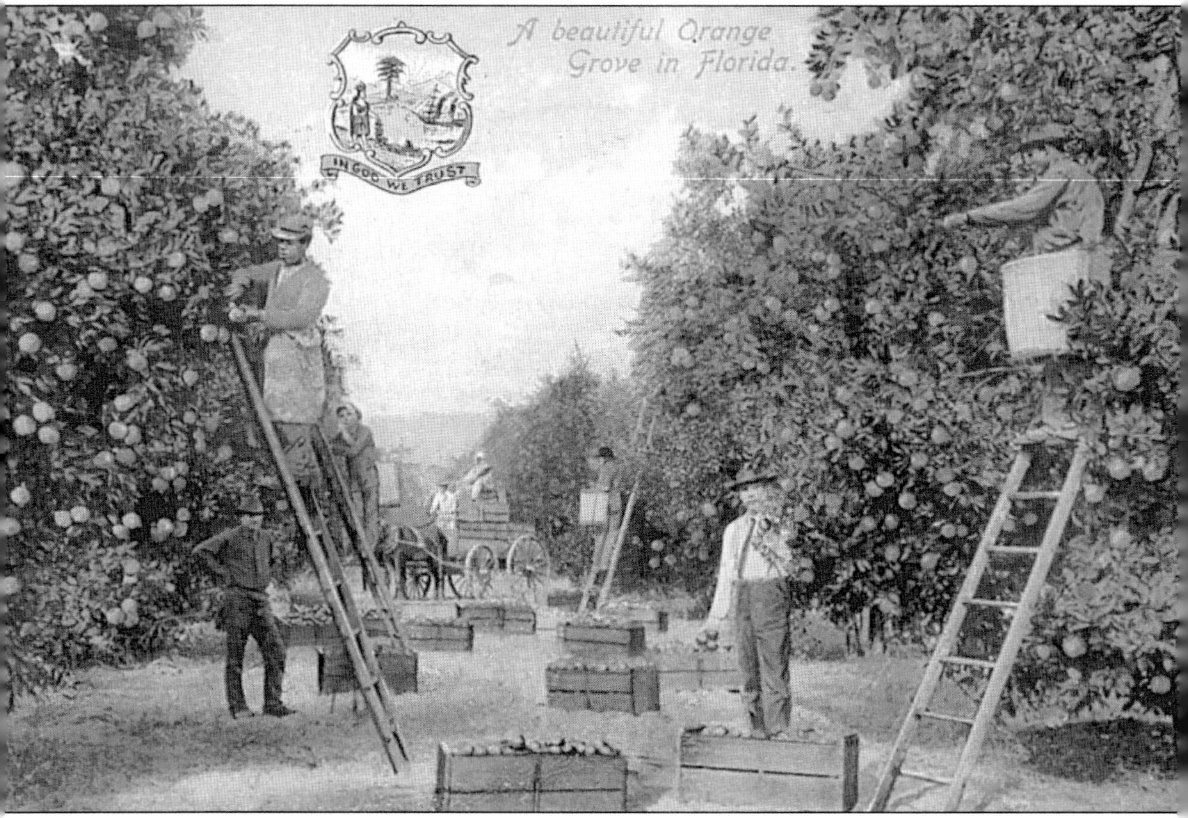

Before 1940 it was common practice for pickers to use clippers to separate the fruit from the trees. However, clipping turned out to be too time consuming for the mass harvesting of fruit, so it was done away with in favor of hand-picking. Various other devices to separate fruit from the trees have been attempted (one of them shook a tree causing the fruit to drop), but none has been successful in consistently obtaining undamaged fruit for consumers. This card is postmarked Jacksonville, December 12, 1910.

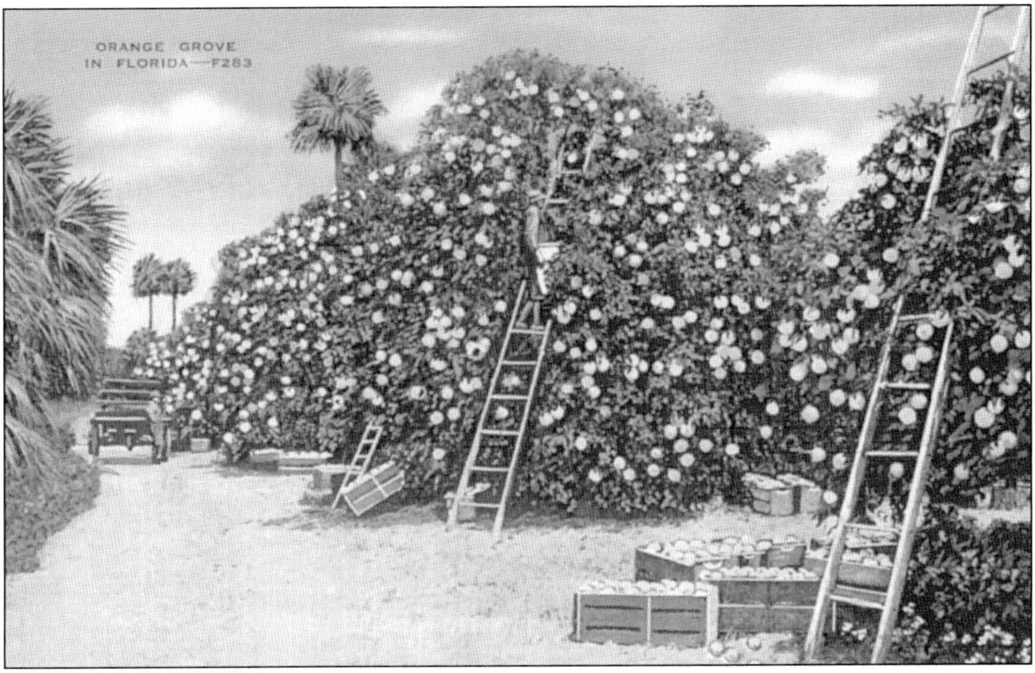

People who pick citrus have to do it a special way. They twist the fruit from the stem with a snap. If this is not done, the fruit will "plug," leaving a hole that can allow decay to set in and make the fruit unmarketable. Harvesting supervisors watch commercial pickers to make sure the fruit is being carefully picked. The below image is postmarked July 24, 1912.

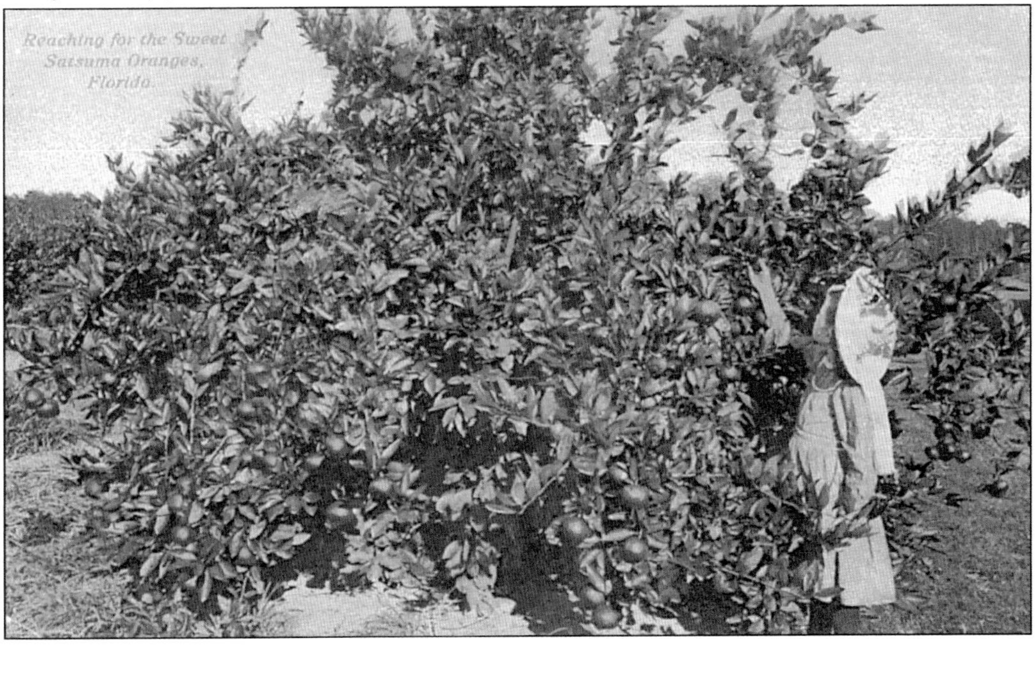

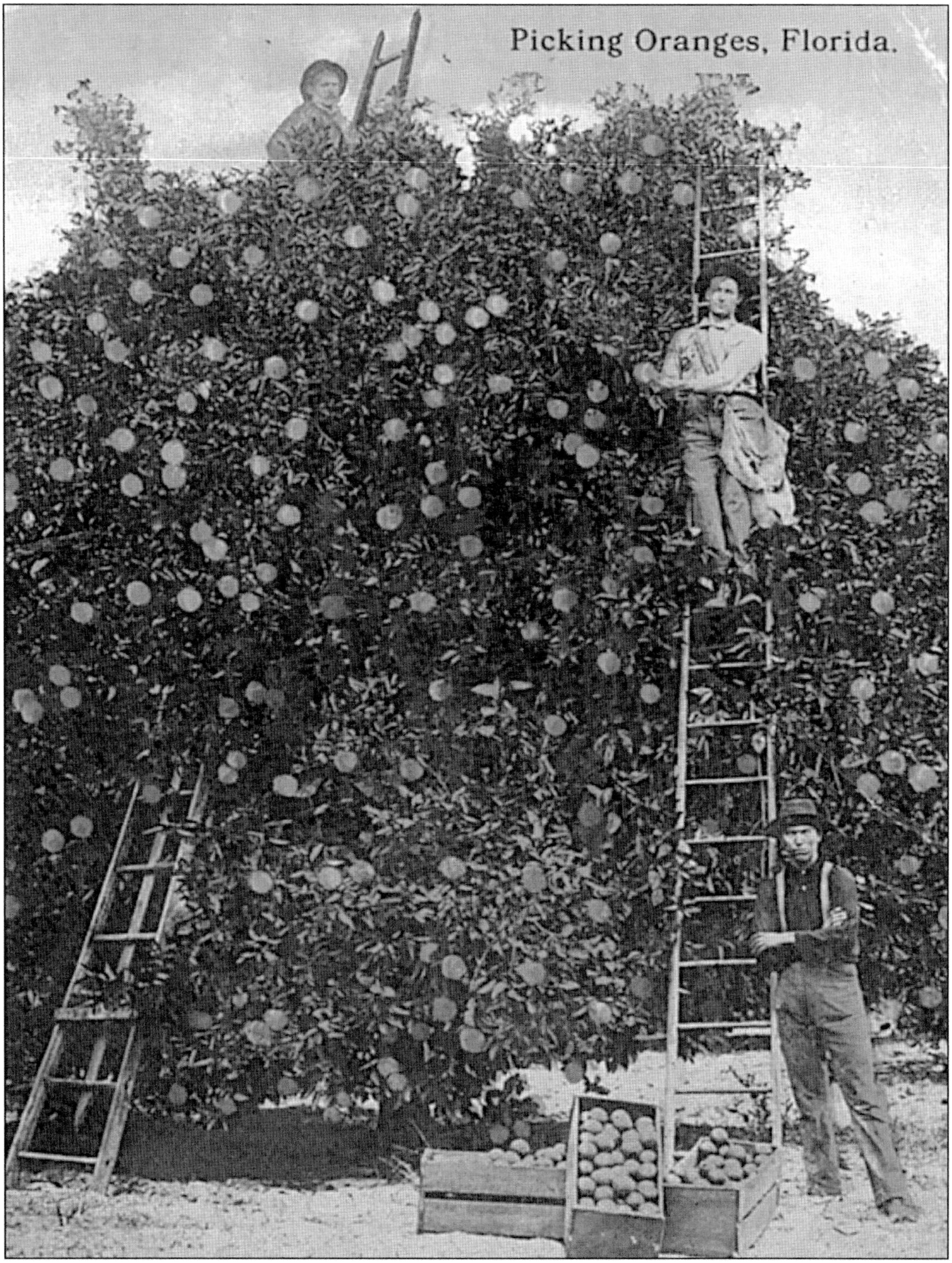

Here, pickers carry bags over their shoulders as they climb ladders to pick fruit. The pickers would have to come down frequently to empty their contents in the field boxes. Because the pickers were working in and out of tree branches, they had to wear long sleeves to prevent being stuck by the tree's thorns as they moved about. The clothes also prevented sunburn, a major problem for people who work in Florida sun. Of course, these clothes only made hot work hotter.

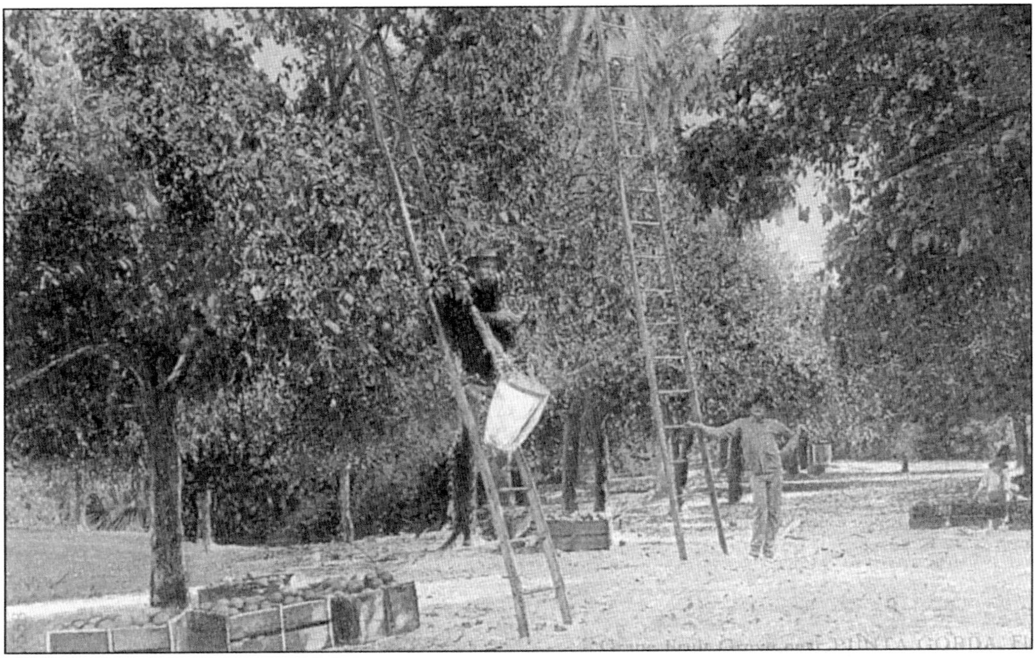

Ladders like these were made of split cypress trees, could be as long as 40 feet, and were very heavy. Workers would lean the tall ladders against the stronger limbs of the tree when they picked. Over the years, it became harder to find workers willing to climb such tall ladders. Trees are kept much shorter now, and so are the ladders used to climb them.

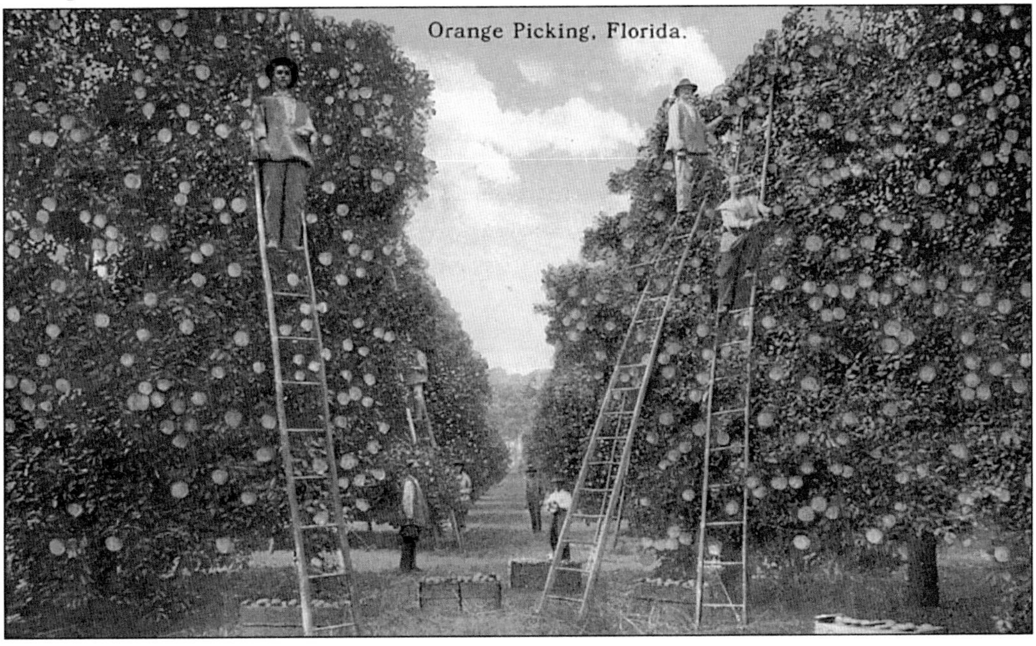

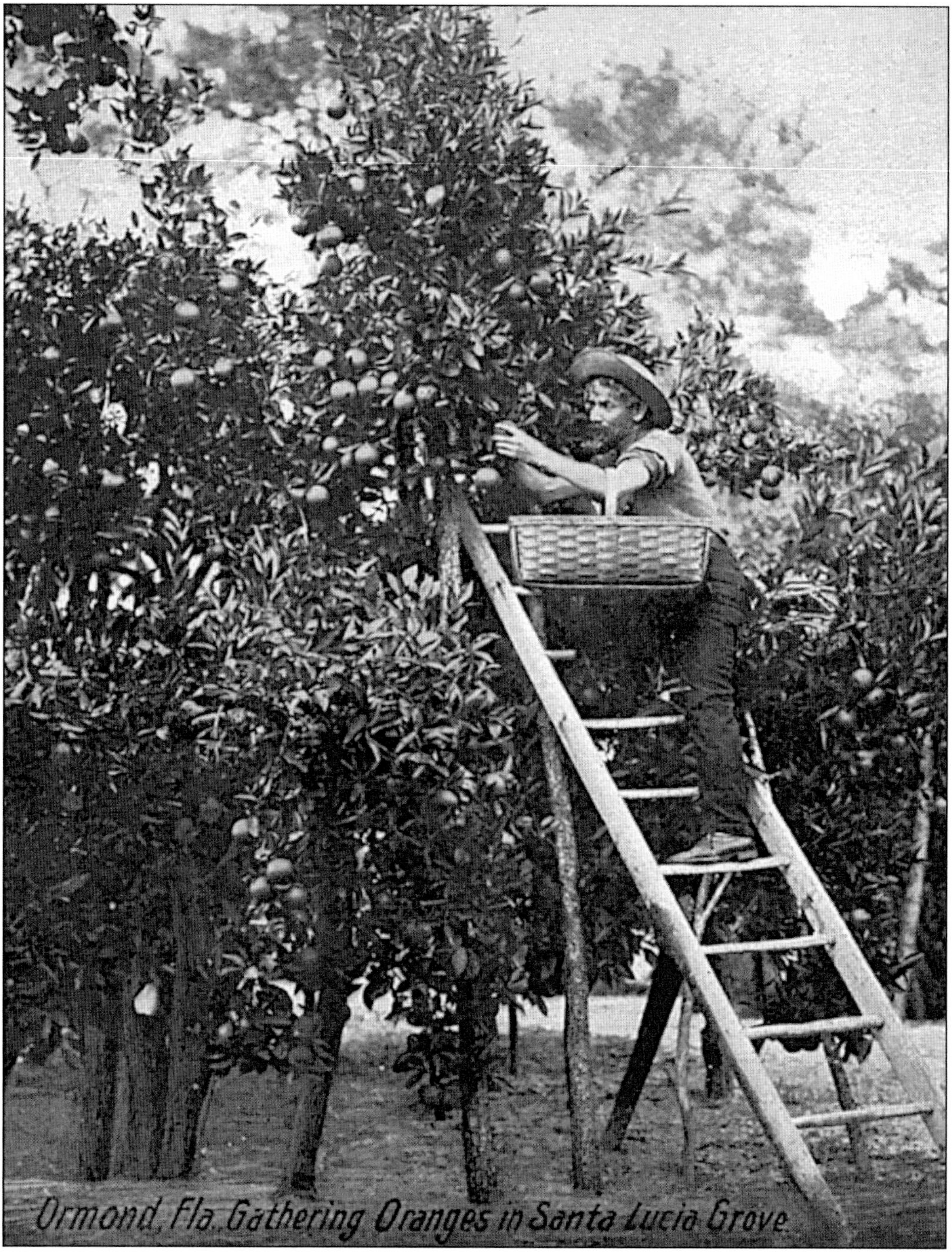

A woven basket like the one shown here may have been useful for homeowners who were lucky enough to have their own citrus right outside their door.

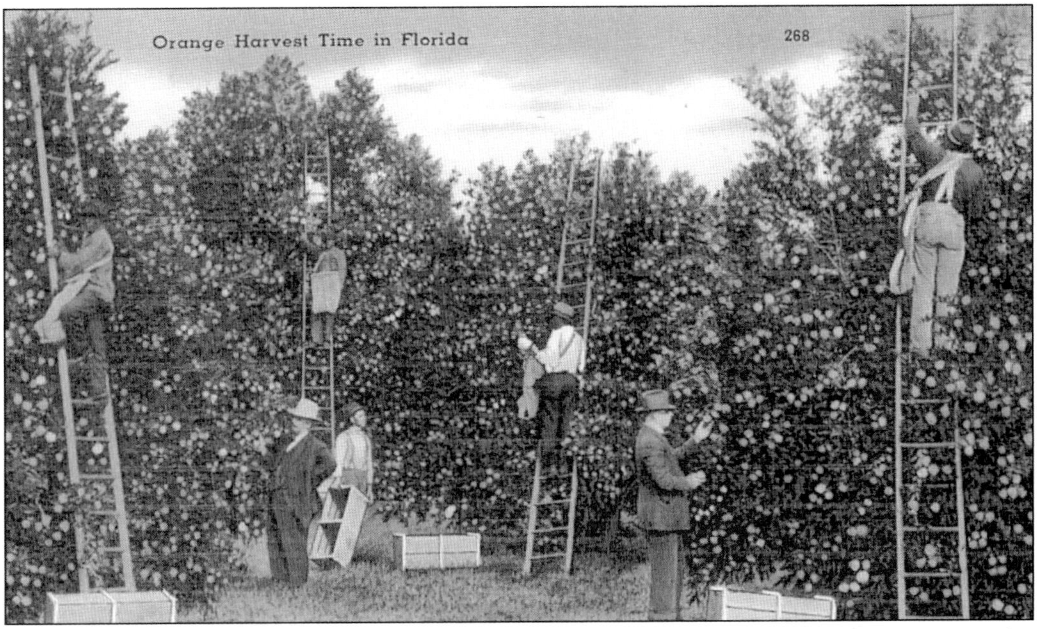

Field supervisors (or field riders, as they were sometimes known) kept the crew in line. This included setting a picking price and insuring that the picking job was done correctly. The above card is postmarked Kendall, April 20, 1950.

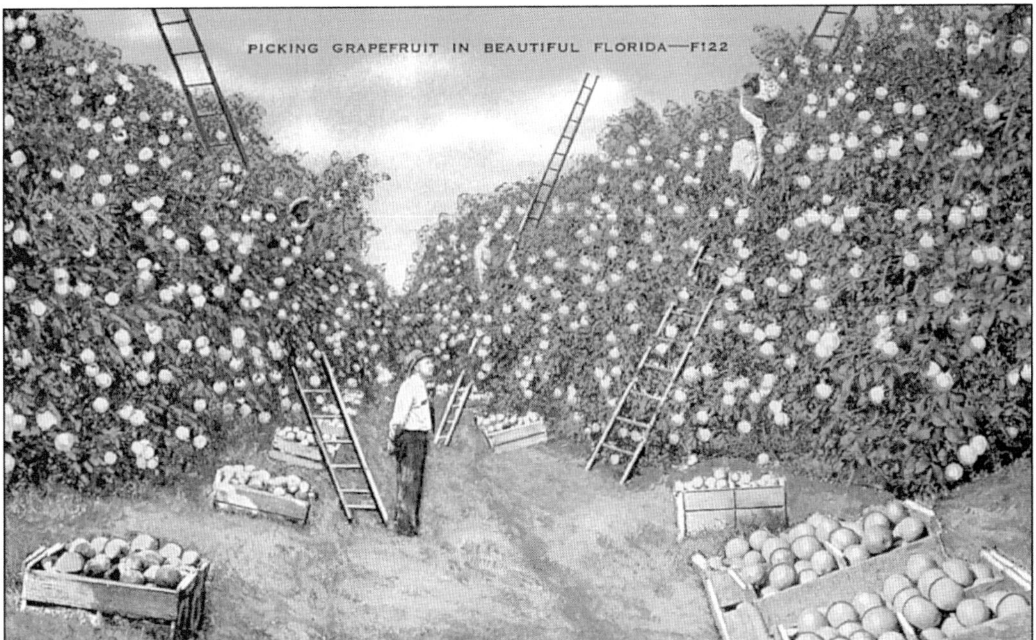

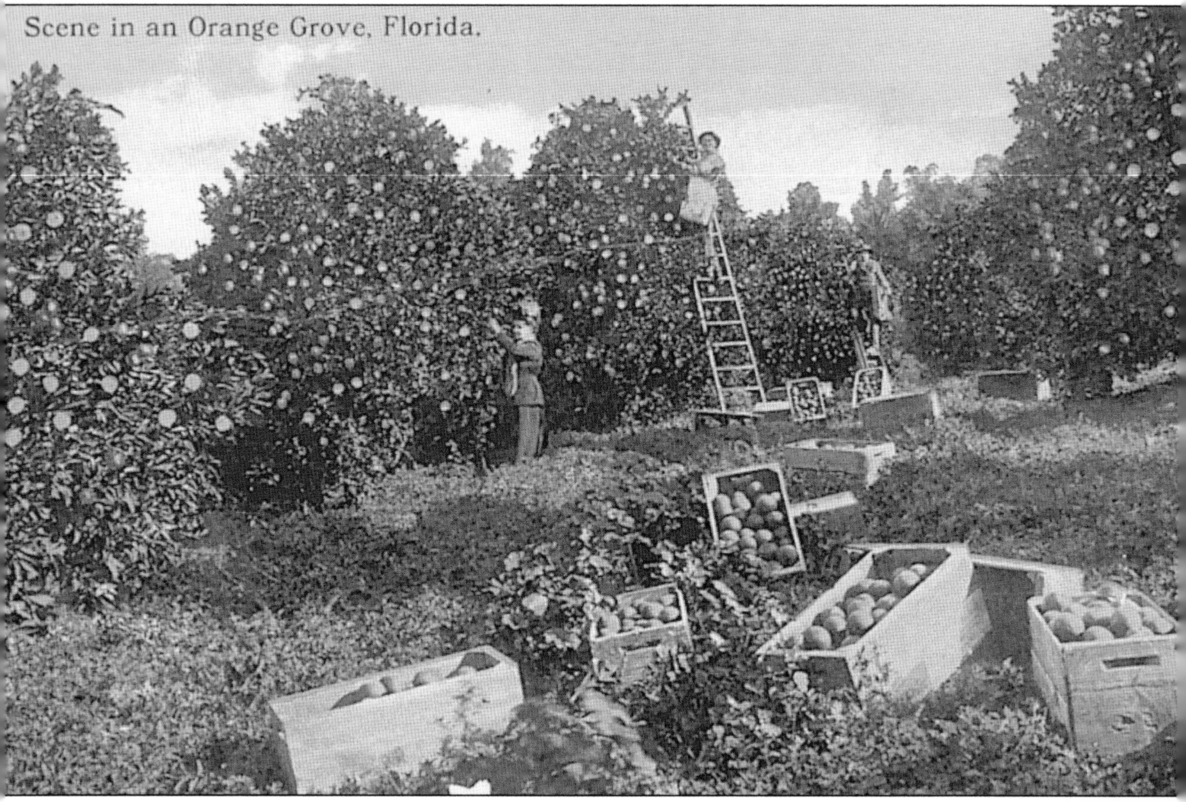

The "field boxes" used by pickers would weigh approximately 15 pounds and would hold 90 pounds of fruit when full. These full boxes, with about 200 pieces of fruit in each, would then be lifted into a truck or wagon to be taken out of the groves. The average worker can pick 70-80 boxes of fruit per day; the pay for picking is negotiated at each grove, and it is based on the volume of each crop. This card is postmarked St. Petersburg, March 9, 1916.

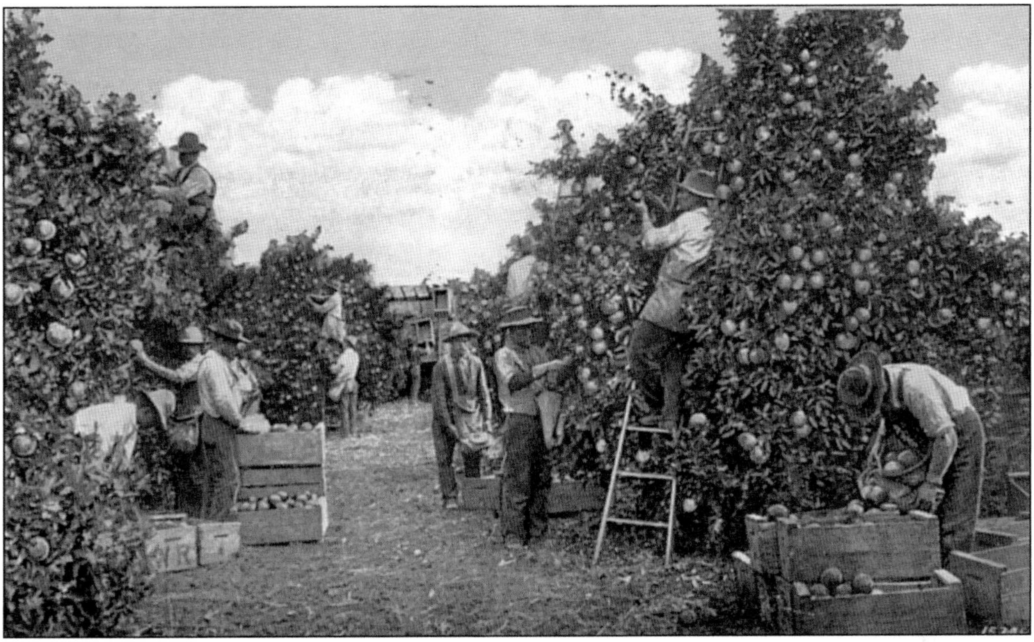

In the 1970s, we owned two adjoining 40-acre blocks of Temple oranges and tangerines along the St. John's Marsh in the northwestern part of Indian River County. White-tailed deer came out of the surrounding woods at night to feed on the tender leaves of the very young citrus trees. Bucks would use their racks and destroy young trees by rubbing their horns against them. We would often see a dozen or more deer when we drove through the groves at night. The postcard above is postmarked Sebring, December 17, 1926.

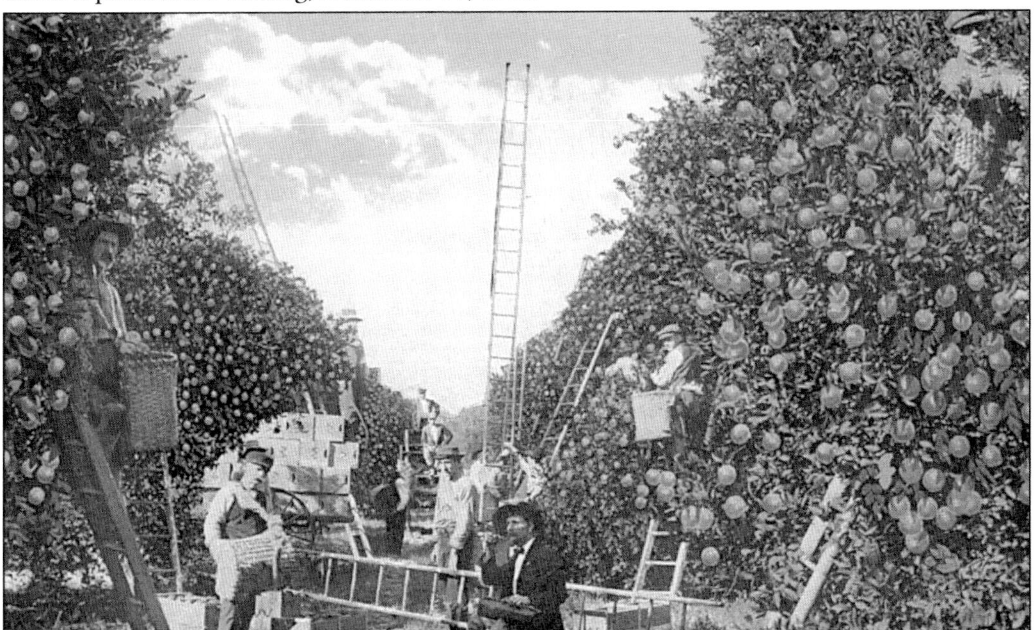

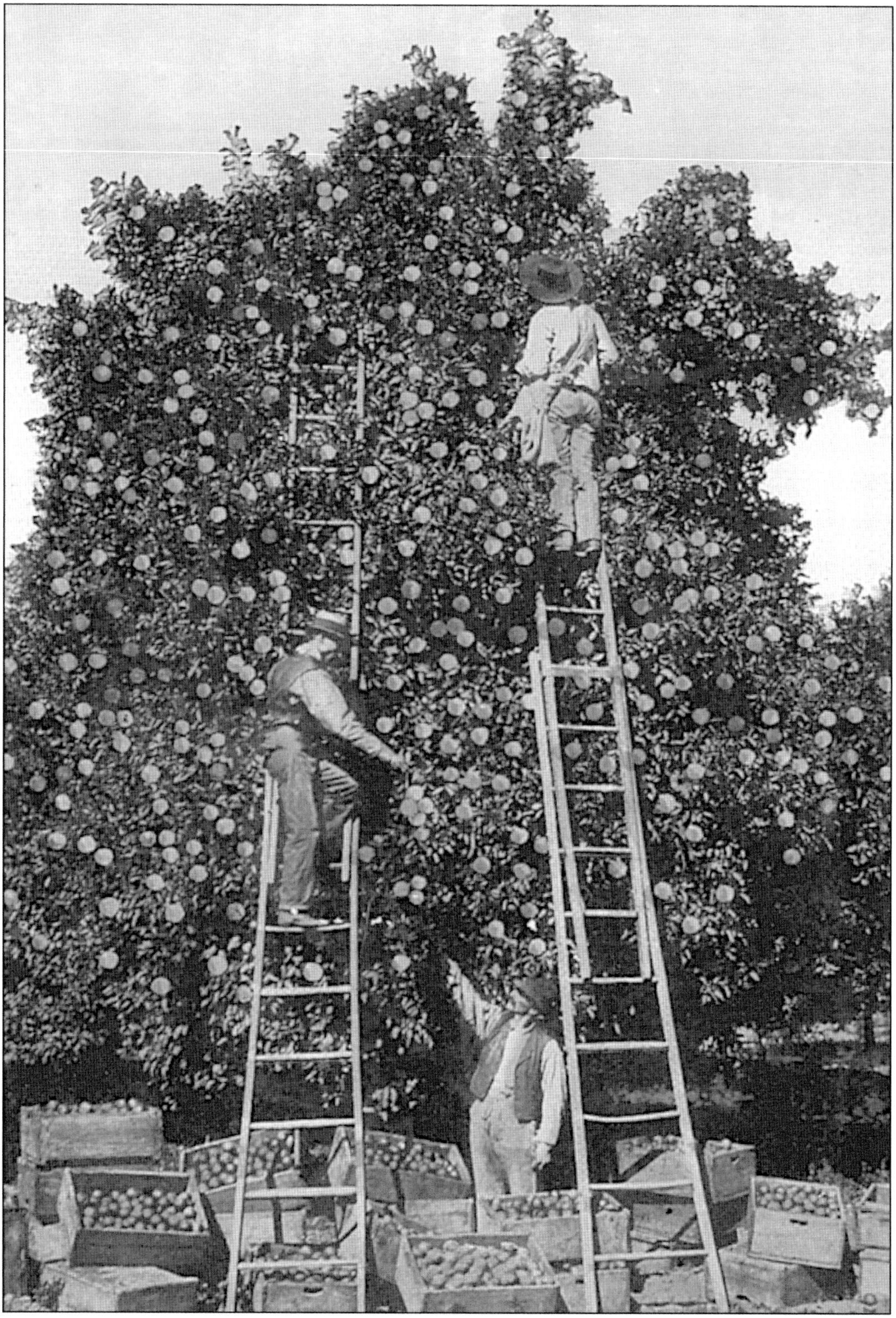

Industrious workers nailed two short ladders together to reach the top of these tall trees.

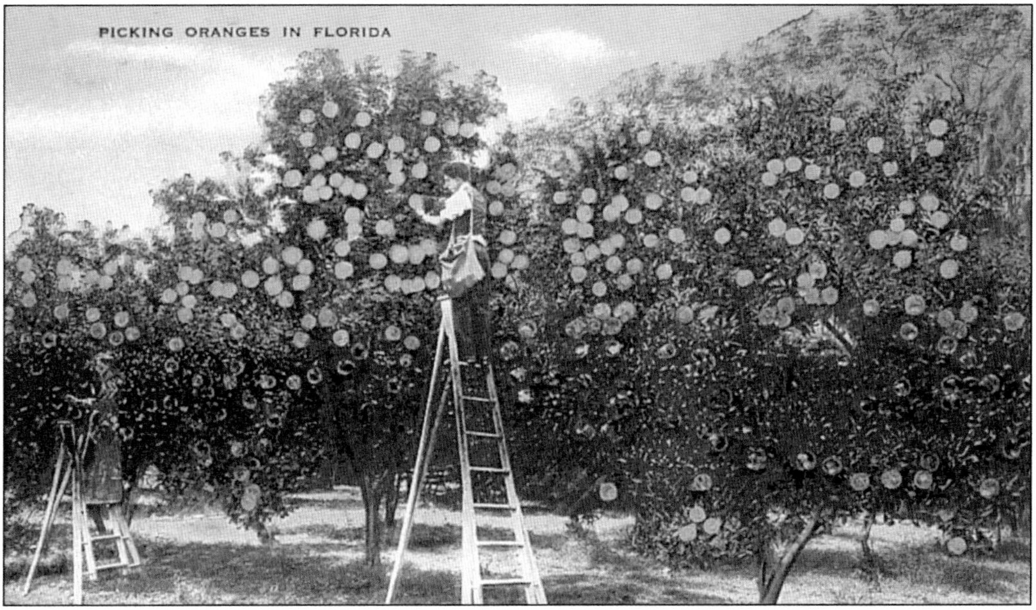

In winter, problems arise when the air dips below 28 degrees for more than four hours. These temperatures can cause leaves and twigs to die back and fruit to be damaged. Sub-freezing temperatures cause the juice sacs within fruit to burst and ultimately dry out. If fruit is damaged, it can be picked and juiced to salvage the crop. The card above is postmarked West Palm Beach, December 30, 1930.

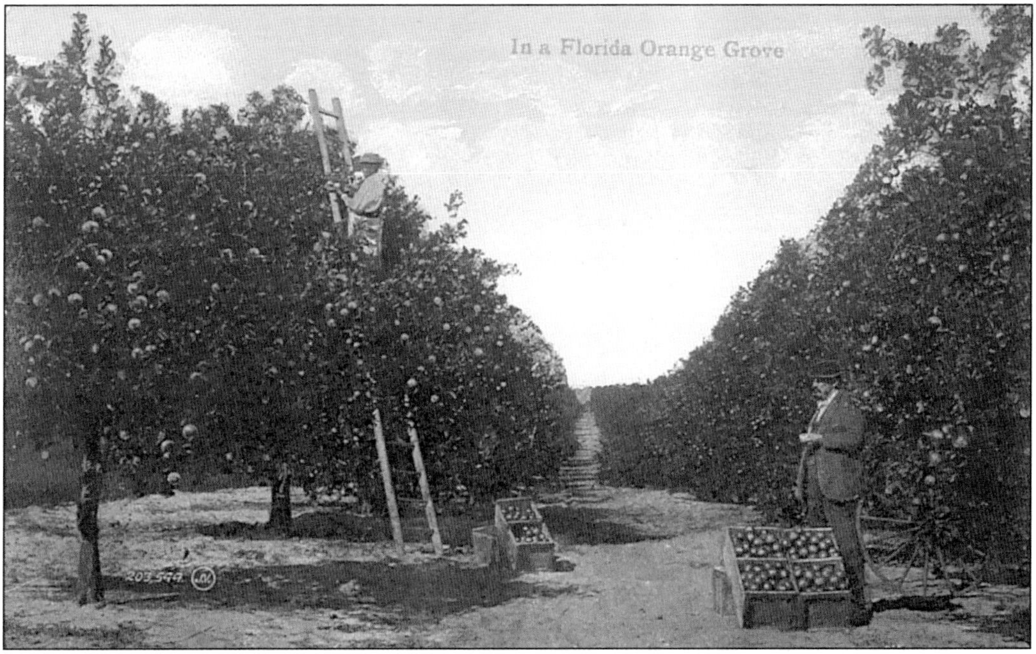

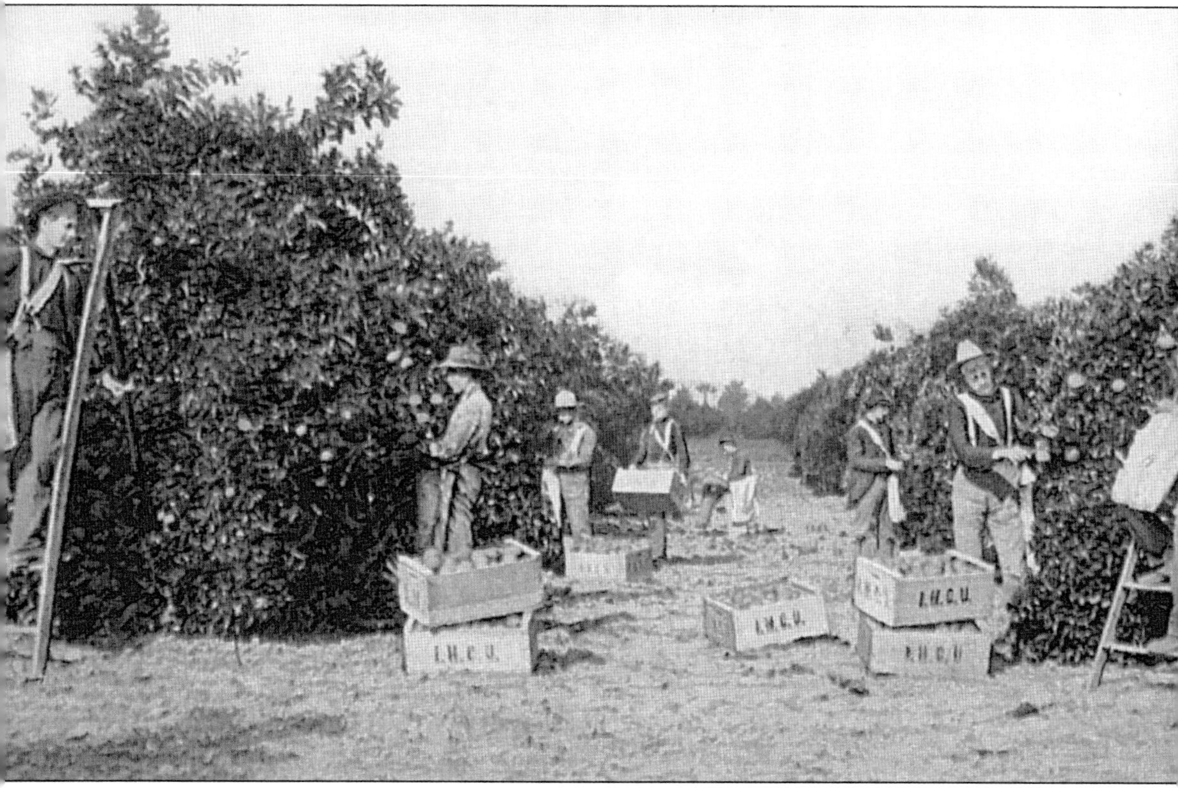

I graduated from Florida Southern College in 1969 with a degree in citrus (my son Randy graduated with the same degree in 1998). The course of study in my day included departmental field trips to groves around Lakeland, Florida. The entire class could ride in Professor Lyle's Rambler.

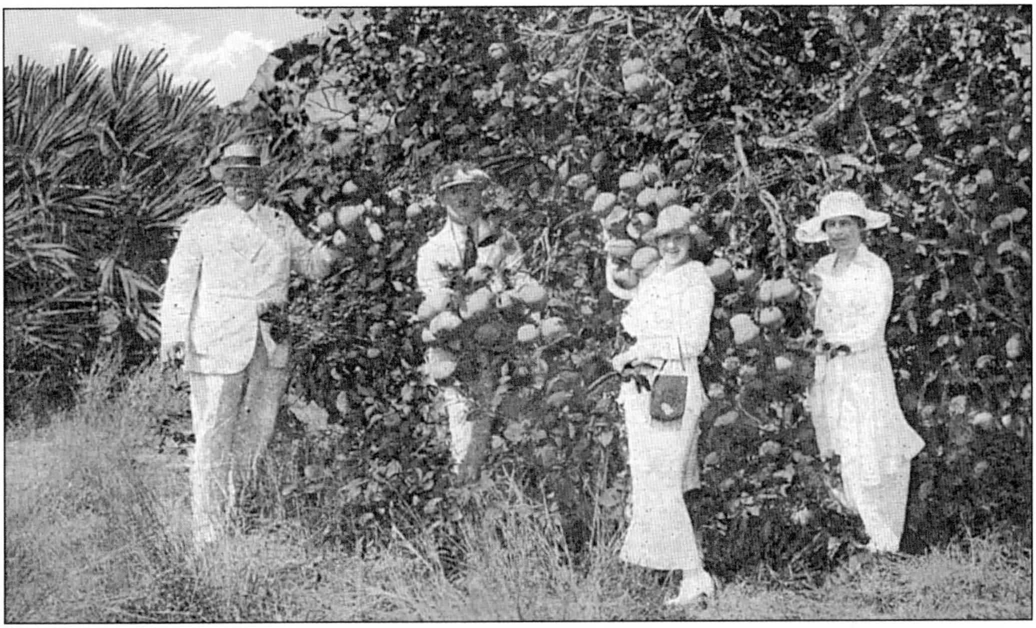

The message on the above image reads, "I see thousands of these Grape-fruit trees every day and have eat several messes of them. Will get all the oranges I want today . . . Dee." This card is postmarked Wabasso, October 24, 1921, and the one below is Sanford, March 2, 1907.

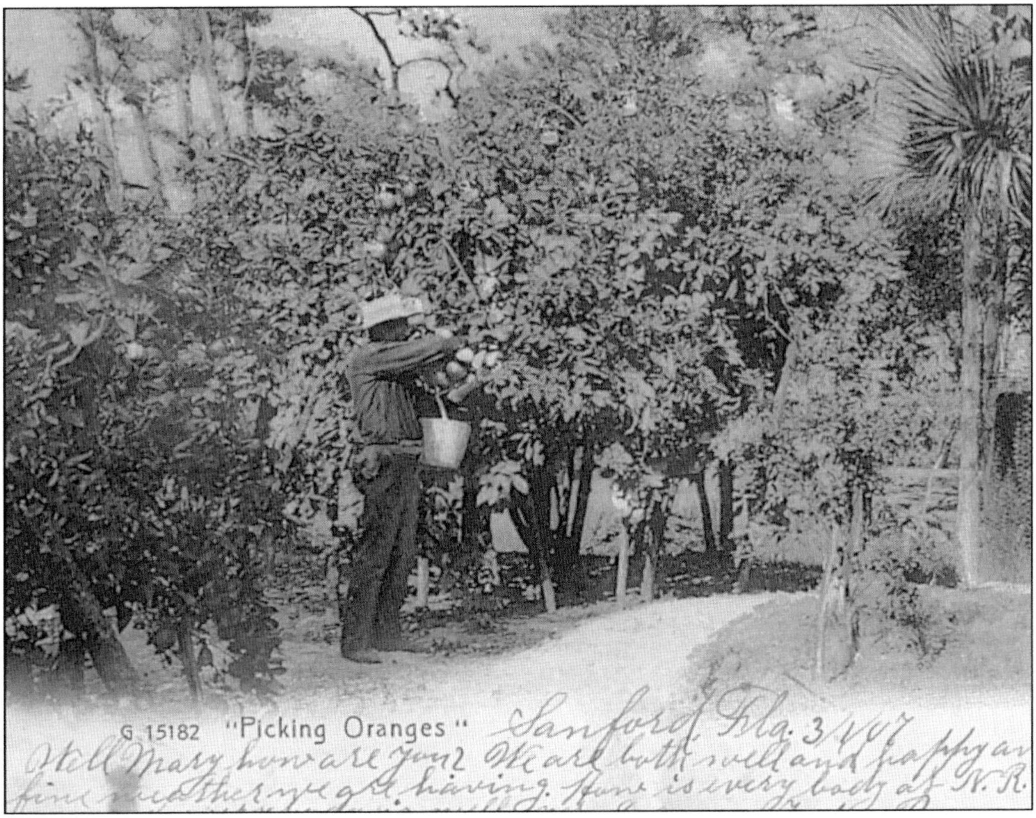

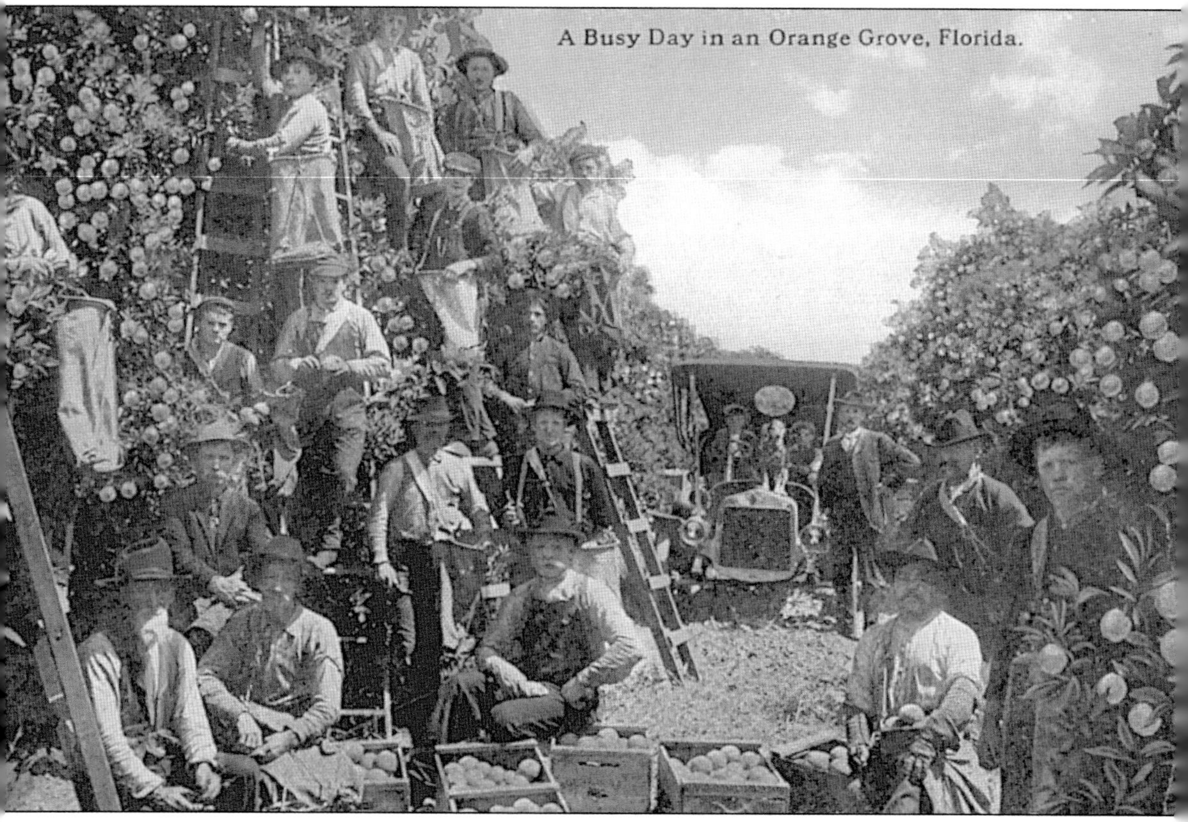

This postcard, like many others, features posed people. Without the camera there never would be this many people grouped together picking fruit. The real workers would be almost certainly men, as this was not considered women's work.

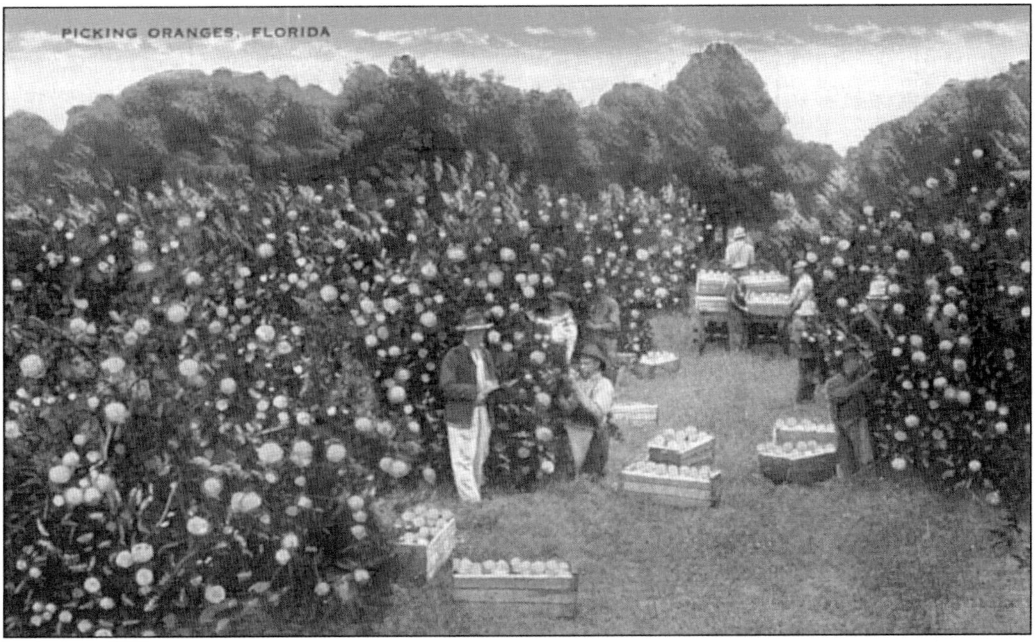

The postcard above says "There are those who like the Northland/ With its cold and its sleet/ Winter winds blowing through you/ As you hurry down the street/ Here we stroll among the roses/ In the sun that shines so warm/ Eating fruit and smelling flowers/ With our coats upon our arm." The postcard below is postmarked Sarasota, January 13, 1914.

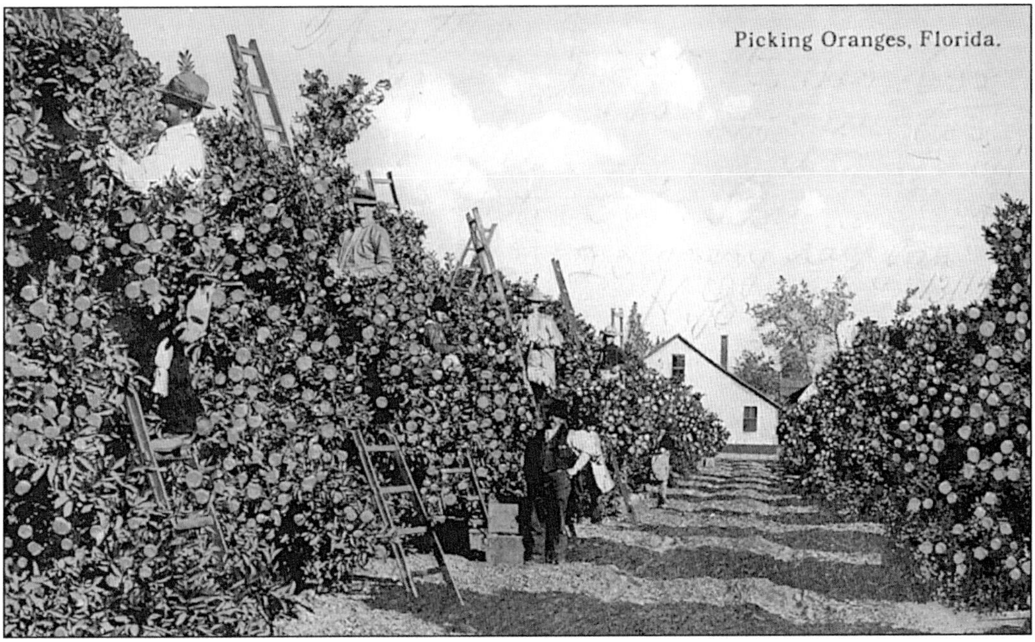

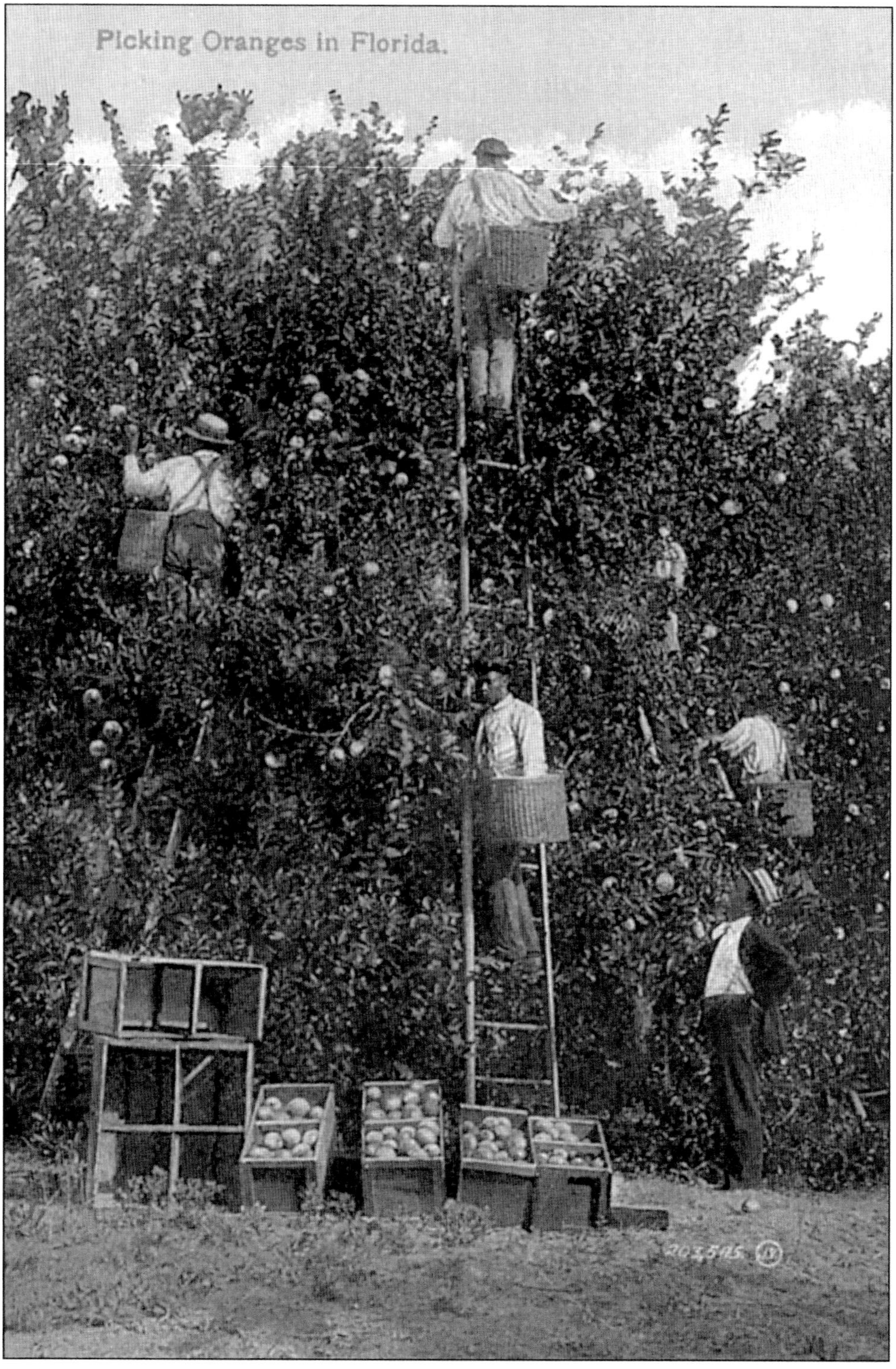

In the late 1900s, Eban B. Bean designed the type of wooden field boxes seen here. The box was called a "nail box," because that is how it was held together. This field box had two equal compartments to divide the pressure on the fruit.

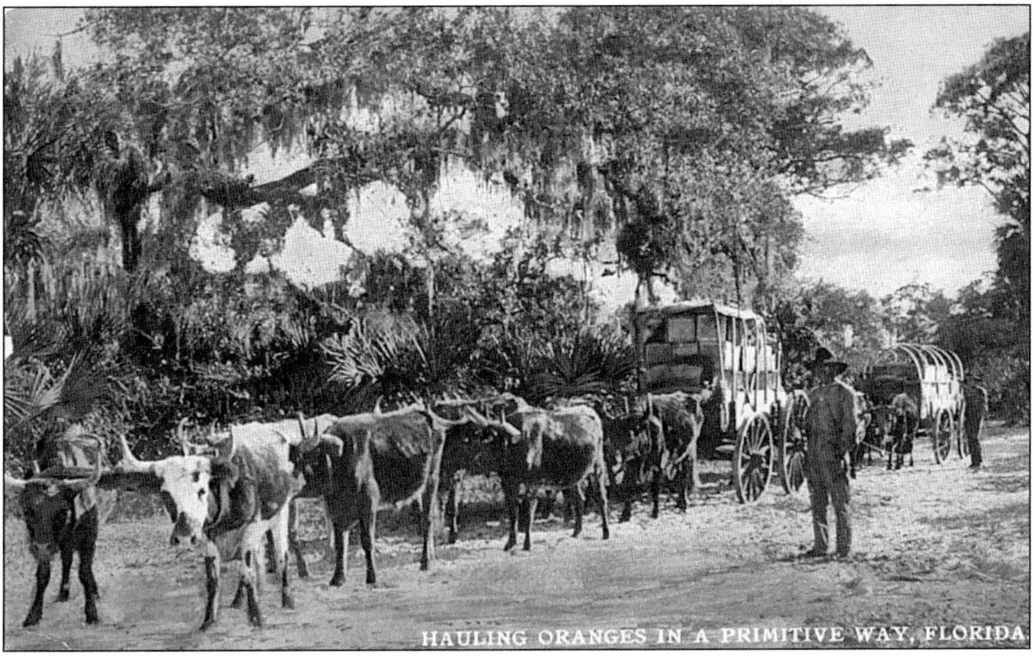

Growers often used oxen to pull the wagons of fruit out of the groves. Mules and bulls were also employed to help; in certain areas, long-horned wild Florida bulls would be captured and put into service. The image above is postmarked Tampa, January 31, 1912.

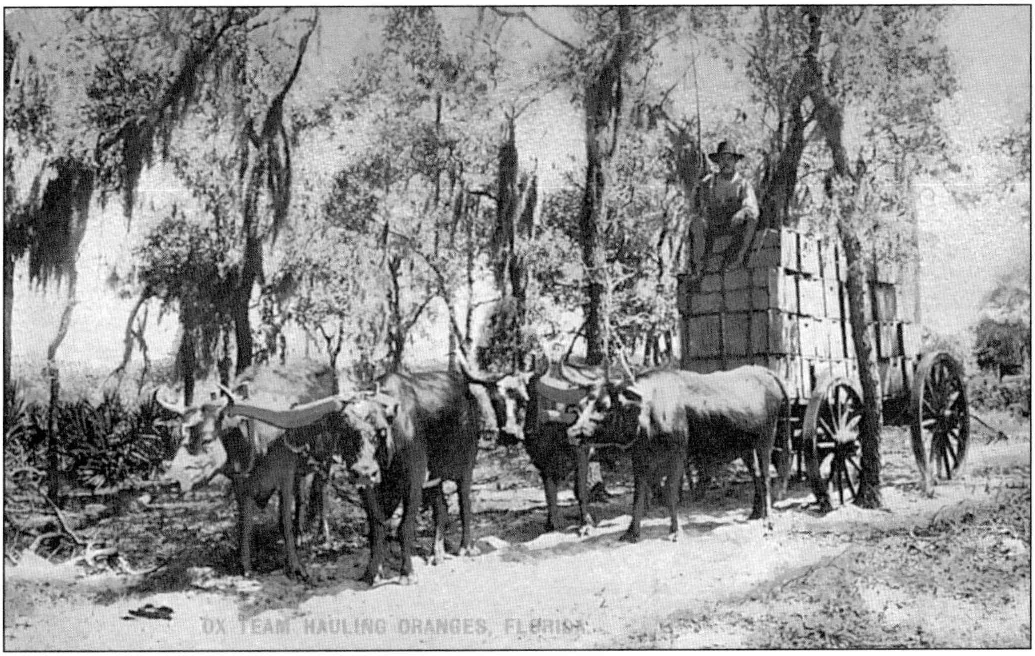

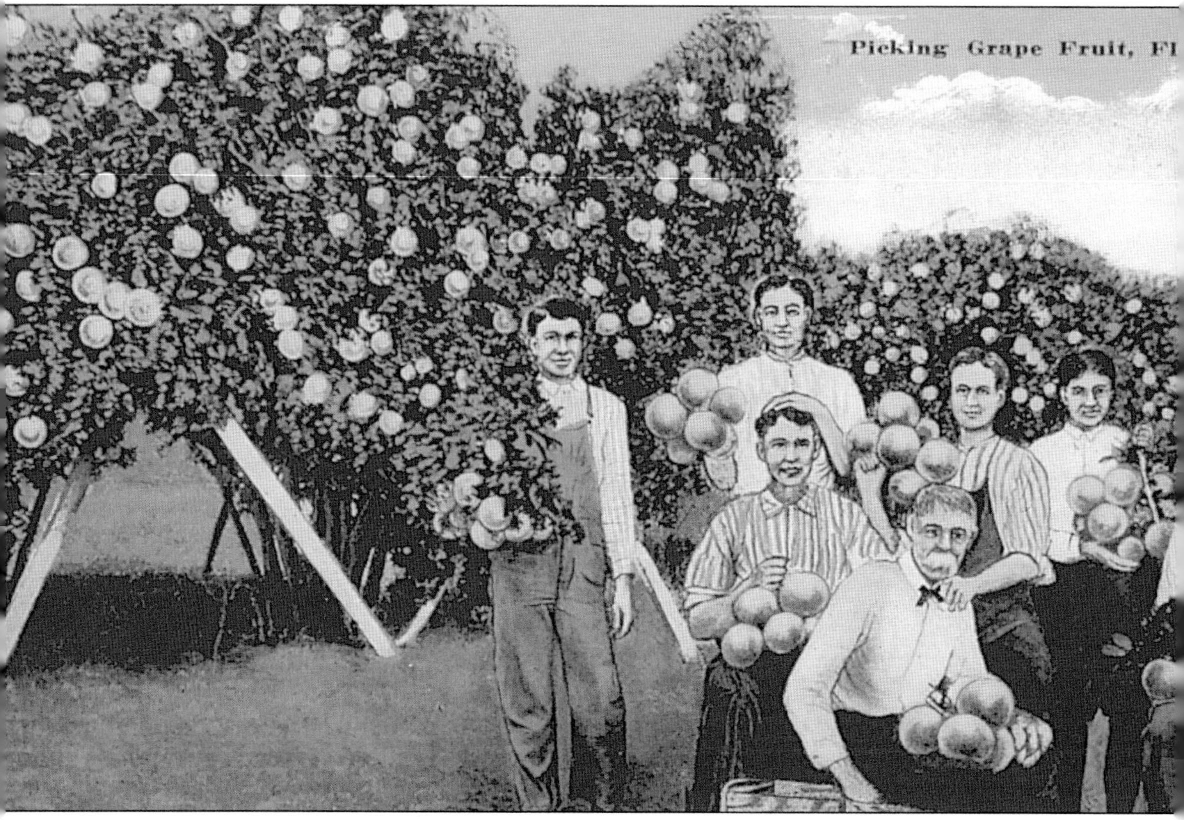

"Can you beat this where you live? How about sugar—can you get any now? We can only get a pound once in awhile. Minnie E. Williams." This image is postmarked St. Petersburg, Florida, December 21, 1917.

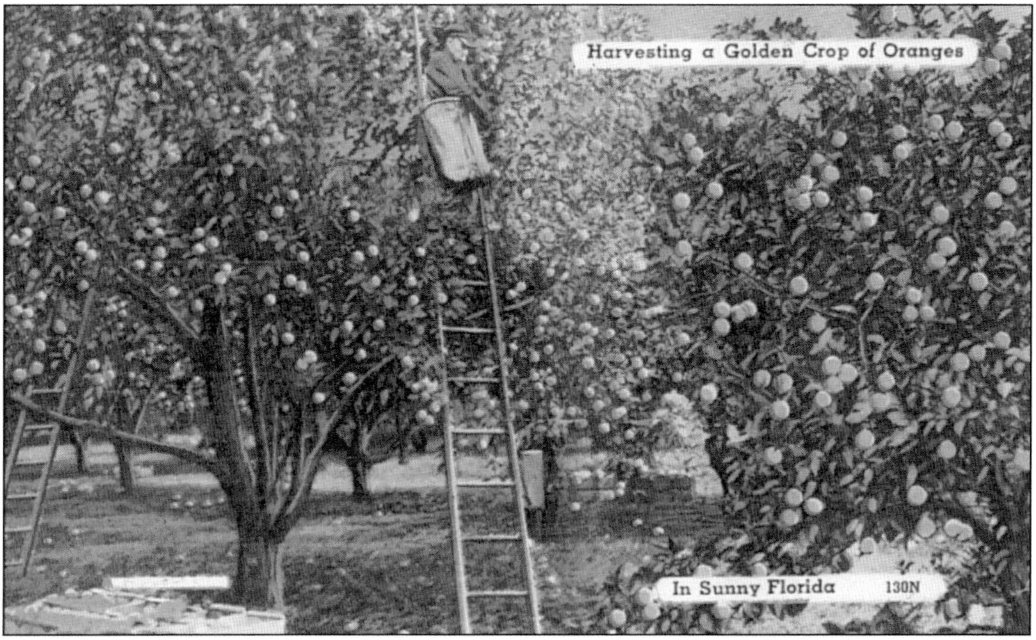

When I was a teenager, my Dad and I would drive from our home in Orlando to check on the family grove in Ft. Pierce. An added bonus to our day was a stop on the way home at the canals along the edge of Highway 60, in the St. John's Marsh, to try our luck at fishing. A typical catch would be 10 to 20 mudfish. What a good way to end our day together. The card below is postmarked Orlando, January 30, 1919.

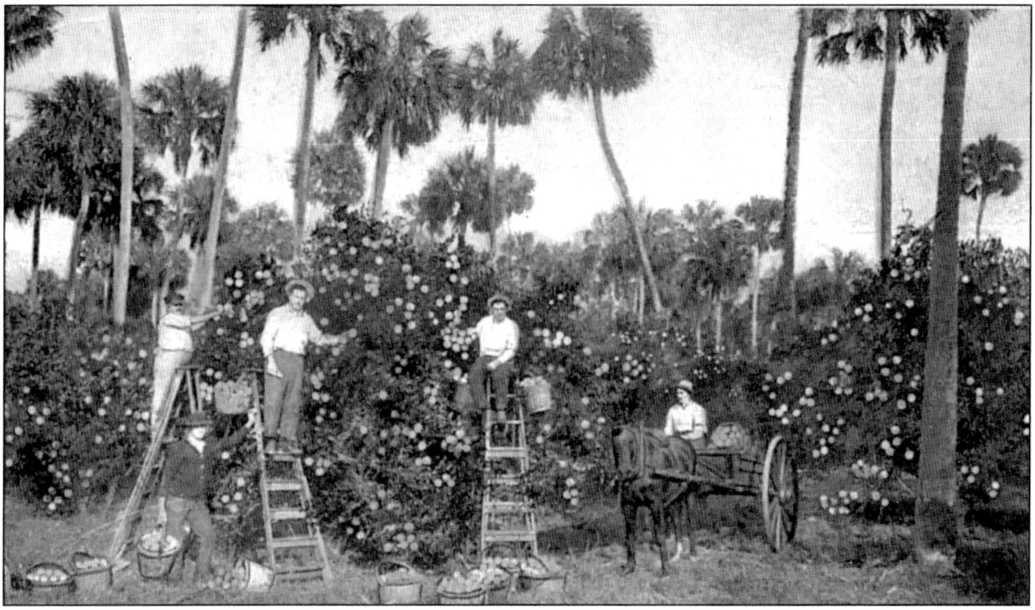

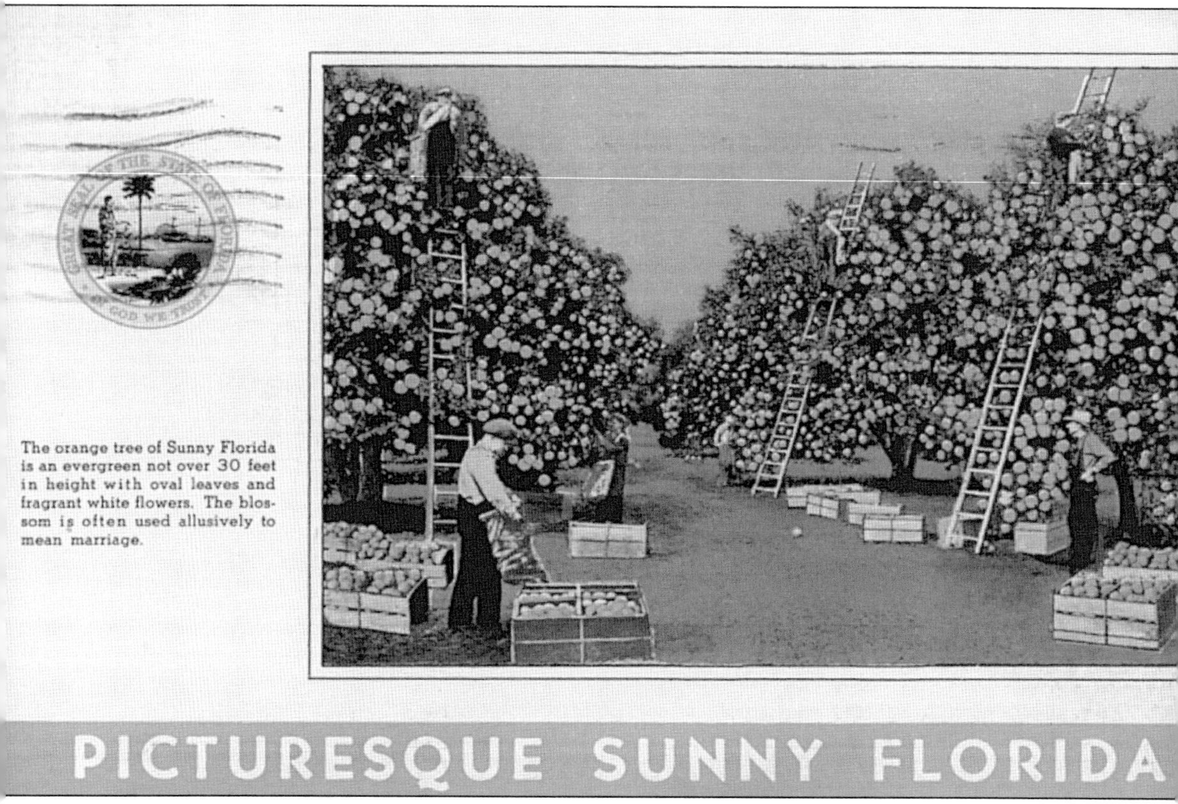

About 26,000 pickers work about eight months a year in the Florida citrus industry. At the end of the season, many of these people move north to work in the peach and apple industries before returning for the next season.

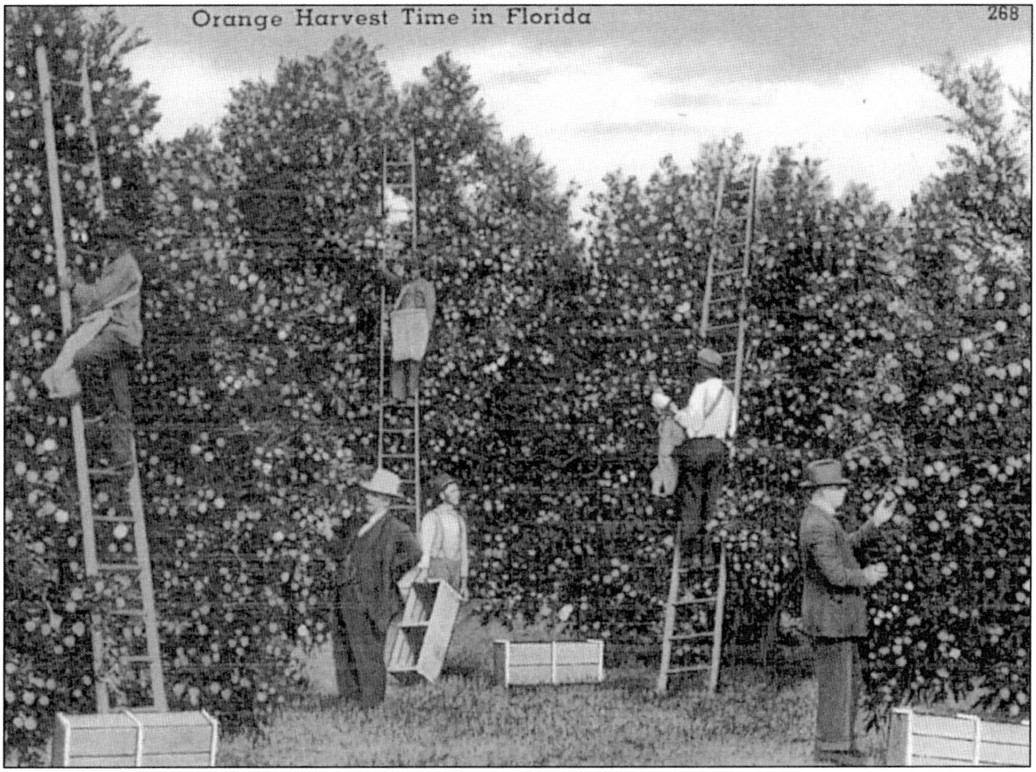

The top postcard is postmarked Lake Helen, January 31, 1910, and contains the following: "Hope this finds you nearly well. We are all right and happy because we don't have to put on rubbers and wraps to go out doors. Emma."

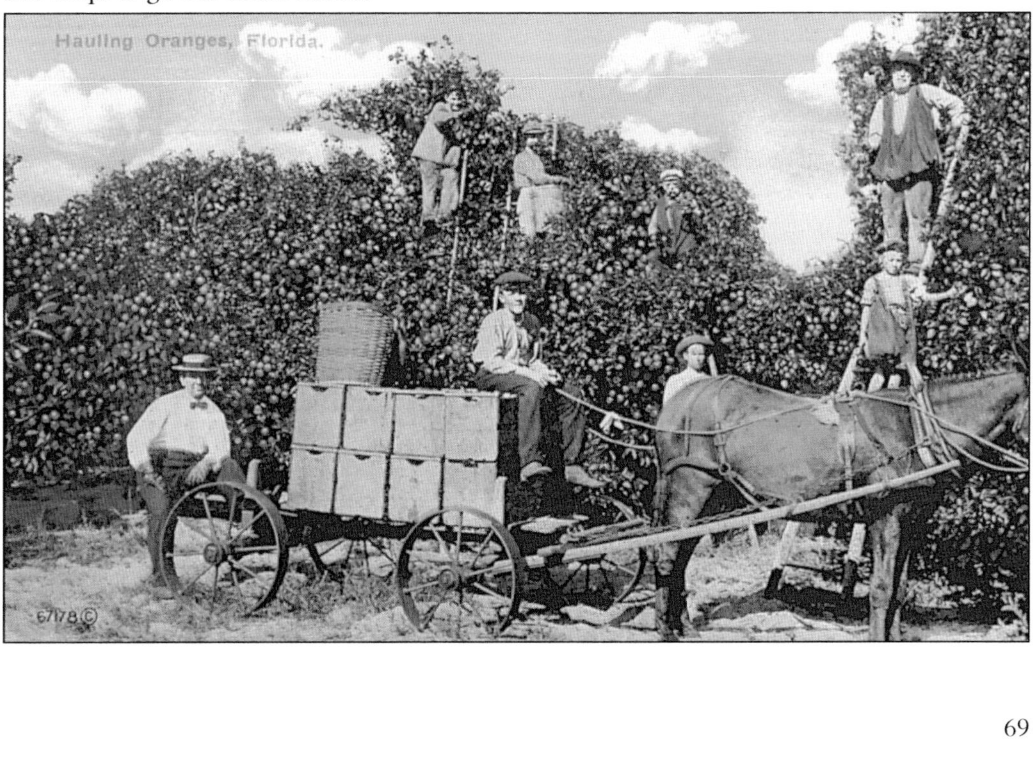

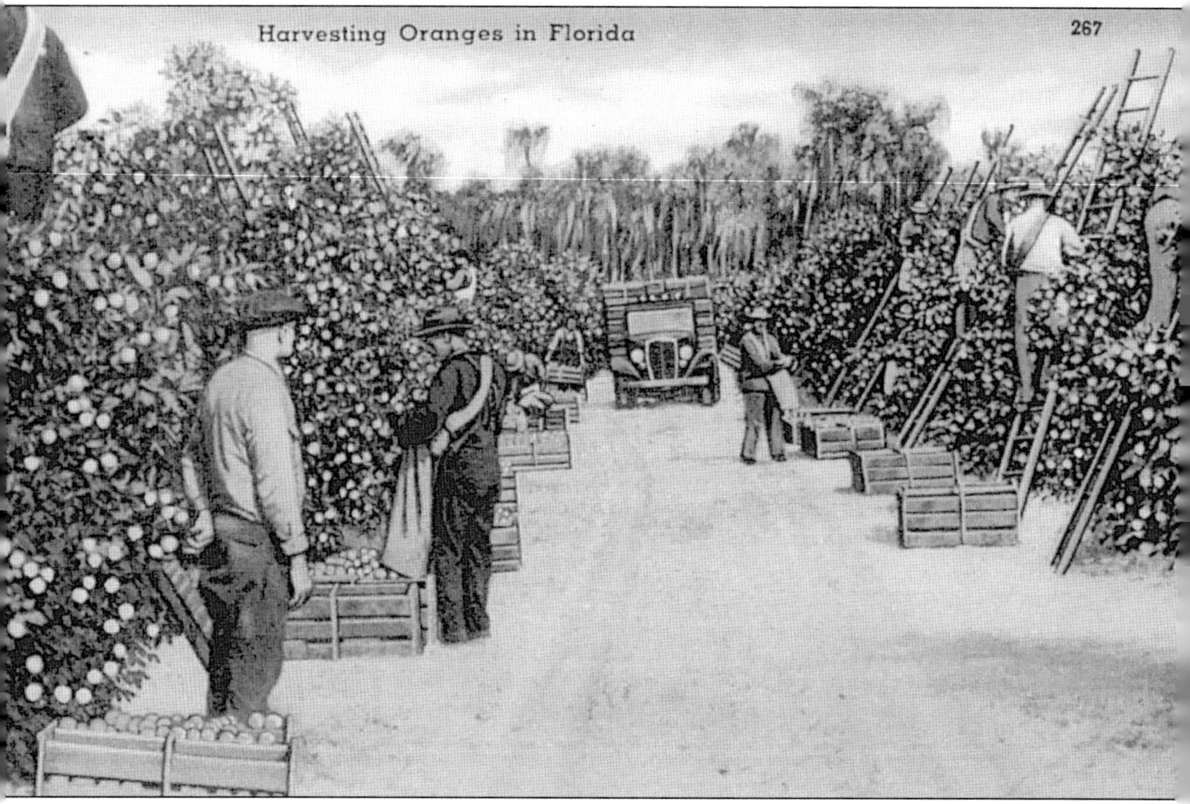

When our boys, Richard and Randy, were very young, a favorite family outing was to go to our Valencia orange grove in Vero Beach and "bump the bunnies." As citrus grove owners know, in the late afternoons, especially after a rain shower or after the grove has just been mowed, Florida cottontail rabbits move out from their hiding places to feed. We would drive in our truck up and down the rows of trees. When we spotted a cottontail, he would freeze as still as a statue. Only when we "bumped" our hands on the sides or top of the truck would the bunny turn his cottontail and scamper away to the squeals of two little boys' laughter. This card is postmarked Jensen Beach, January 25, 1951.

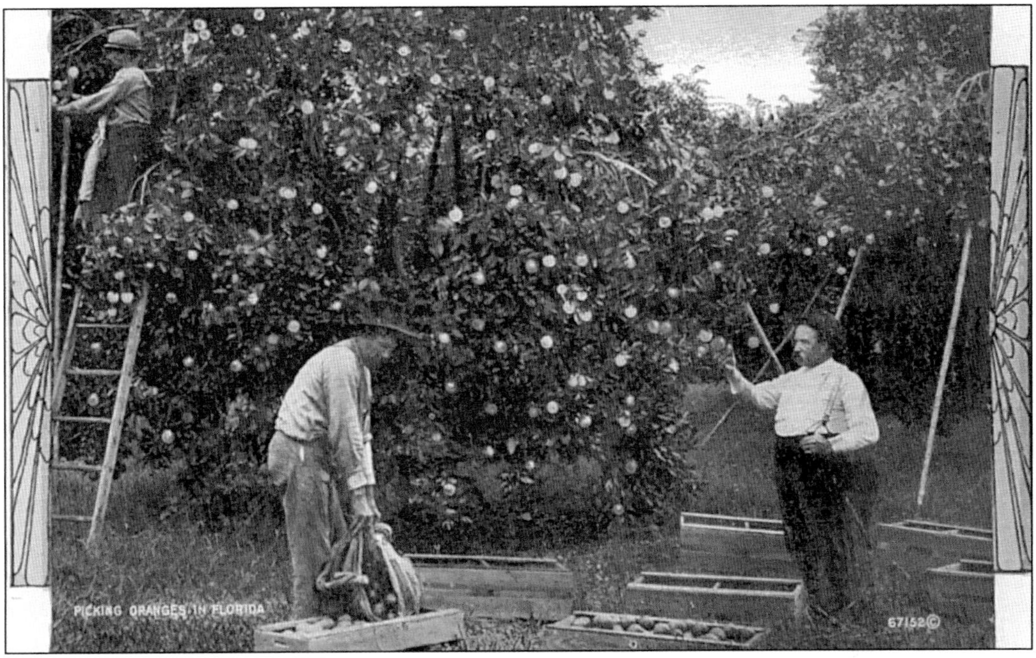

The above postcard contains the following message: "Hello Herbert . . . Now if you want a good job, come down and pick oranges. Beats trapping all to pieces. Grandma."

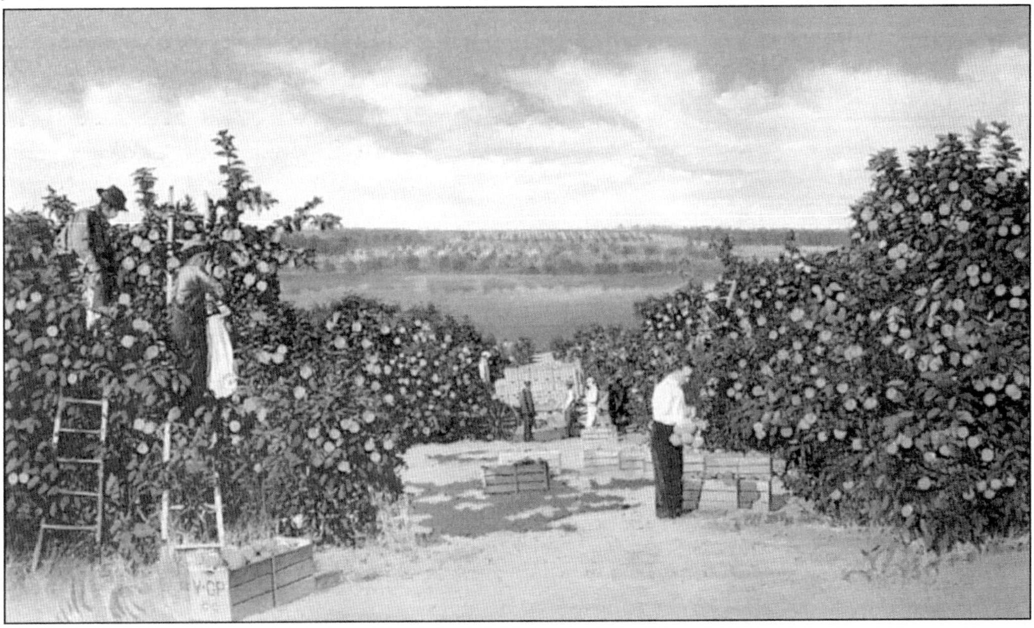

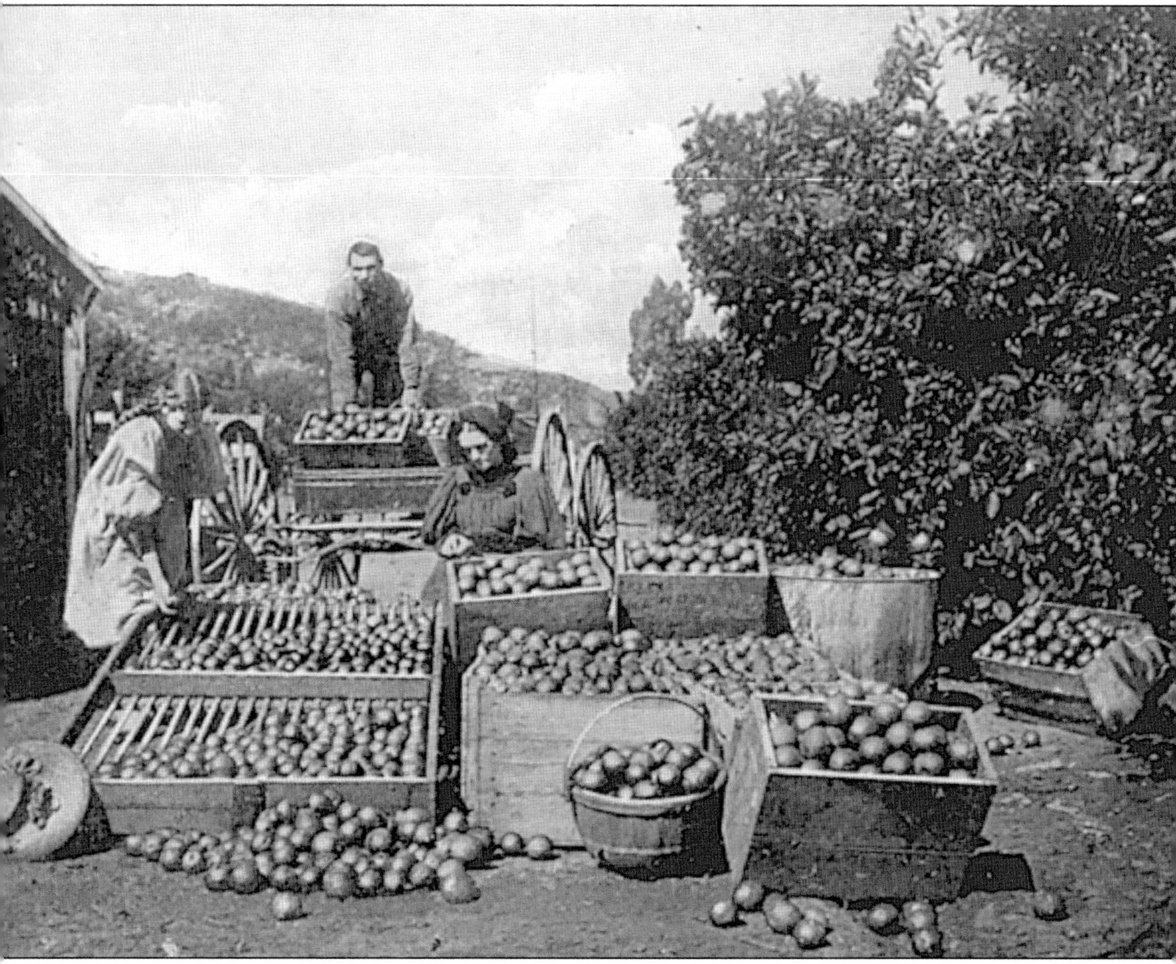

In the days before mechanized sorting, workers divided fruit by size and quality in the groves. They would place fruit in wooden devices with slats placed in varying lengths apart from one another for easier division. "Grading" in the field made it easier for fruit to be packed on the spot and then sold to merchants or given to distributors.

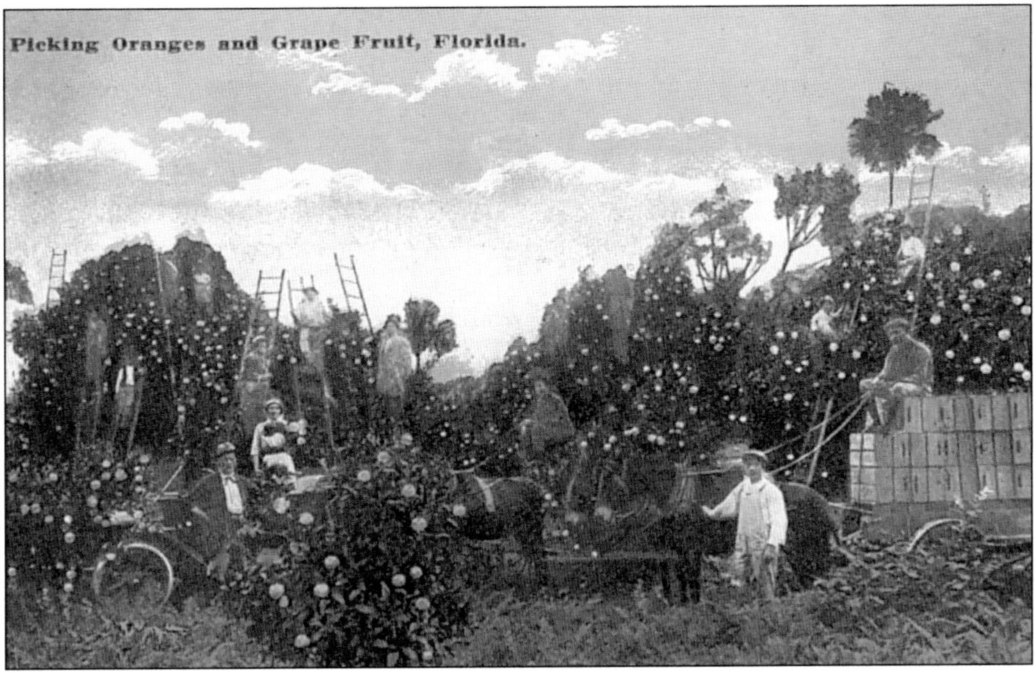

The postcard above is postmarked Fort Meyers, December 18, 1920. It reads, "Hello Sis, We are having a swell time and seeing a lot of pretty sites. Think I will try to bring Florida back with us. Fred and Evelyn."

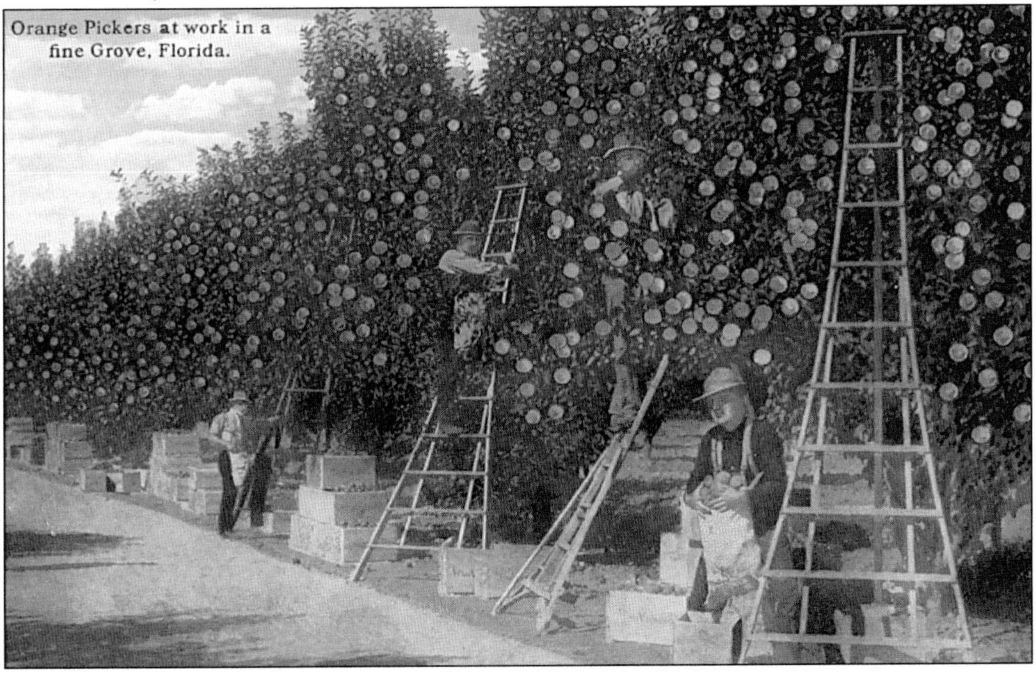

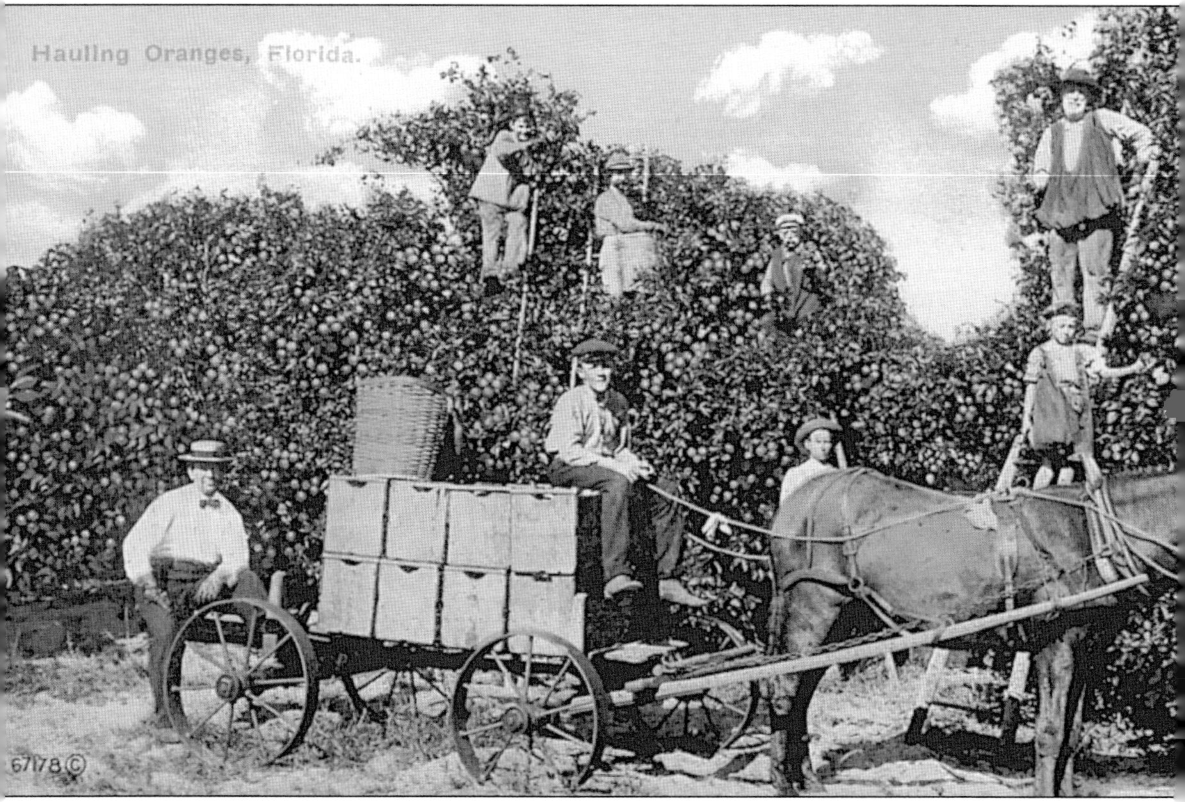

Fall and winter bring cooler temperatures and shortened periods of daylight. When there is less sunshine, citrus trees have less energy to derive from photosynthesis, and they become dormant and less vigorous. That state makes them less susceptible to the cold. Lower temperatures are welcome to a degree because they cause chlorophyll to leave a fruit's peel, bringing out the orange color. This card is postmarked McGraw, April 6, 1912.

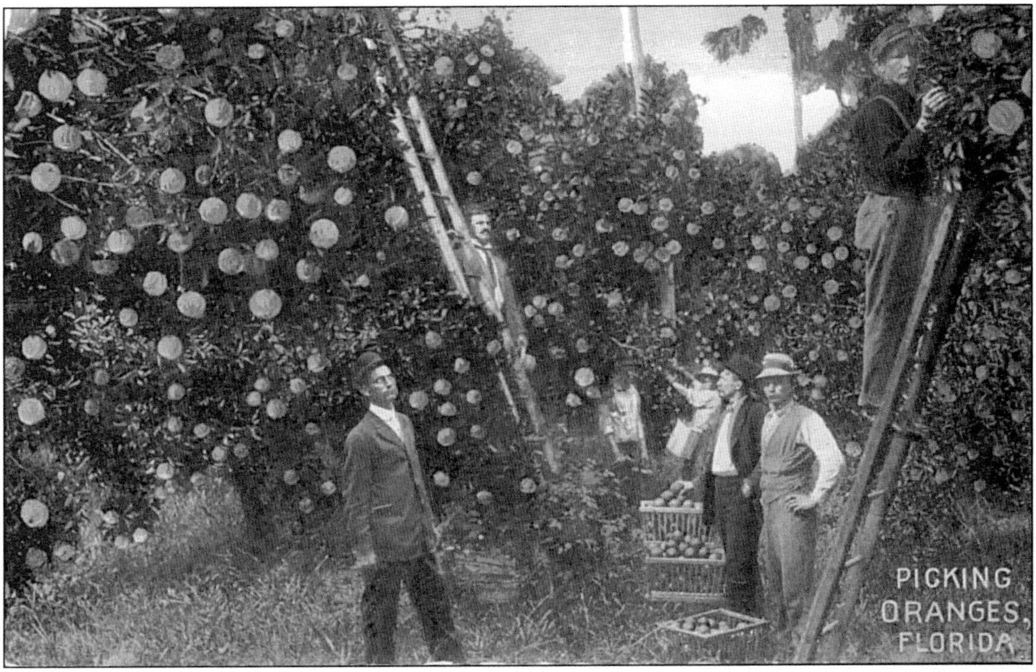

The top postcard is postmarked Hilliard, February 2, 1946, and its caption reads, "Dear Alice—We are just over the Florida line. Boy it is beautiful. Nice and warm. My cold is feeling lots better. Boy, what a time I had for a couple of days. Dr. D. put me on fruit juice and cod liver oil, but I was glad to take it. I was coughing like no body's business. Hope you are well again. Mother and Fred."

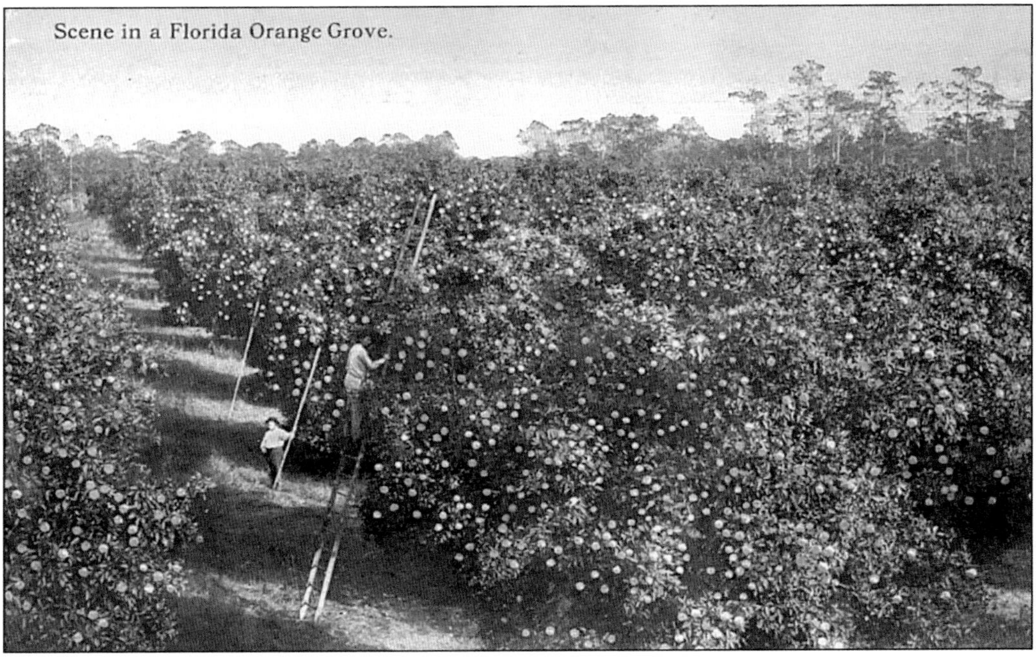

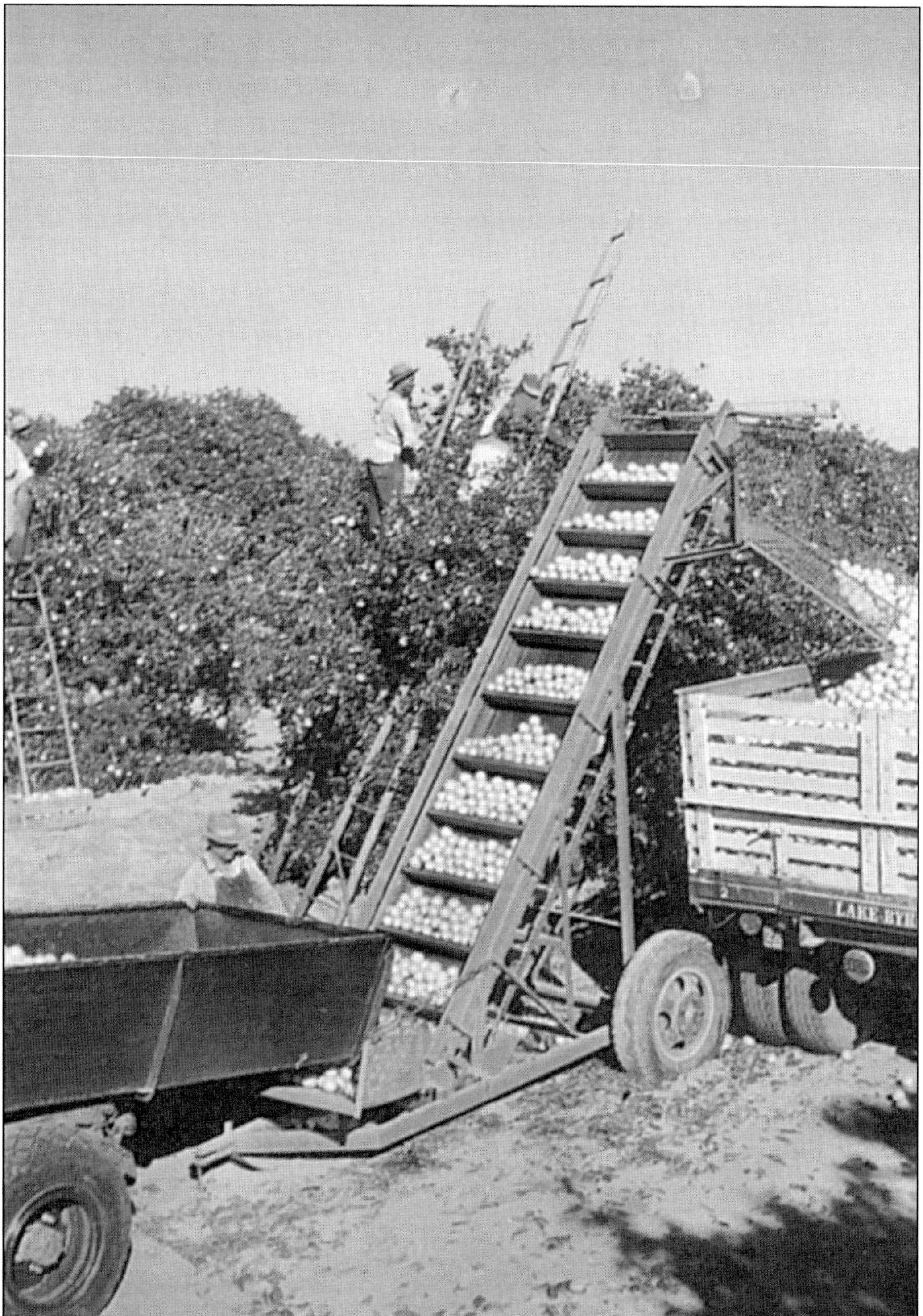

Machinery began to replace the strong arms and backs of the men who loaded fruit by hand. This fruit elevator loads fruit into a trailer destined for a juice plant.

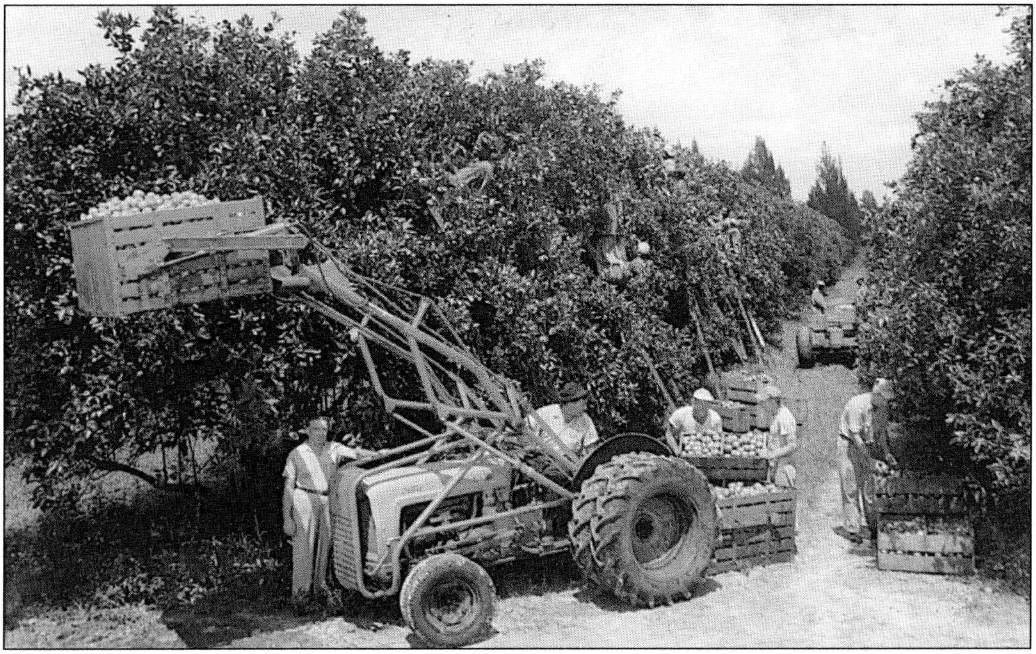

The evolution of harvesting saw individuals loading single boxes of fruit by hand change to the increasing use of larger harvesting equipment and containers. These containers held 8-10 boxes of fruit. The improvements helped the expanding industry move volume more quickly and efficiently to both packing houses and processing plants.

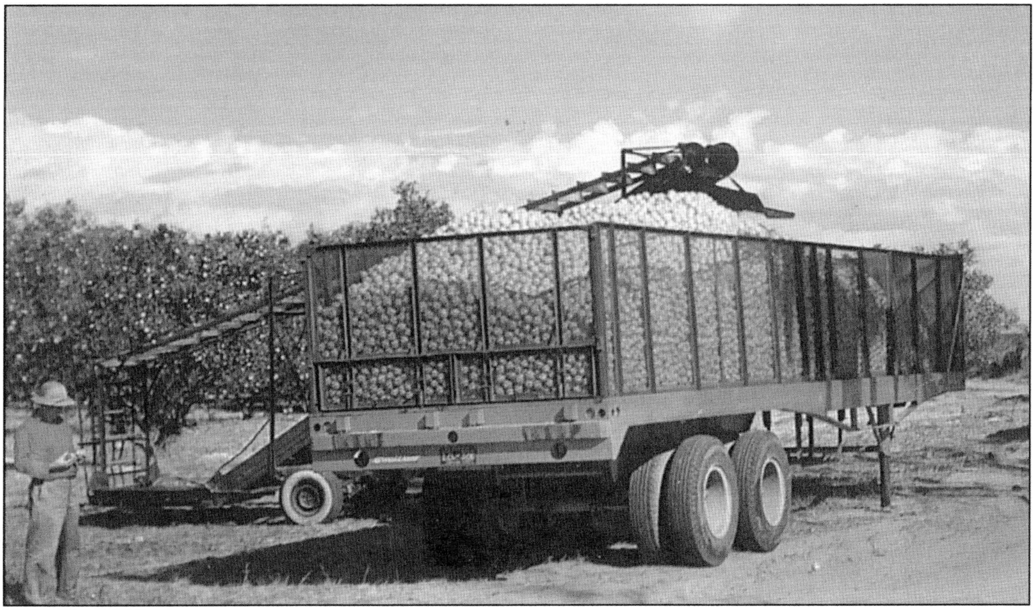

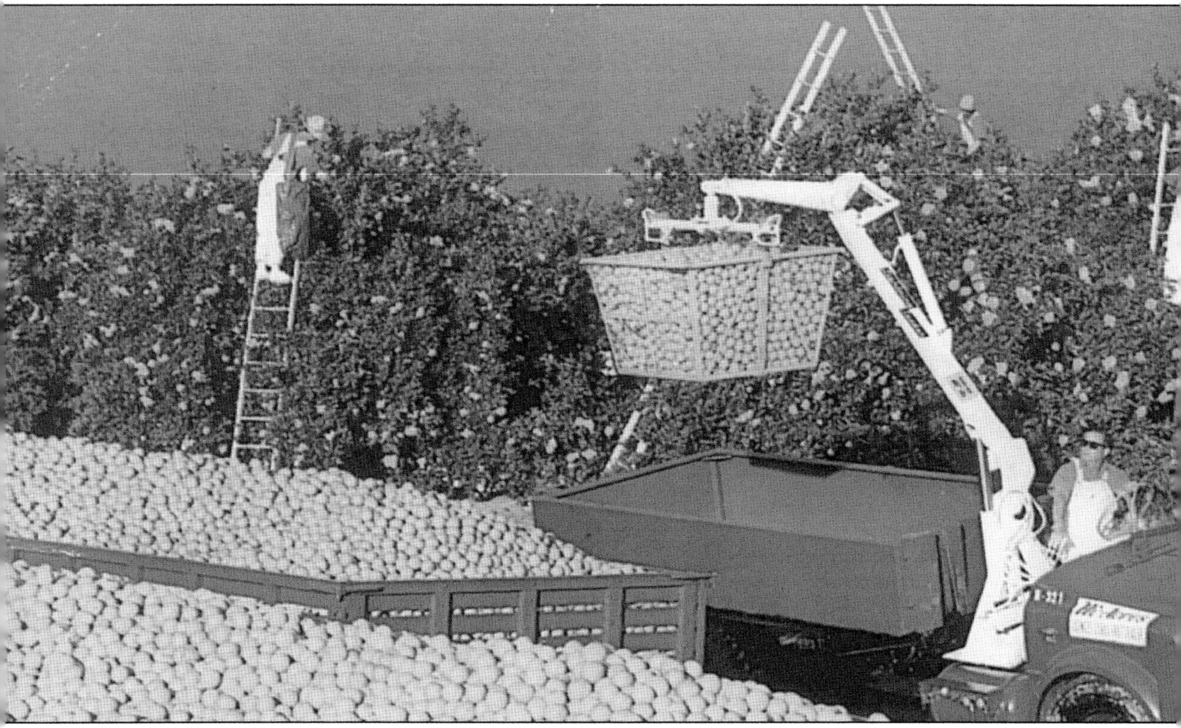

The advent of the "lightning loader" brought mechanization in harvesting to the present day. Despite these advancements, the industry still relies on the individual laborer to pick its crop.

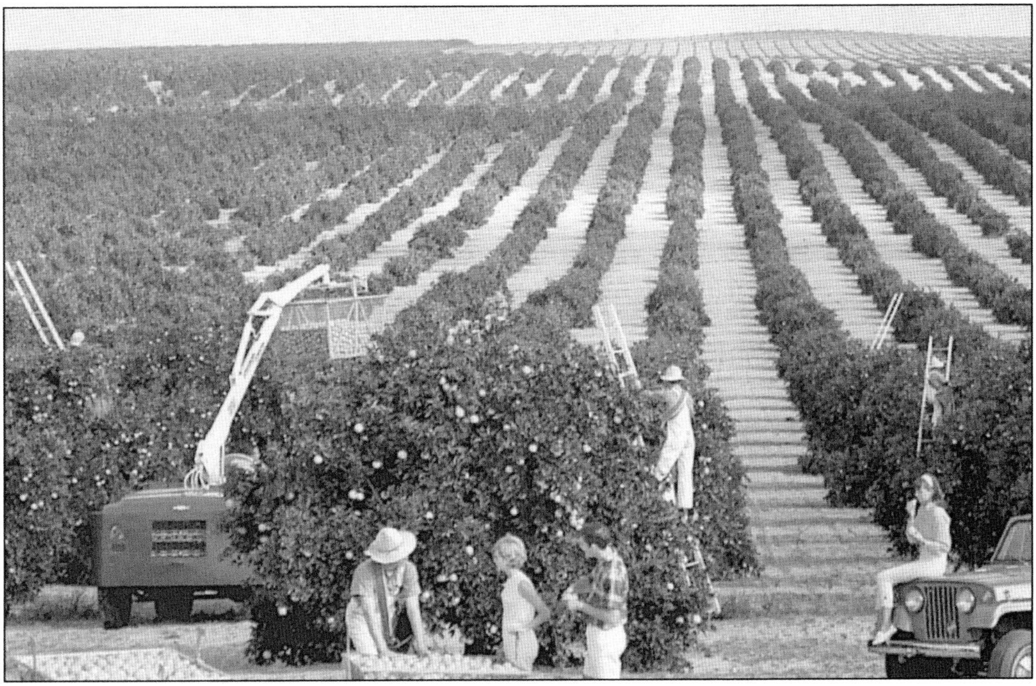

The bulk trailers pictured below can hold 500 or more boxes of juice oranges. Ninety-five percent of Florida's orange crop is processed into juice products.

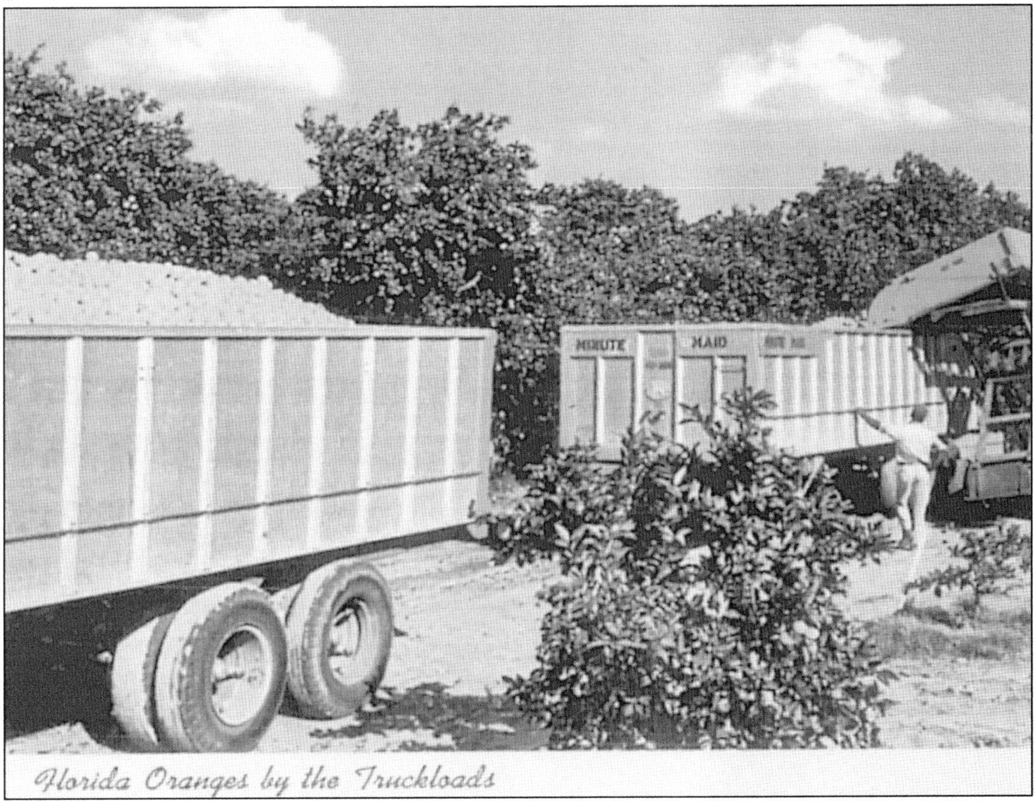

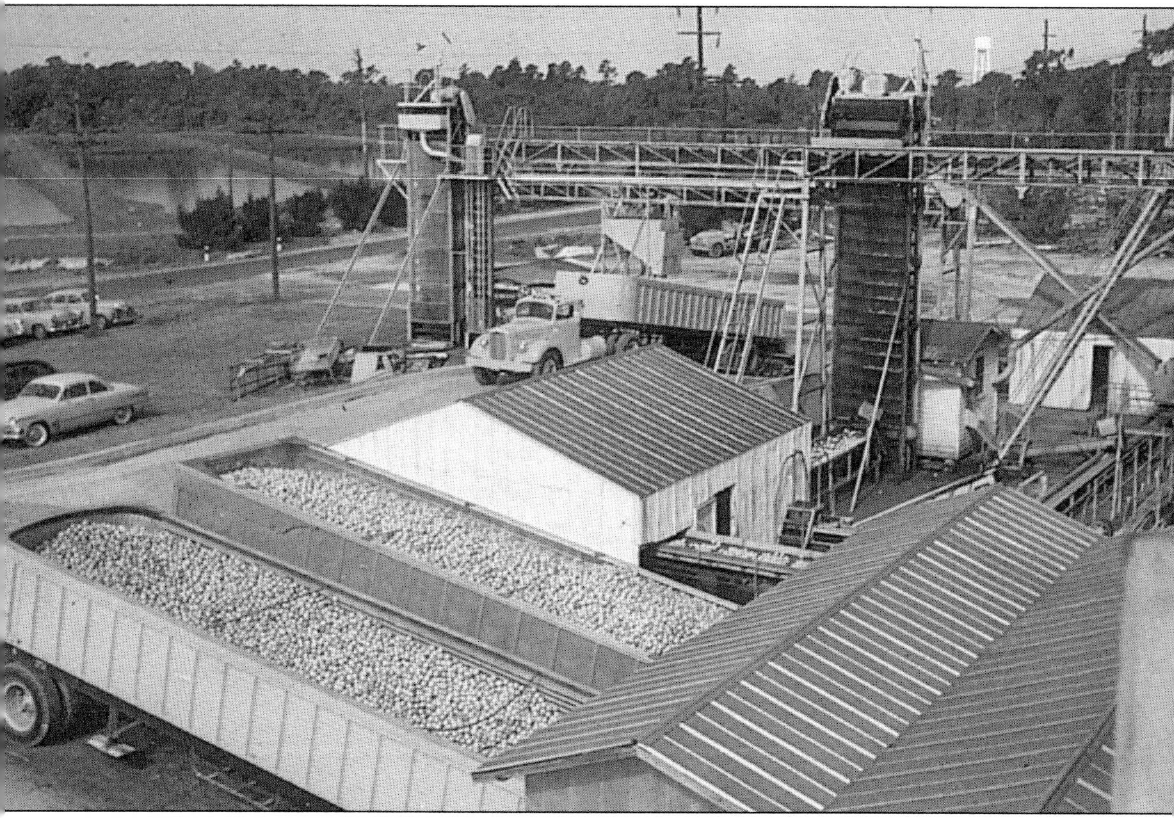

The state of Florida runs a computerized test on each load of fruit upon its arrival at juice plants. The fruit is graded and placed in storage bins within the facility, and then it is washed and goes through the extraction process.

Four

PACKING THE FRUIT

The citrus industry employs a large number of people to handle fruit after it has left the groves. Packing houses, juice processing plants, and gift fruit outlets all have a role in getting the finished product to the consumer.

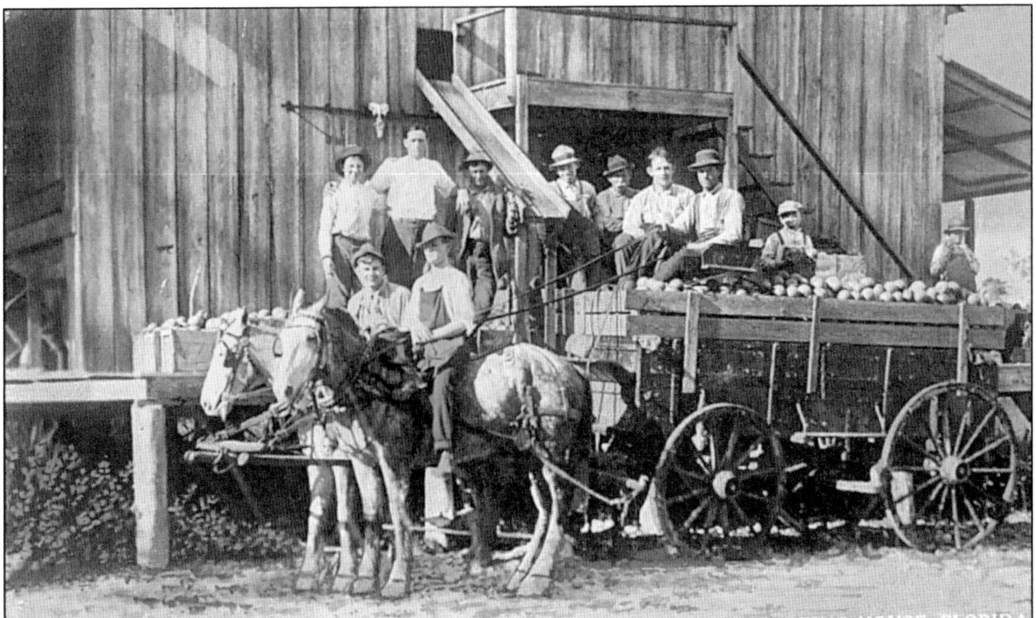

Early packing houses did little to sort picked fruit other than removing noticeably soft pieces of fruit. Workers placed the fruit in whatever wooden barrels or boxes they could find. They also used Spanish moss to cushion the fruit. However, there was nothing workers could do to estimate or guarantee the fruits' freshness when it arrived at the destination. The card is postmarked Tampa, August 9, 1920.

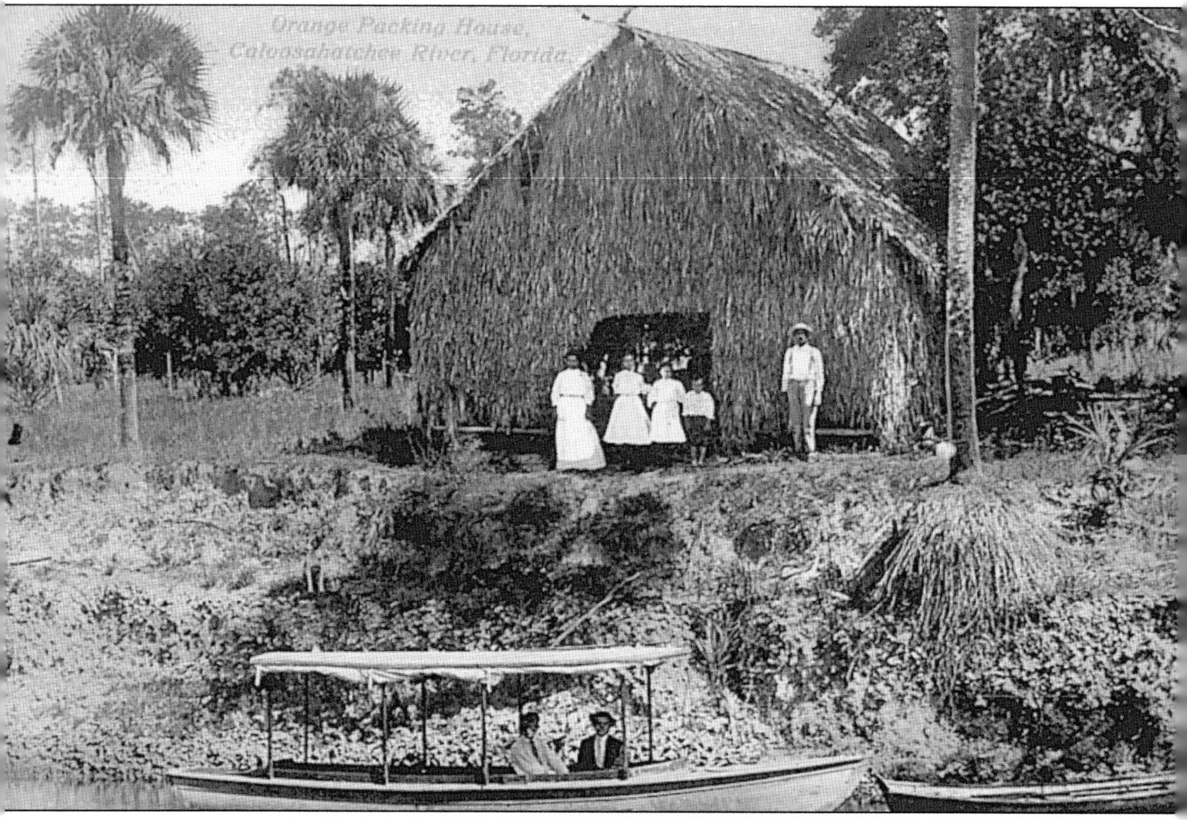

The first packing houses were often temporary structures, built for easy access to transportation that would pick up the packaged fruit. Itinerant packers would sometimes bring tents to groves and set them up for temporary use. Sheets of canvas would be pulled up between trees. The image is postmarked Tampa, January 9, 1915.

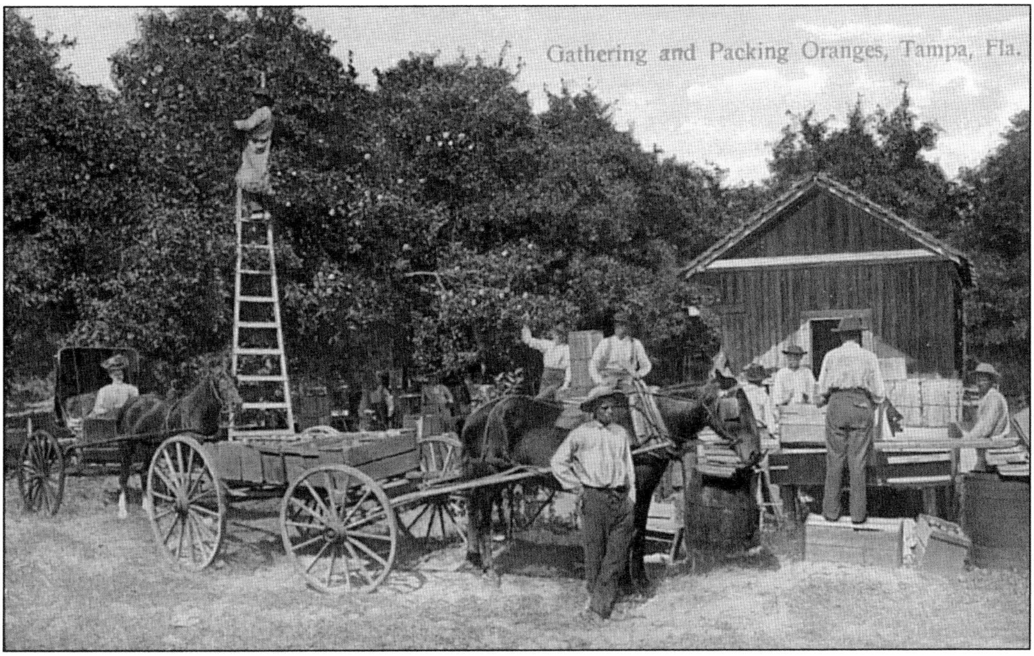

The top postcard has a message that reads, "Dear Jamie: I forgot to tell you about the snakes, spiders, frogs and bugs. There are plenty of them. I can stand them all but the snakes. Snakes kill dogs if the dogs run out—into the country, as dogs love to do. So you see there is good and bad here—L.C.W." This card is dated June 20, 1909, while the card below is dated March 1912.

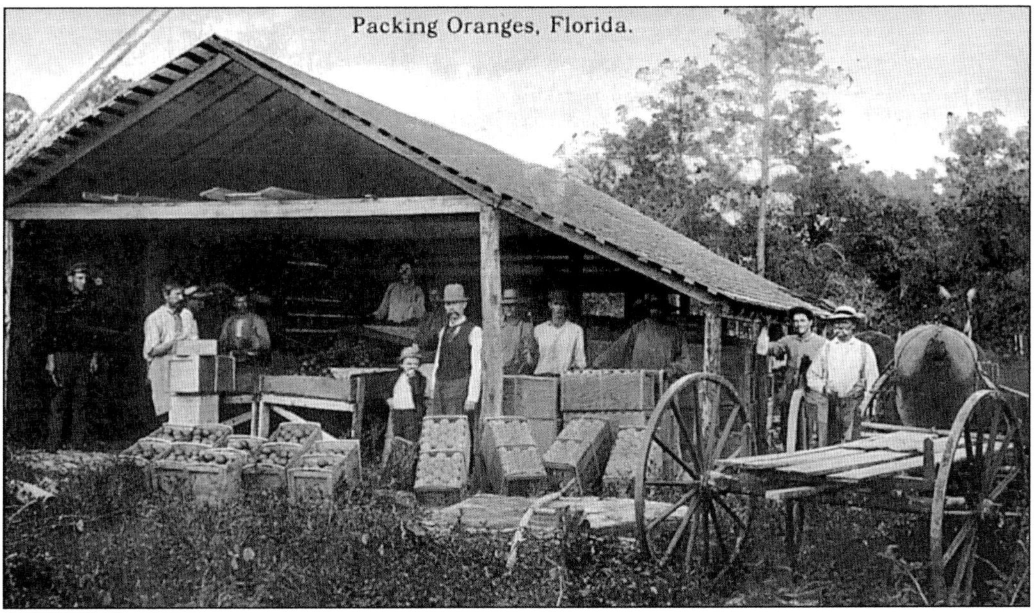

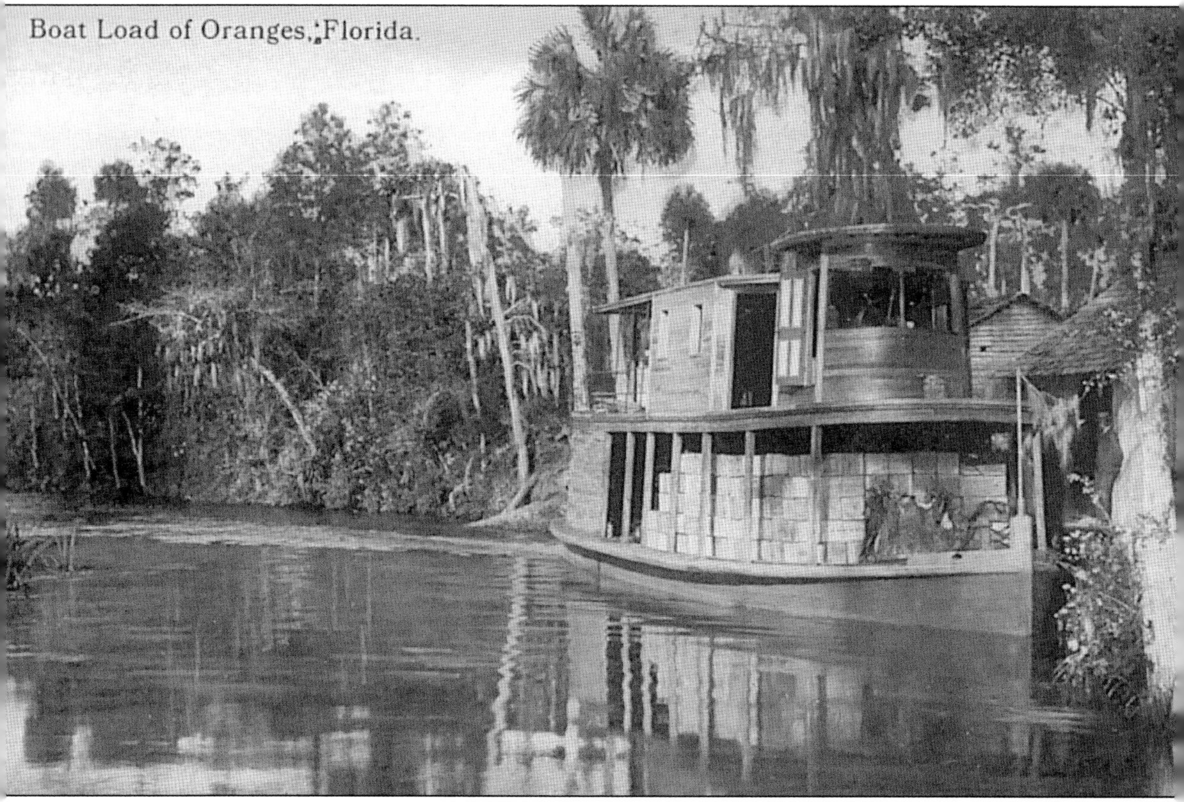

Shipping companies were a crucial link in getting oranges and grapefruit to market. It is likely this boat would travel the waterways of north central Florida near Ocala and Silver Springs, picking up boxes of fruit hauled to the docks by grove owners. The boats would pick up these boxes and take them north on the St. John's River to Jacksonville, where they would be loaded onto other boats or trains for transport beyond Florida.

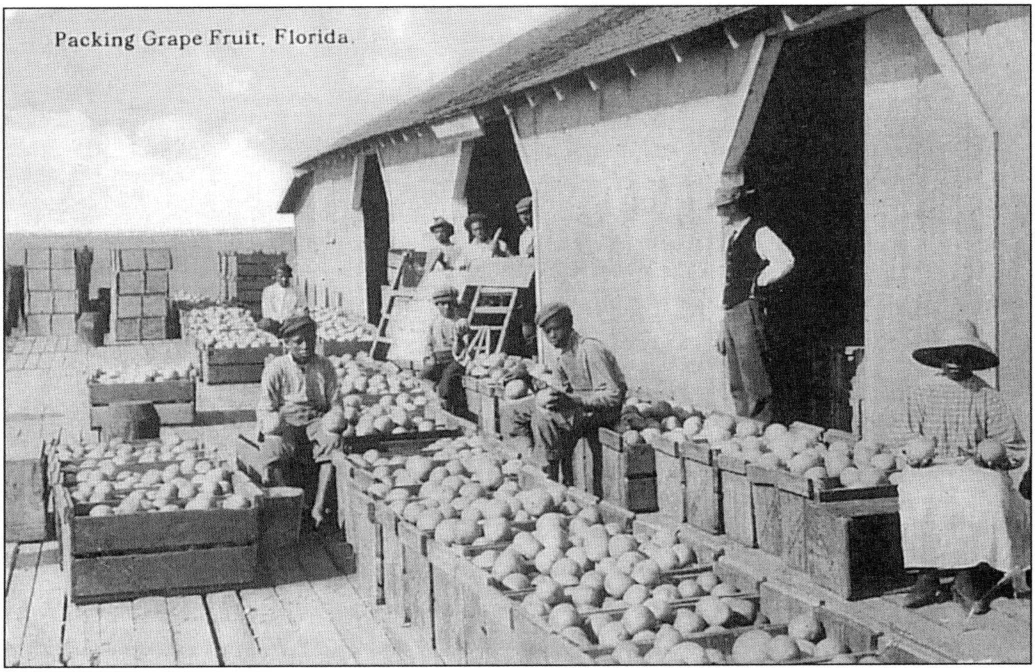

Once fruit arrived at permanent packing houses, workers would go through the piles and sort them by size and appearance. A pile like the one shown below would likely take a worker an hour to go through. While the adults worked, their children would be put to work affixing labels to fruit boxes. With swipes of paste, the children would attach a label at each end of the box, taking home 15¢ an hour for their labor. The postcard below is postmarked Winter Park, February 20, 1912.

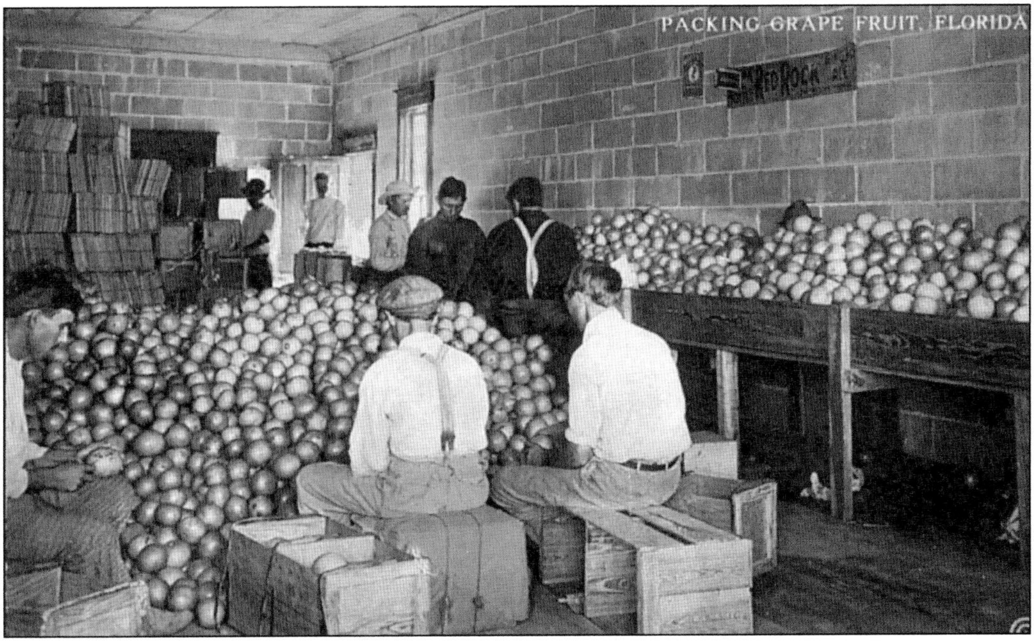

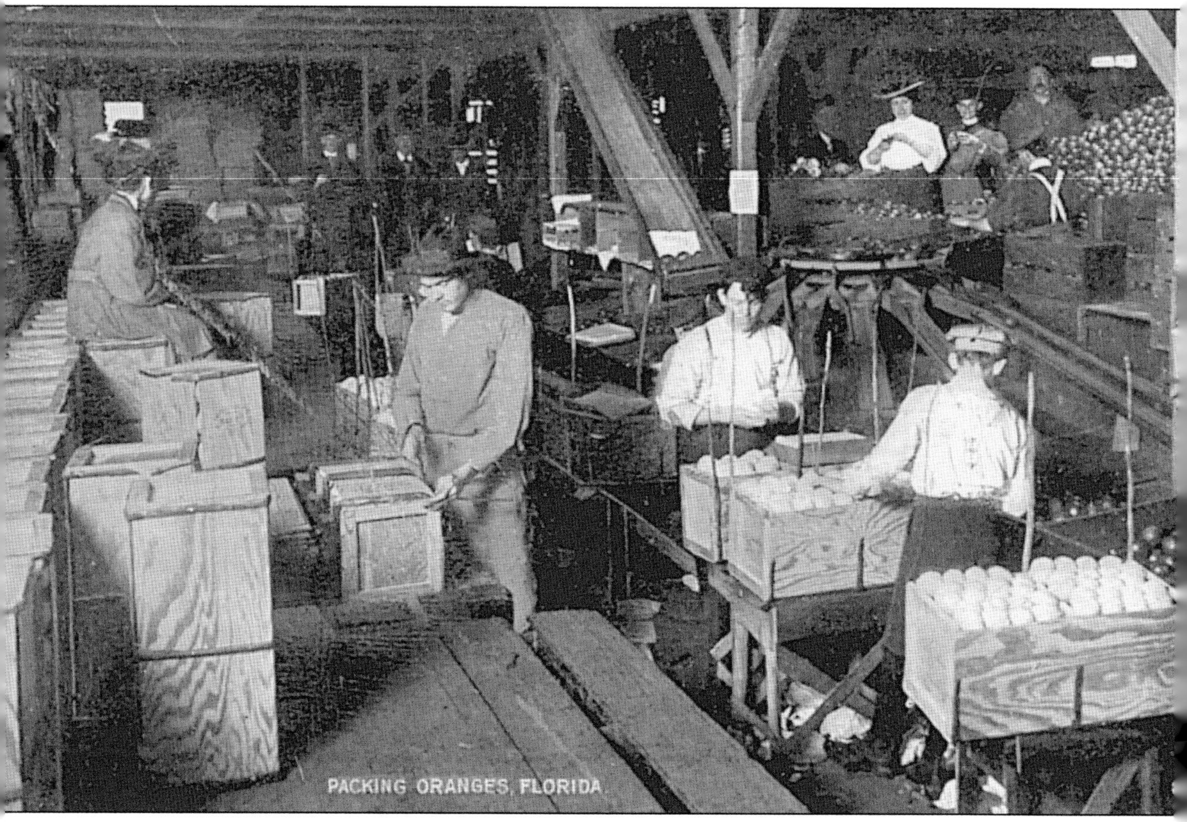

Fruit box labels had significance beyond the particular design of the logo of the packing house or distributor. Use of the color "blue" meant the fruit inside was the best quality possible. Red meant the fruit was of "second grade" or medium quality. Black, gold, or yellow indicated the fruit was either damaged or of poor quality. This card is postmarked Dade City, December 23, 1911.

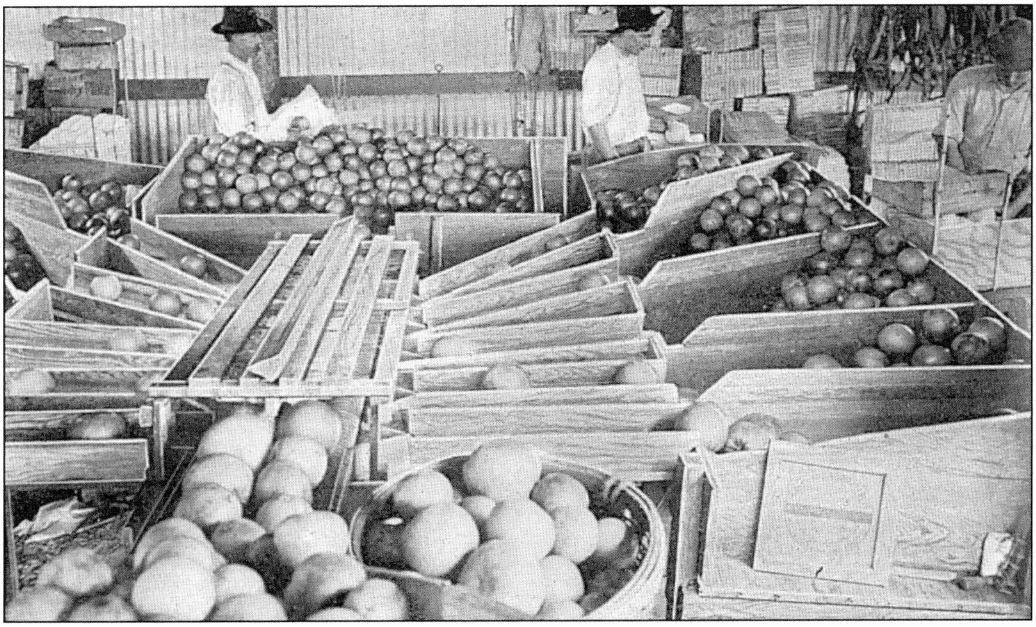

Some packing houses used wooden dividers to allow fruit to drop into bins depending on their size. Their "automated" sorting system required fewer workers and allowed for quicker sorting. However, human eyes were still needed to pick out the best looking fruit. Any oranges or grapefruit with discoloration were set aside to be squeezed for juice. Their appearance has nothing to do with the quality or taste of their contents.

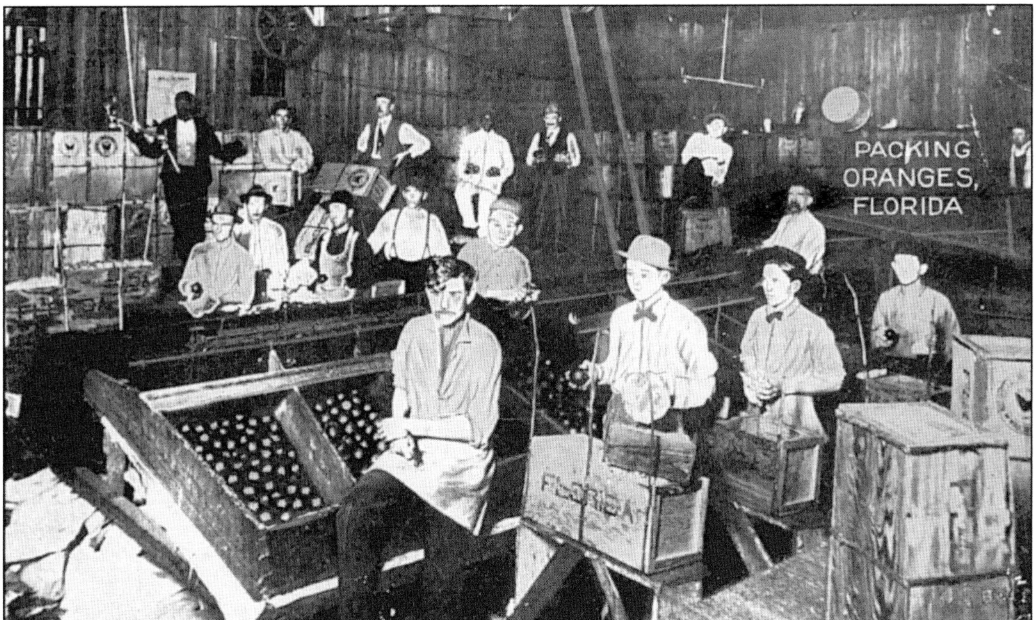

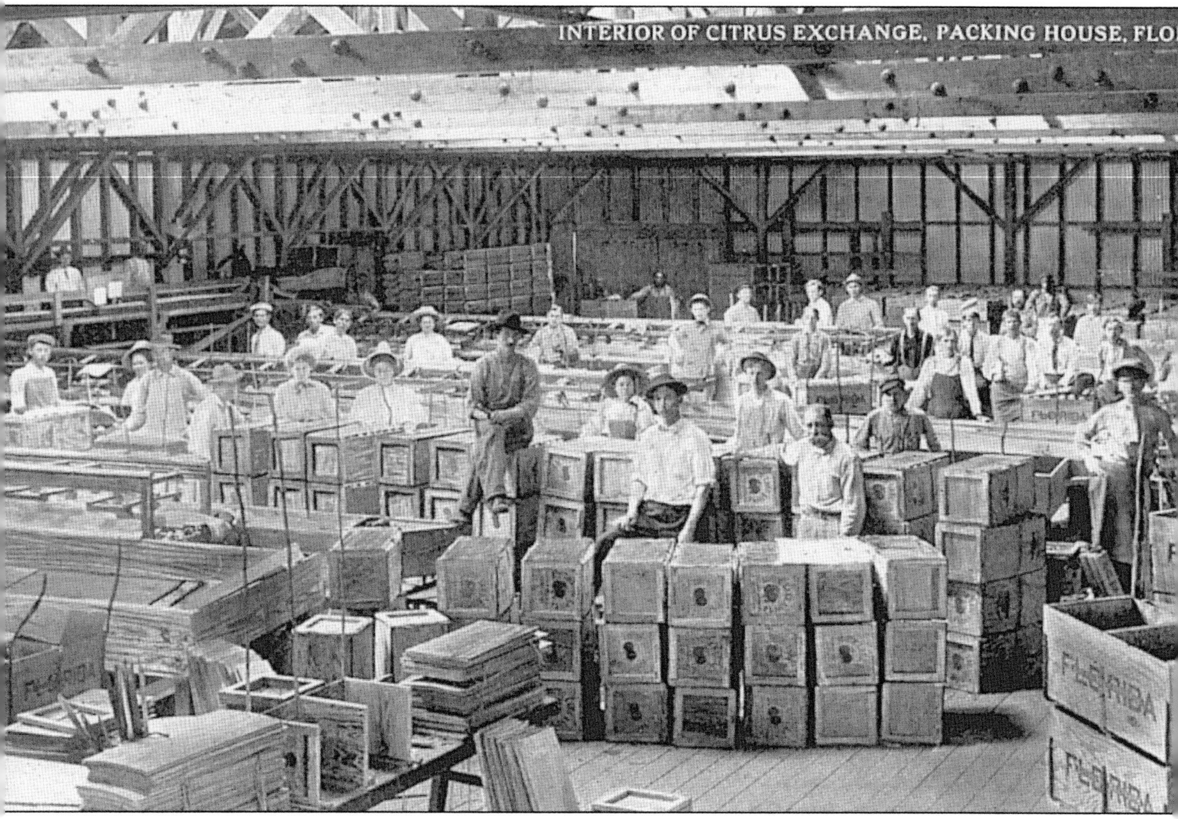

Picked oranges may not always appear "orange" on the outside. Once it is determined that an orange is ready "on the inside," it spends 36-72 hours in a "degreening room" in a packing house, where ethylene gas is added to speed up the natural process of fruit respiration. The procedure turns the orange the color shoppers expect ripe fruit to be.

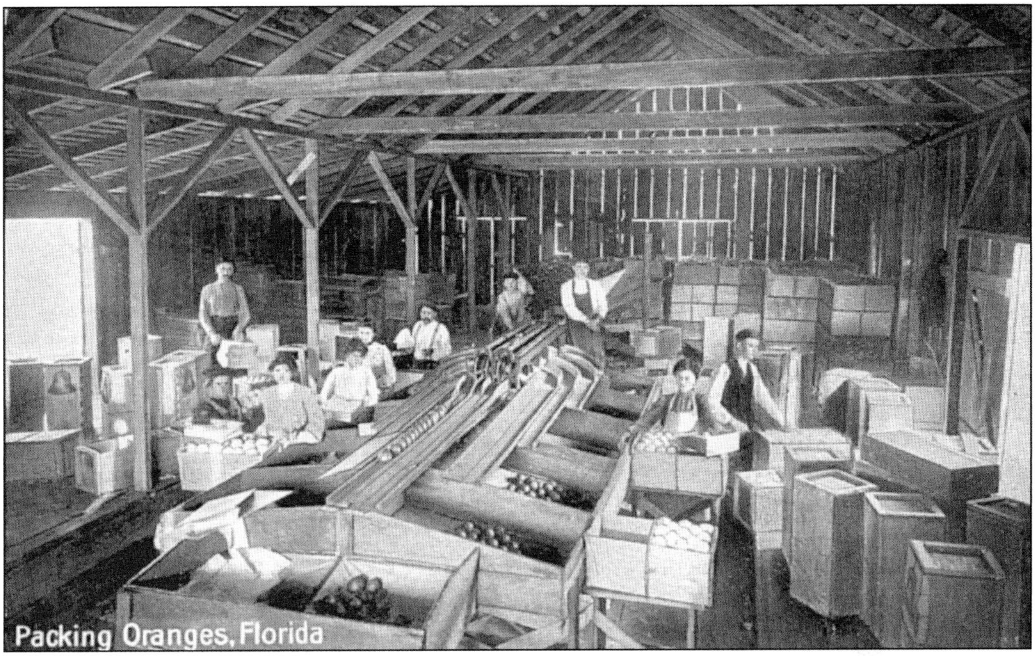

Oranges are packed by size. The sizes are designated by the numbers 163, 125, 100, 80, 64, and 48. These numbers indicate how many individual fruit it takes to fill a four-fifths bushel.

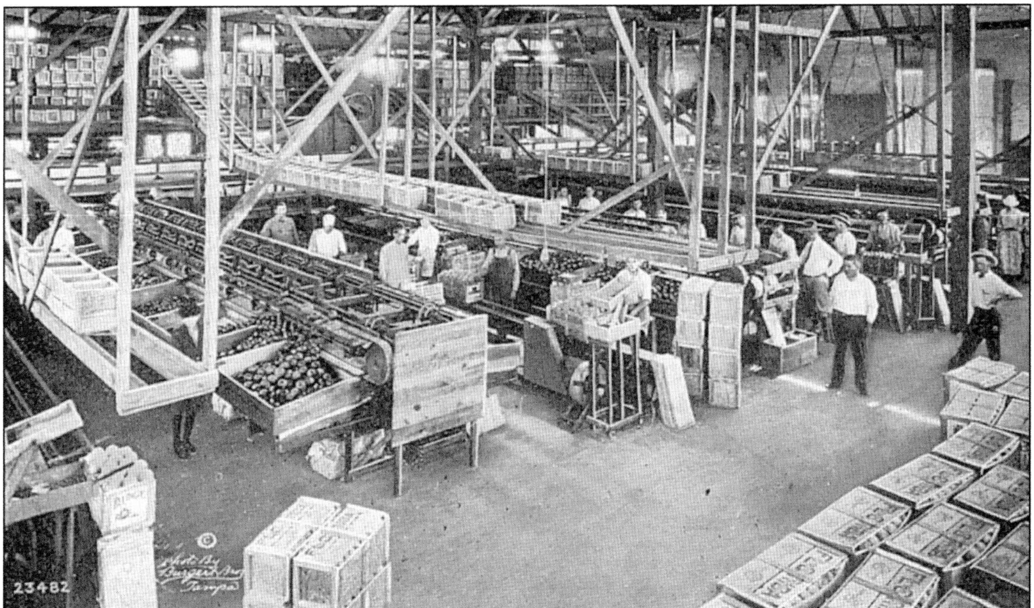

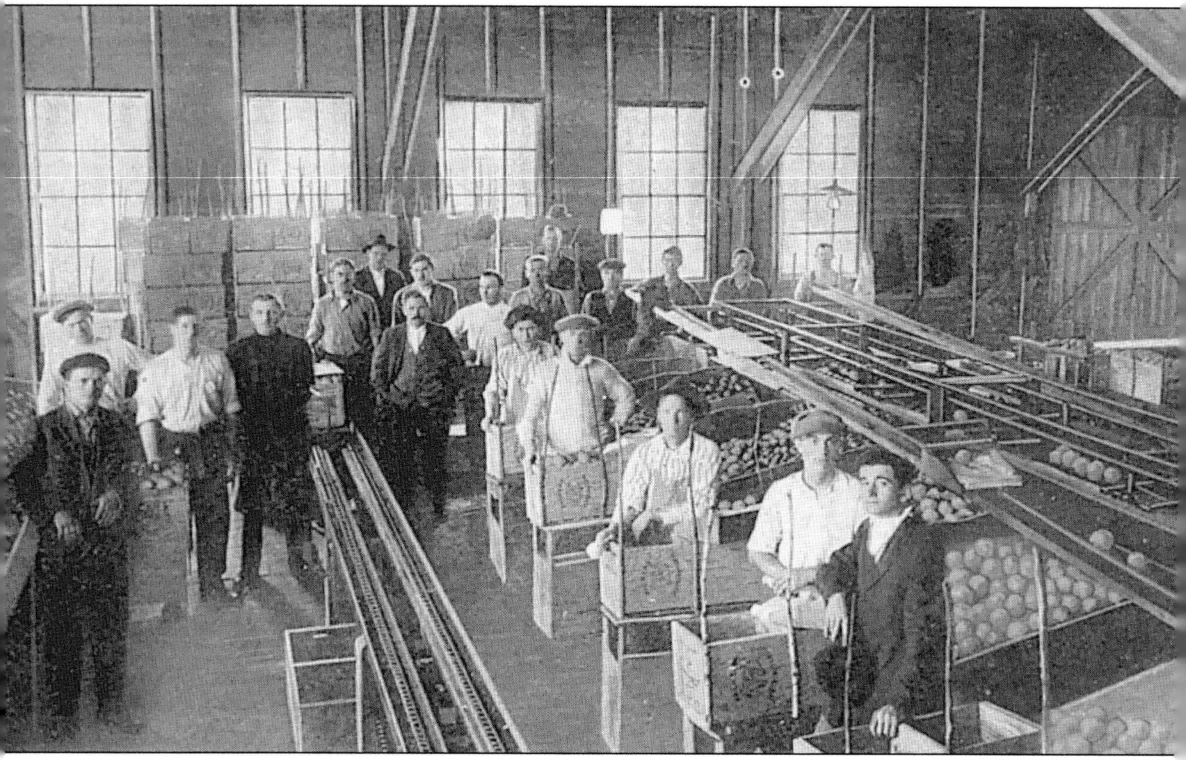

The wooden packing houses of the past were made of heart pine, a wood so tough it was difficult to drive a nail through it. These buildings occasionally caught fire, and once they started burning there was no stopping the flames.

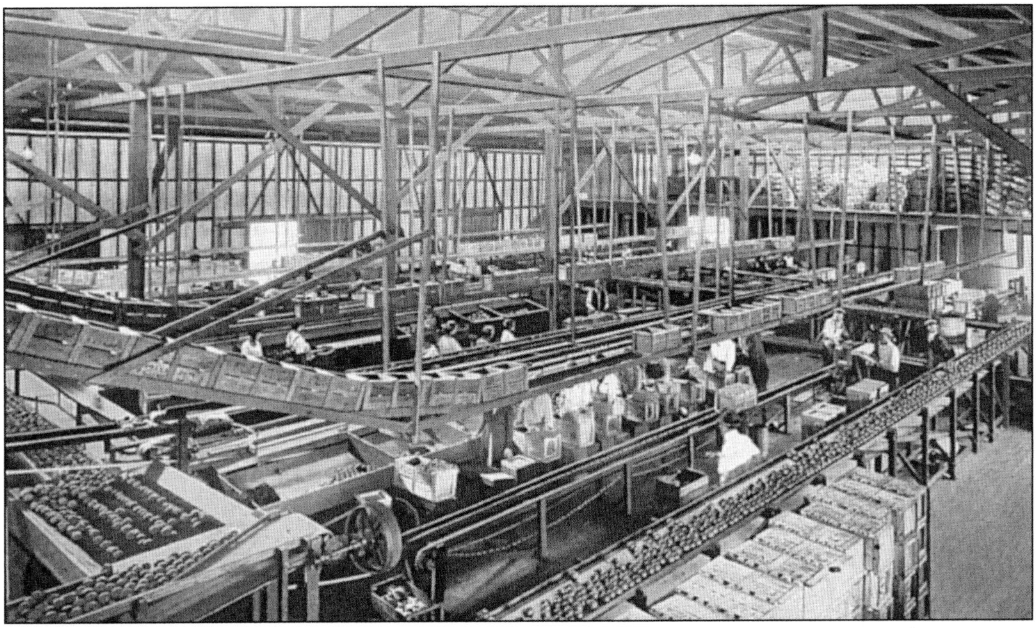

The average modern packing house can handle 1,500 boxes of fruit or more every hour. Once the fruit is dumped into the packing line, it takes about ten minutes for it to be washed, waxed, graded, sized, and packed into cartons for shipment.

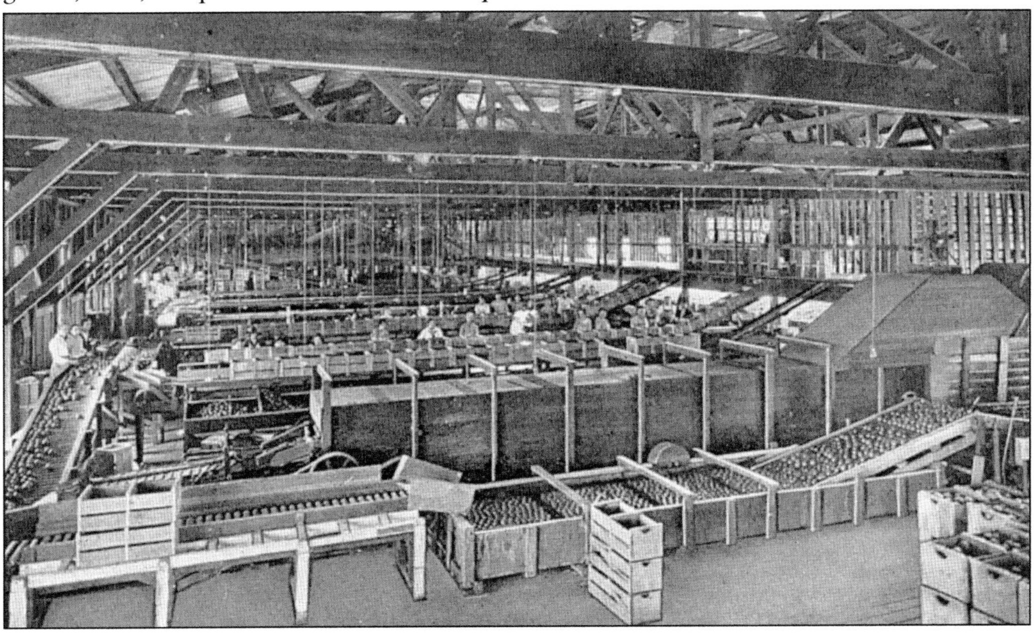

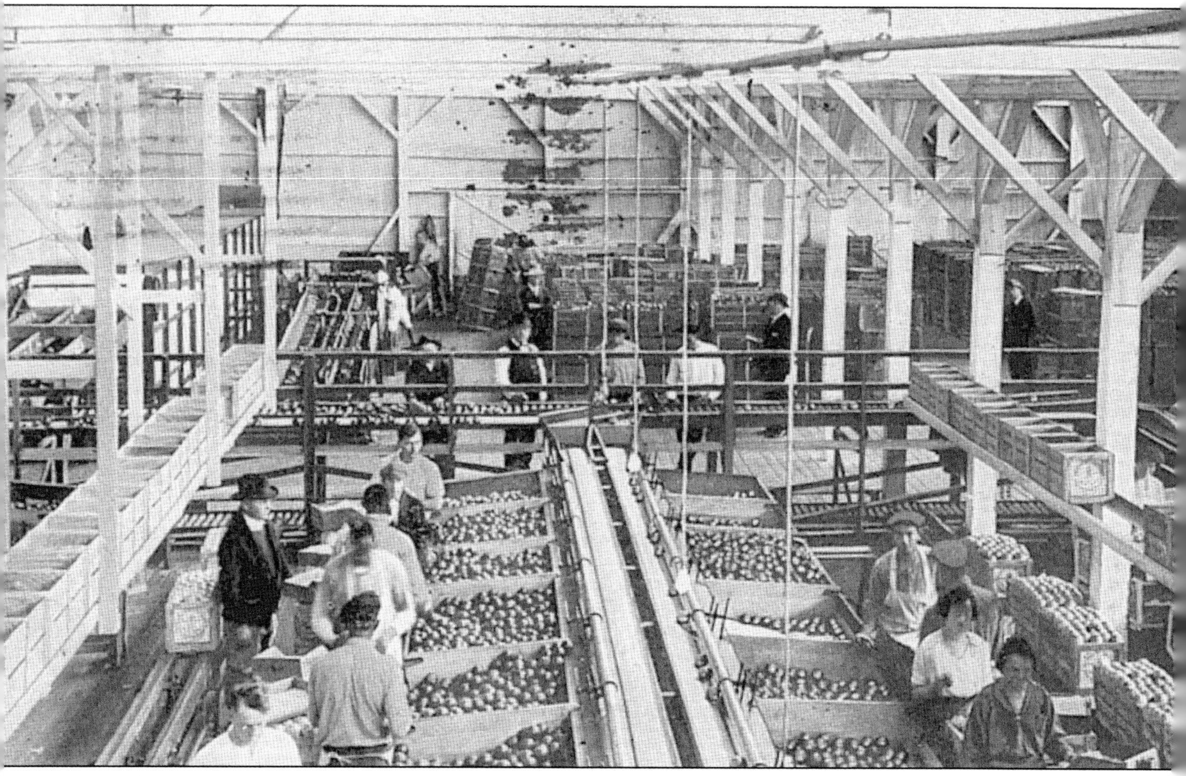

This card, postmarked Daytona, March 20, 1924, has the following message written on it: "Dear Teachers—I am sending a box of orange blossoms. They may not keep but I am taking a chance. One of the school children brought them to me this morning. They are very fragile and drop off easily. Even though they are faded, the scent will still be there . . . Yours sincerely, Ruth C. Earle."

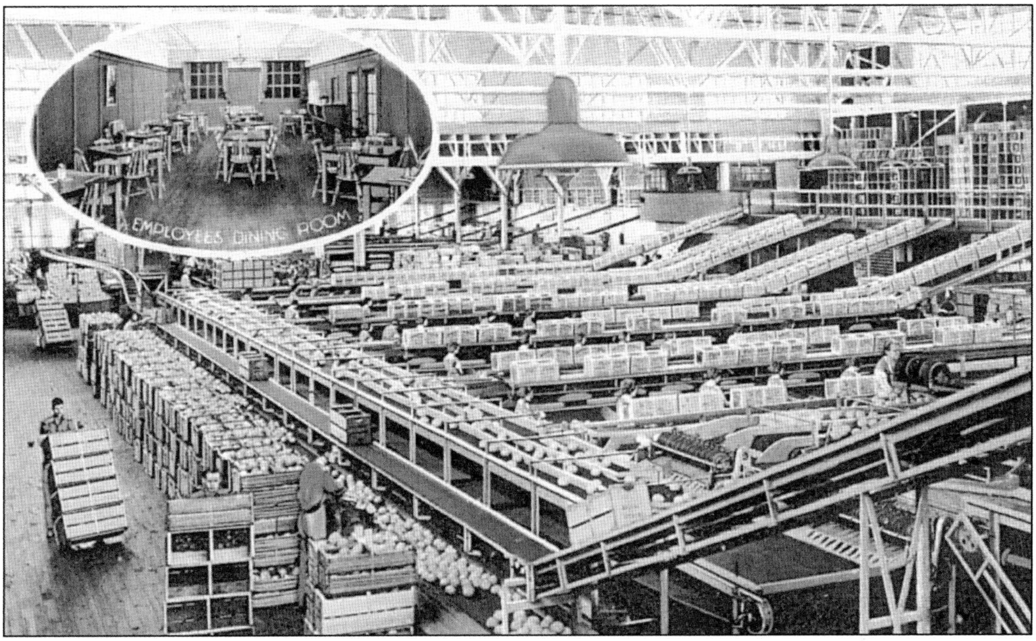

In modern packing houses, like the one pictured below, tractor trailers pull up to a designated off-loading dock, where hydraulic ramps lift up the entire trailer at an angle, allowing the fruit to roll off for transfer to storage bins. From there the fruit is cleaned and sent through the plant for processing. The postcard below is postmarked Fort Myers, January 29, 1963.

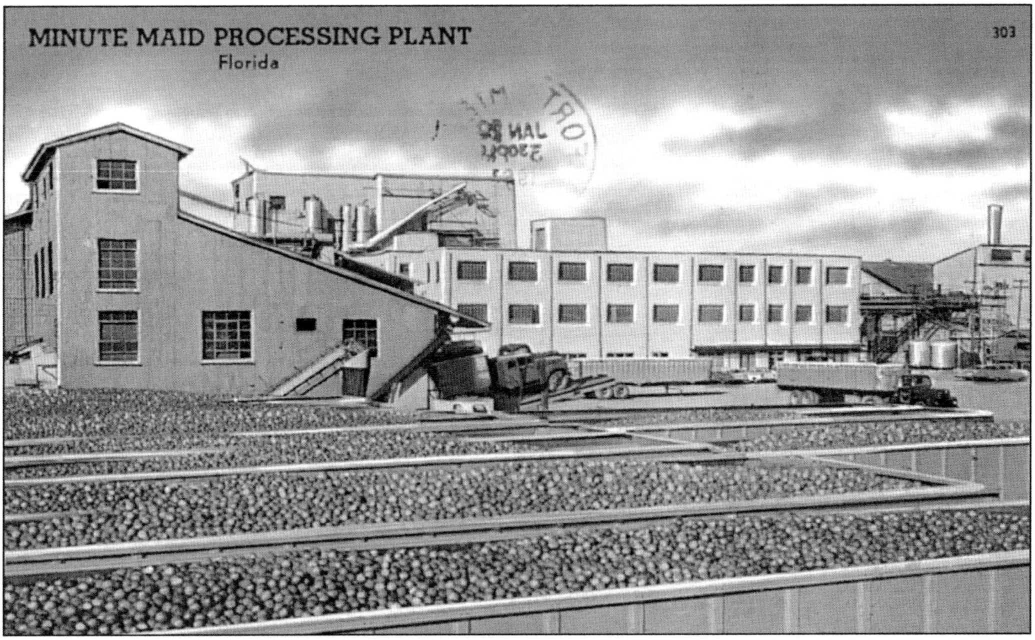

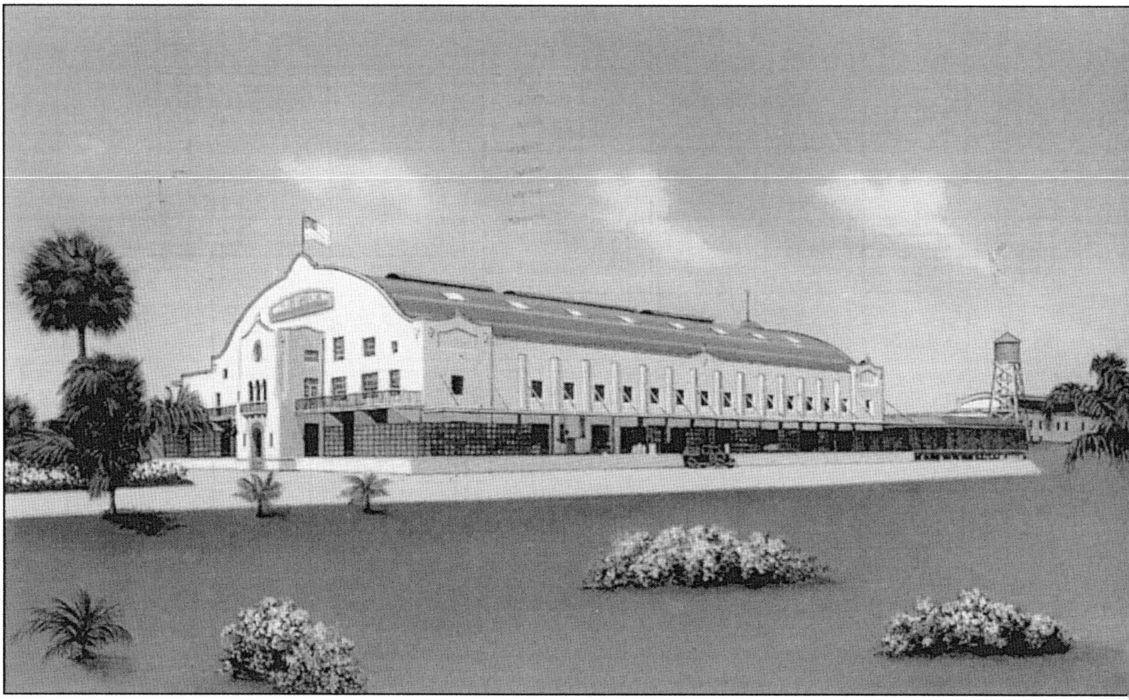

Dr. Phillips' Packing House is located at Dr. Phillips, Florida. This great packing house is in the center of miles of wonderfully kept groves, and it is the largest individually owned, modern, sanitary plant in Florida. Here the luscious, tree-ripened fruit is carefully prepared and packed for the markets. "Dr. Phillips oranges, grapefruit, and tangerines are always fresh, uniform, jucier, and sweeter, and rich in vitamin C."

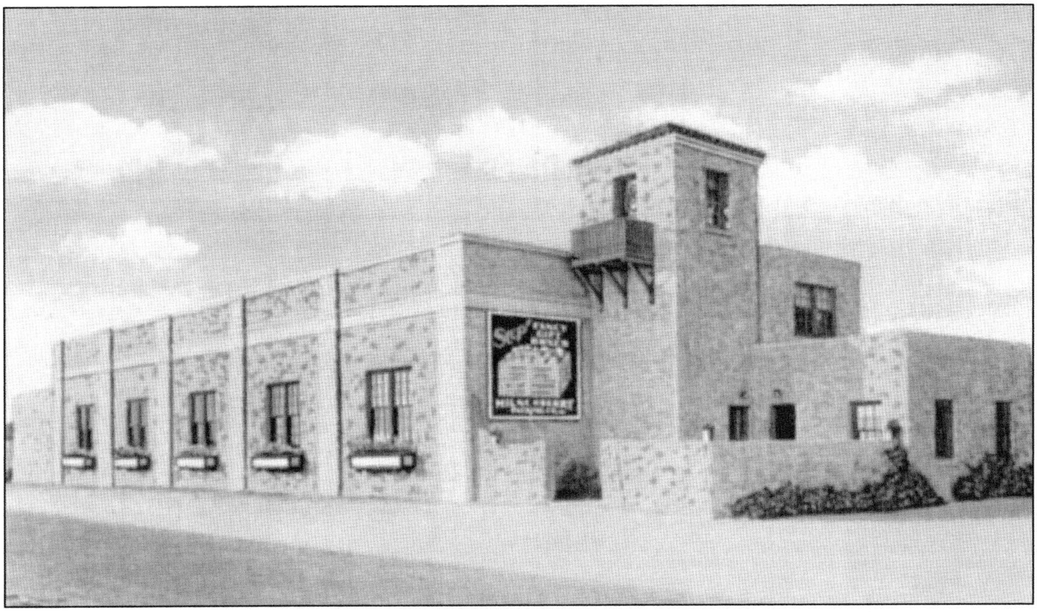

Some packing houses have become tourist attractions in their own right. The above postcard was sold by the Milne-O'Berry Packing Company in St. Petersburg, Florida. Other houses operate their own stores to sell fruit they have processed. These stores are often located along main roads frequented by tourists who may want to take some fruit back home with them. The packing houses also sell souvenirs, jellies, postcards, and maybe even this book! (Both cards courtesy of Barbara Eggleson.)

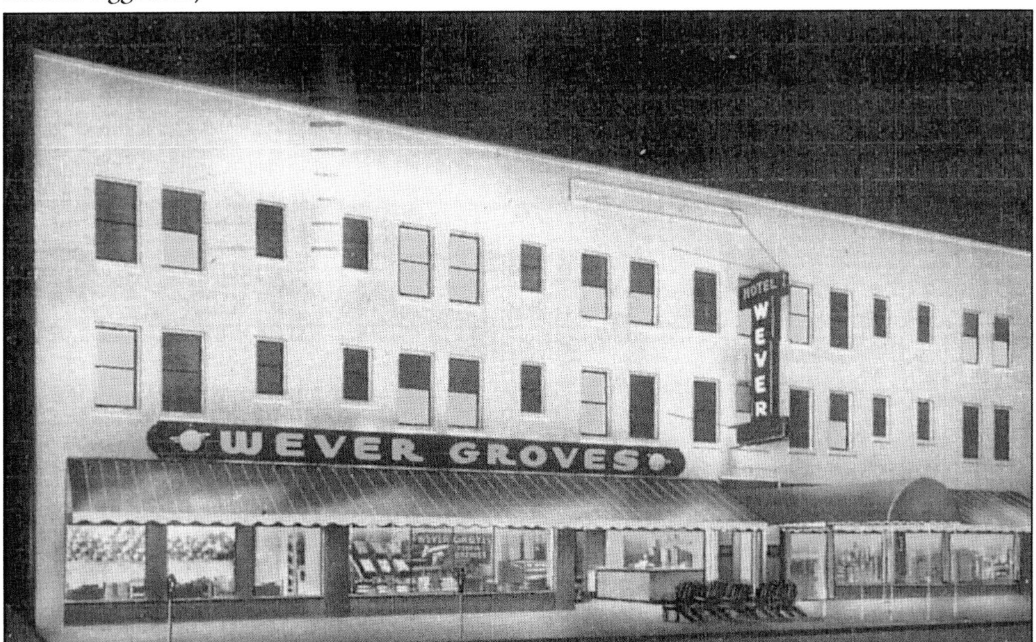

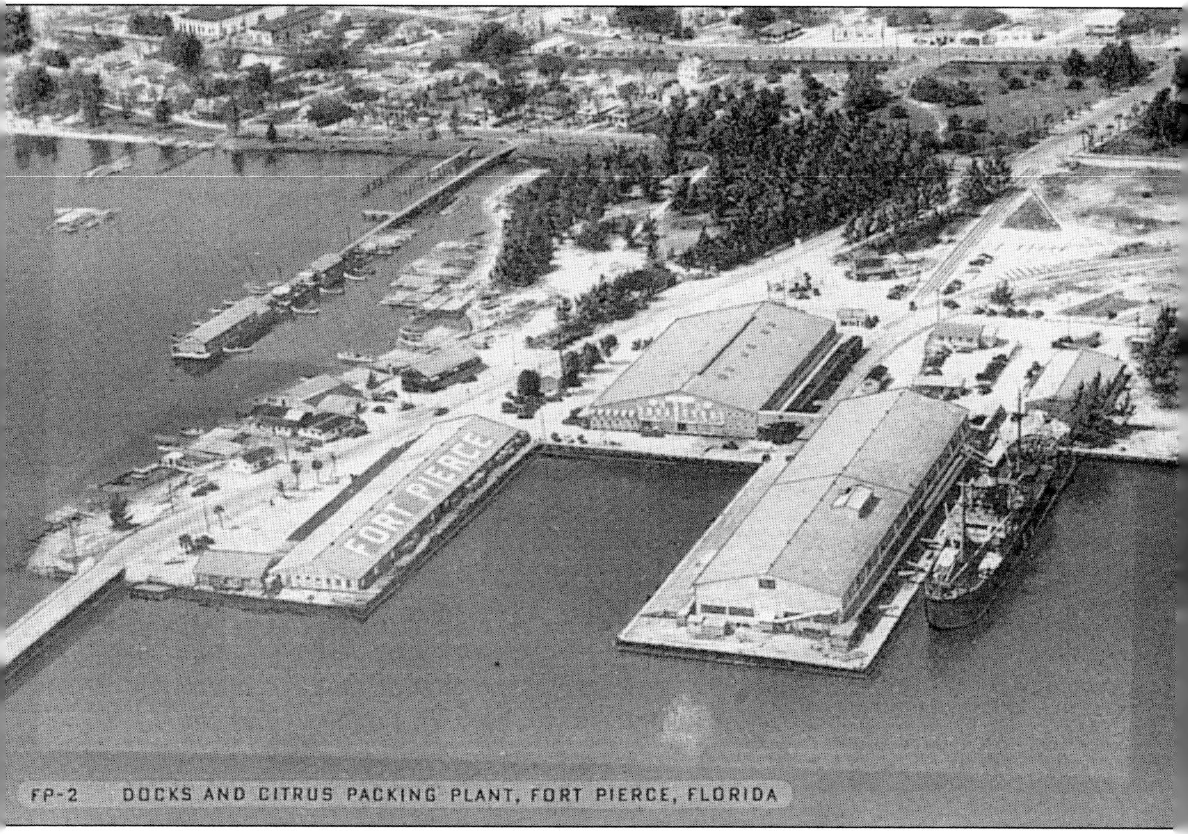

My office is located in the center building, which was the original Ft. Pierce Growers packing house, a growers' co-op built in the 1930s. At this location, fruit was packed and transported by conveyor belt to the terminal building at the right to be loaded onto steamships. Today, the building is owned by Bernard Egan and Company, the largest fresh fruit shipper in Florida.

Five

Touring the Groves

Many people in the citrus industry say oranges and grapefruit are a lot more interesting than some multi-colored cartoon mouse. Before there were theme parks, tourists would stop alongside the road to have a look at citrus trees. Visitors were encouraged to stop and smell the blossoms.

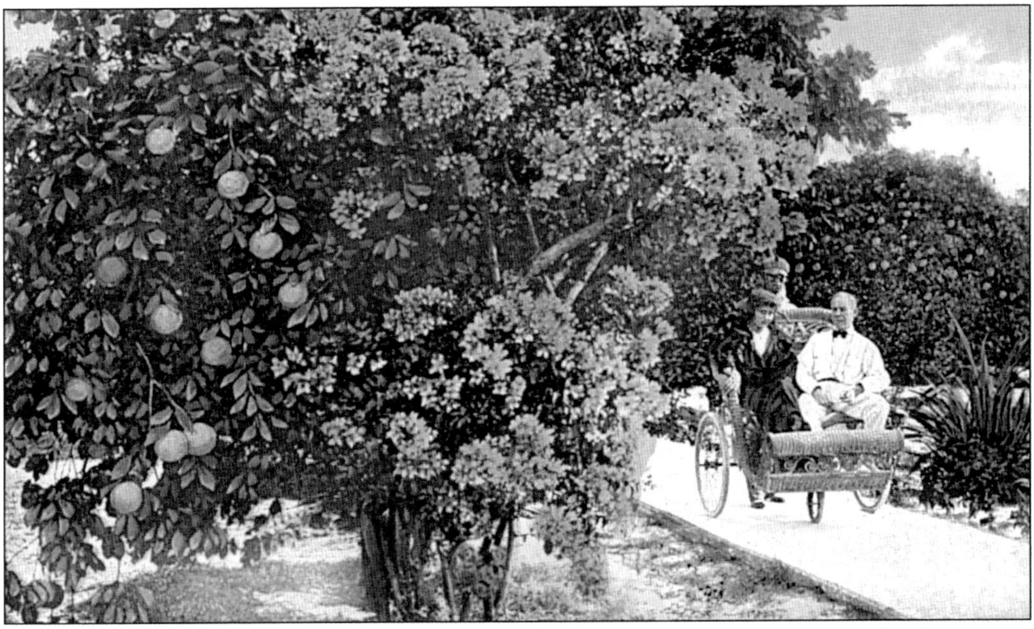

Many old hotels and restaurants in Florida planted orange trees on their grounds for their guests to enjoy. Concrete walkways were laid to allow carriage rides and tours that would not soil the shoes of the tourists. Lucky guests were even allowed to pick a few oranges and grapefruit to enjoy there or to take home.

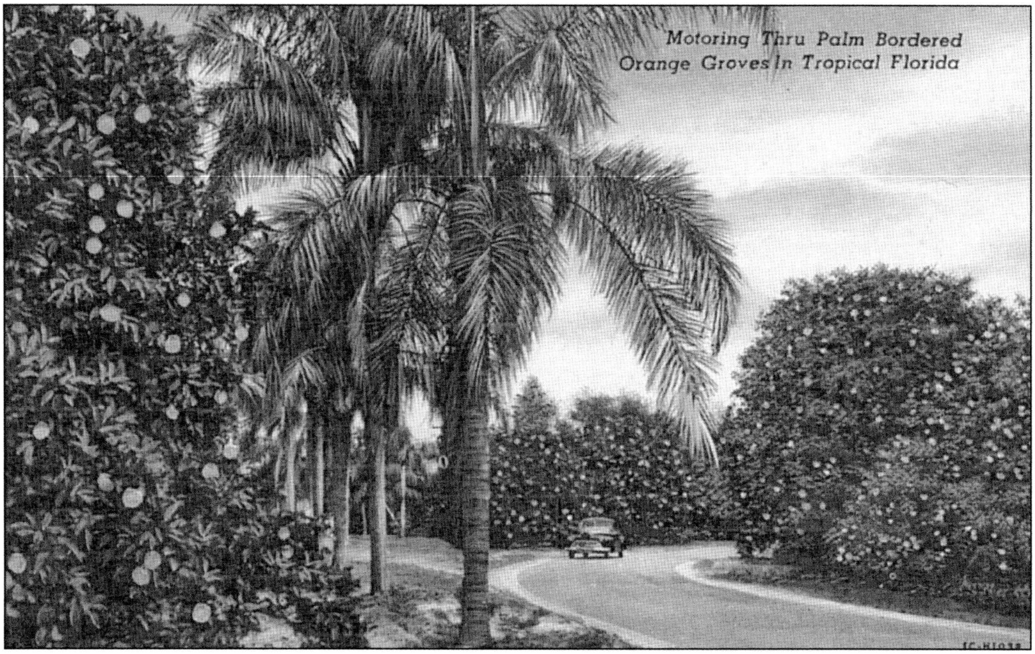

Many growers note a "mysterious" disappearance of fruit on trees located next to highways. On the flip side, acres of healthy orange trees are a far better advertisement for the industry than any billboard or commercial could be. The card below is postmarked Miami, February 20, 1935.

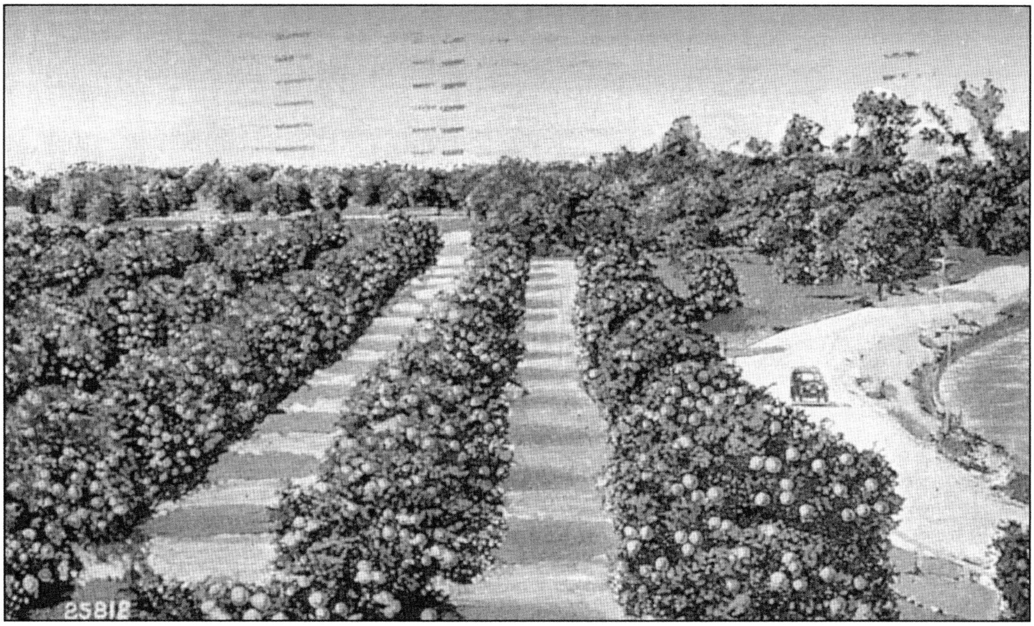

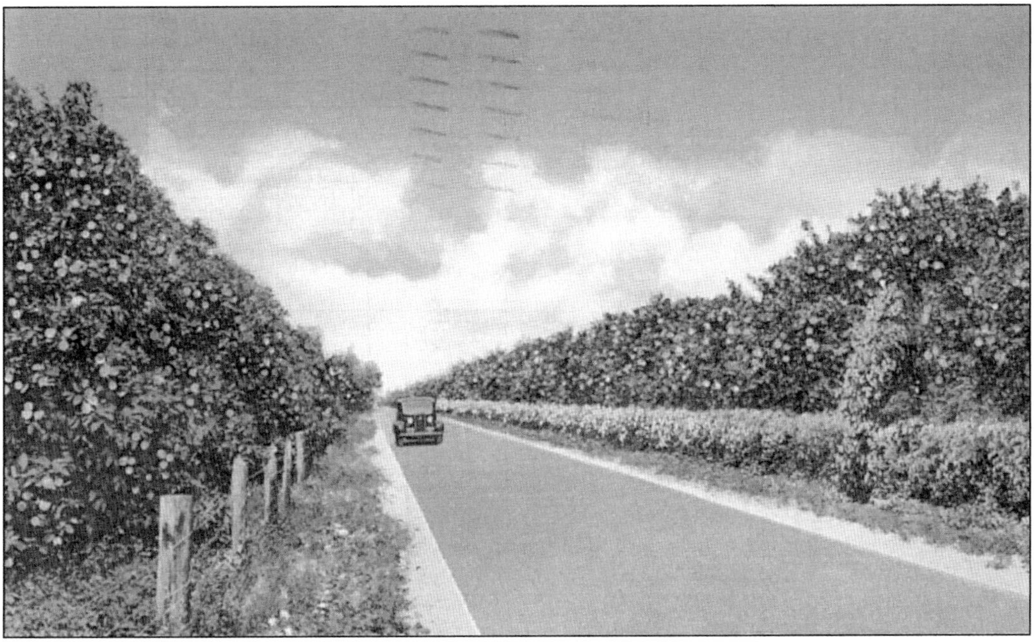

Rural Florida afforded visitors a close-up view of the citrus industry. Riding through the groves was recommended as a proper way to spend a Sunday afternoon. The above postcard is postmarked St. Petersburg, April 14, 1940.

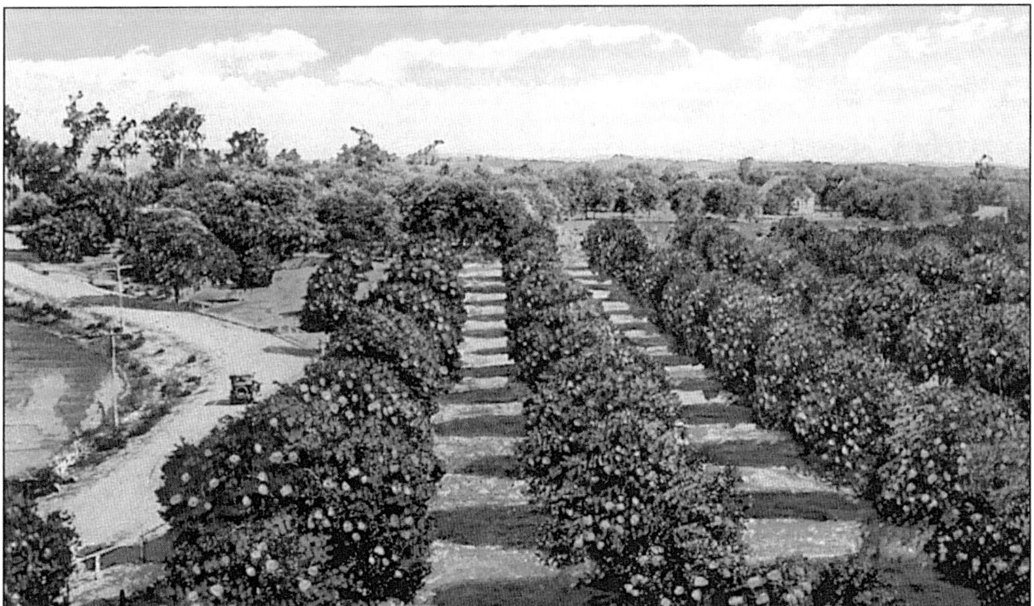

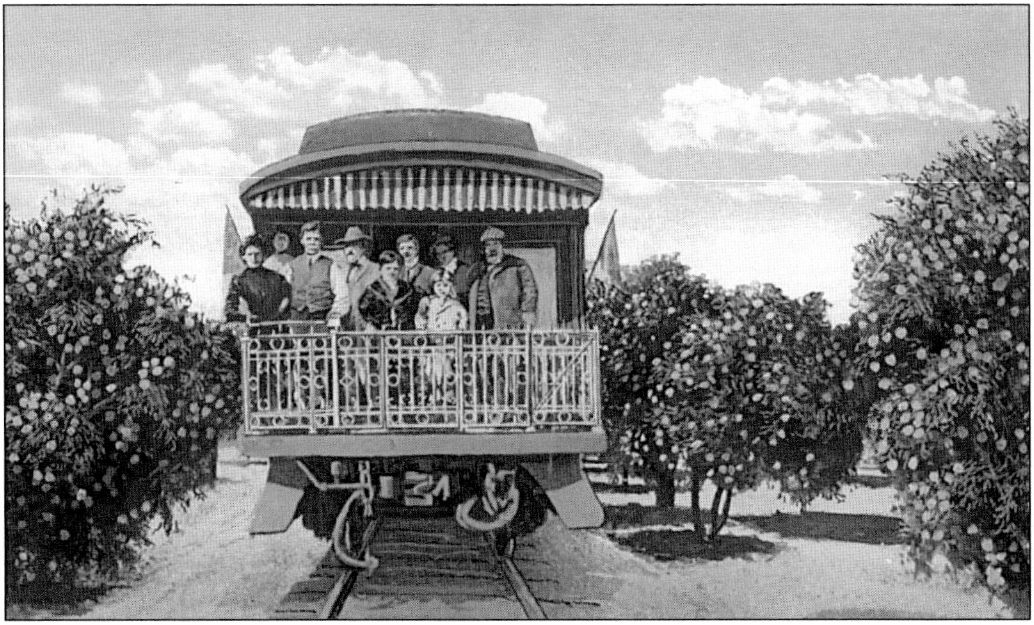

It's unlikely that these postcards are accurate representations of trains that passed through citrus groves. Growers probably would not have planted trees this close to the rails. The postcard below is postmarked Palatka, December 26, 1910.

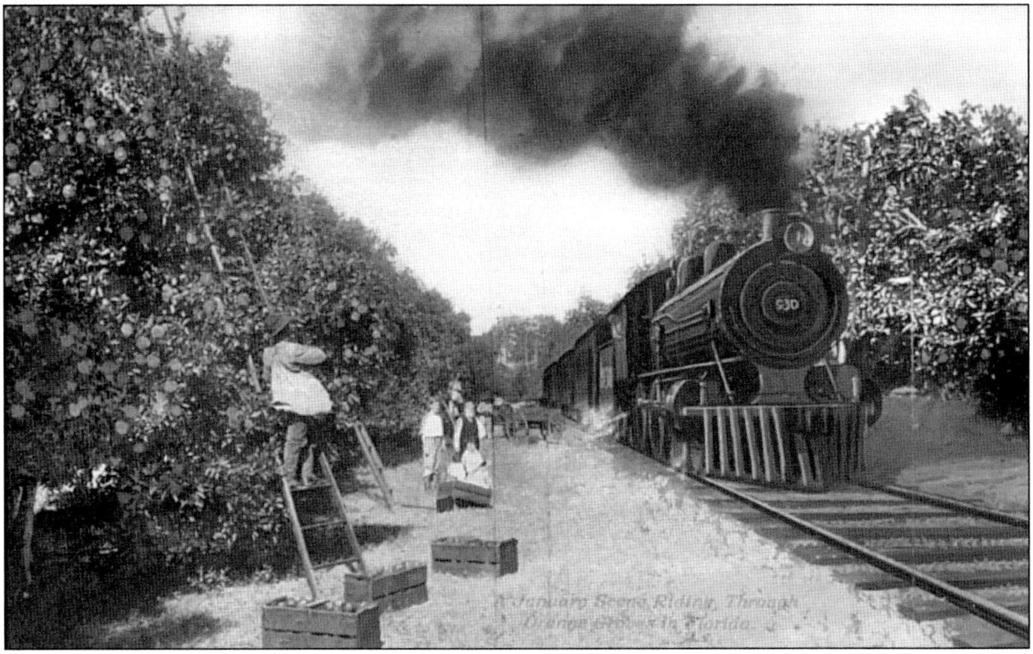

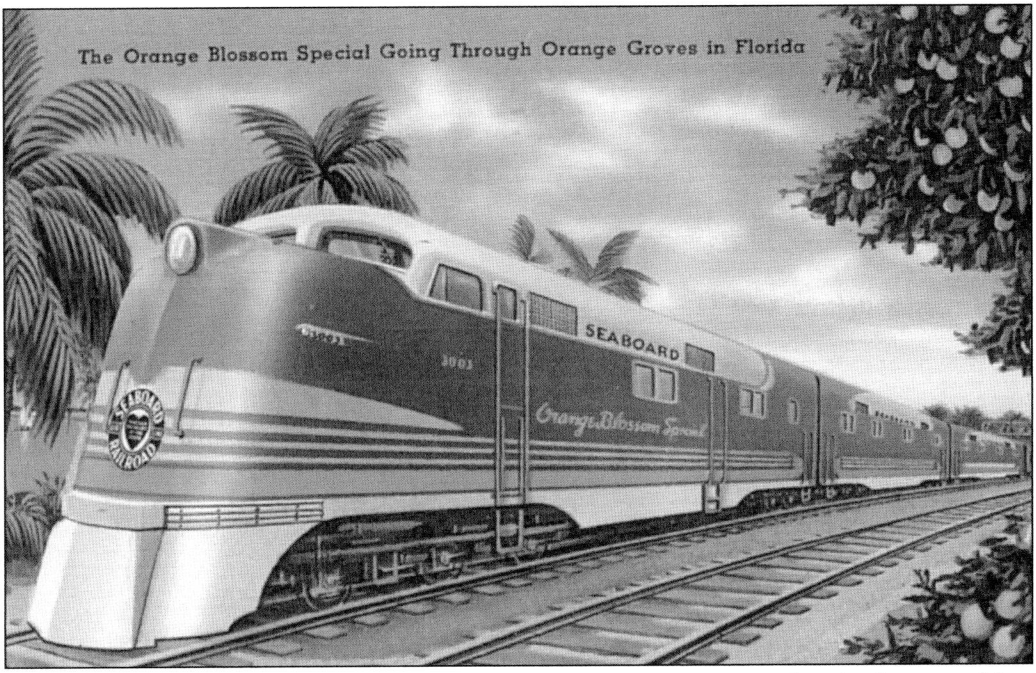

"The Diesel-powered Orange Blossom Special, deluxe winter-season favorite between New York and Florida resorts, follows the route of the Silver Meteor and the Silver Star, leaders of Seaboard's popular Silver Fleet." The postcard above is addressed to author Brian Weaver and was postmarked Miami, April 27, 1956.

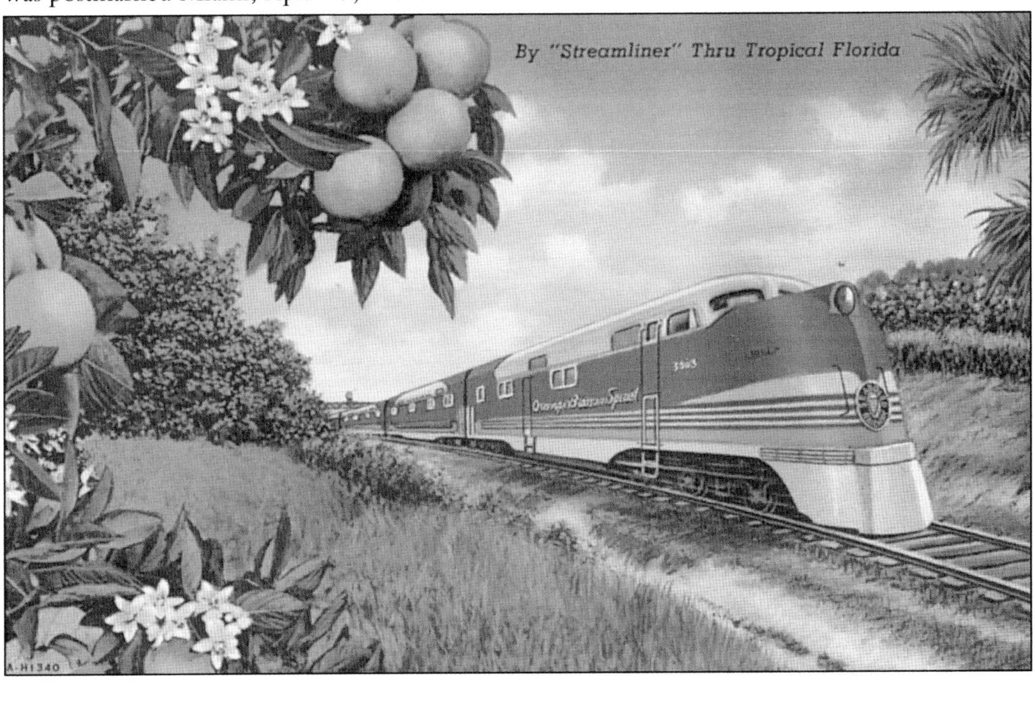

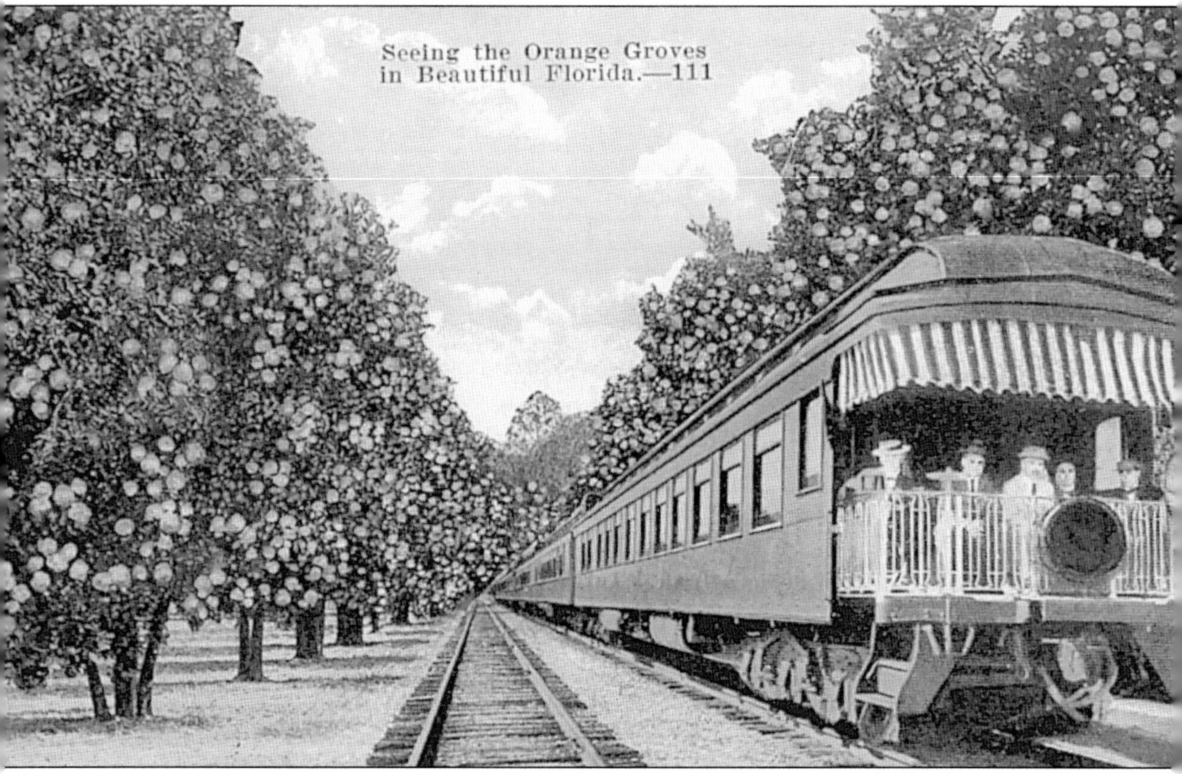

Before the days of parcel post, the railroad was the prime shipper of commercial citrus. My Dad would fill bushel baskets with the fruit he picked from our backyard or from one of our groves, and then he would take it to the railway station. Eventually, the fruit would make it to our family and friends in the North.

Six

"How's This for a Peach among the Oranges?"

There are many delightful things that emerge from groves, but our favorites include the ingredients for two special family recipes. The first is Mema's orange fruit cake. Helen Meriwether's cake is a family Christmas tradition (we've been known to tuck pieces in the freezer so we can enjoy it throughout the year). The second is Roberta Weaver's orange cake; she has been making it since before I was born. We hope you enjoy Mema's and Nana's recipes.

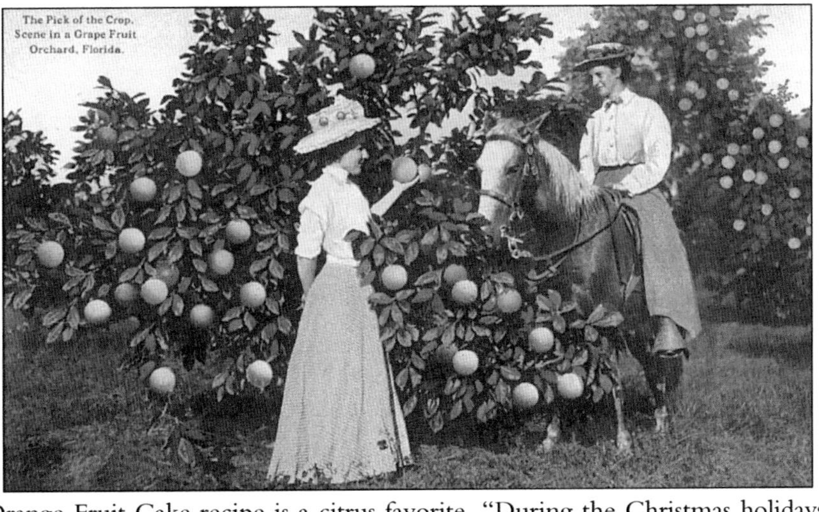

Mema's Orange Fruit Cake recipe is a citrus favorite. "During the Christmas holidays I like to make this orange fruit cake to give to our family and friends. I first tasted this cake at the home of Mrs. Brodie Williams, here in Sanford, Florida. She was the mother of a good friend. This was before I was married, almost 58 years ago." This card is postmarked Daytona, January 23, 1915.

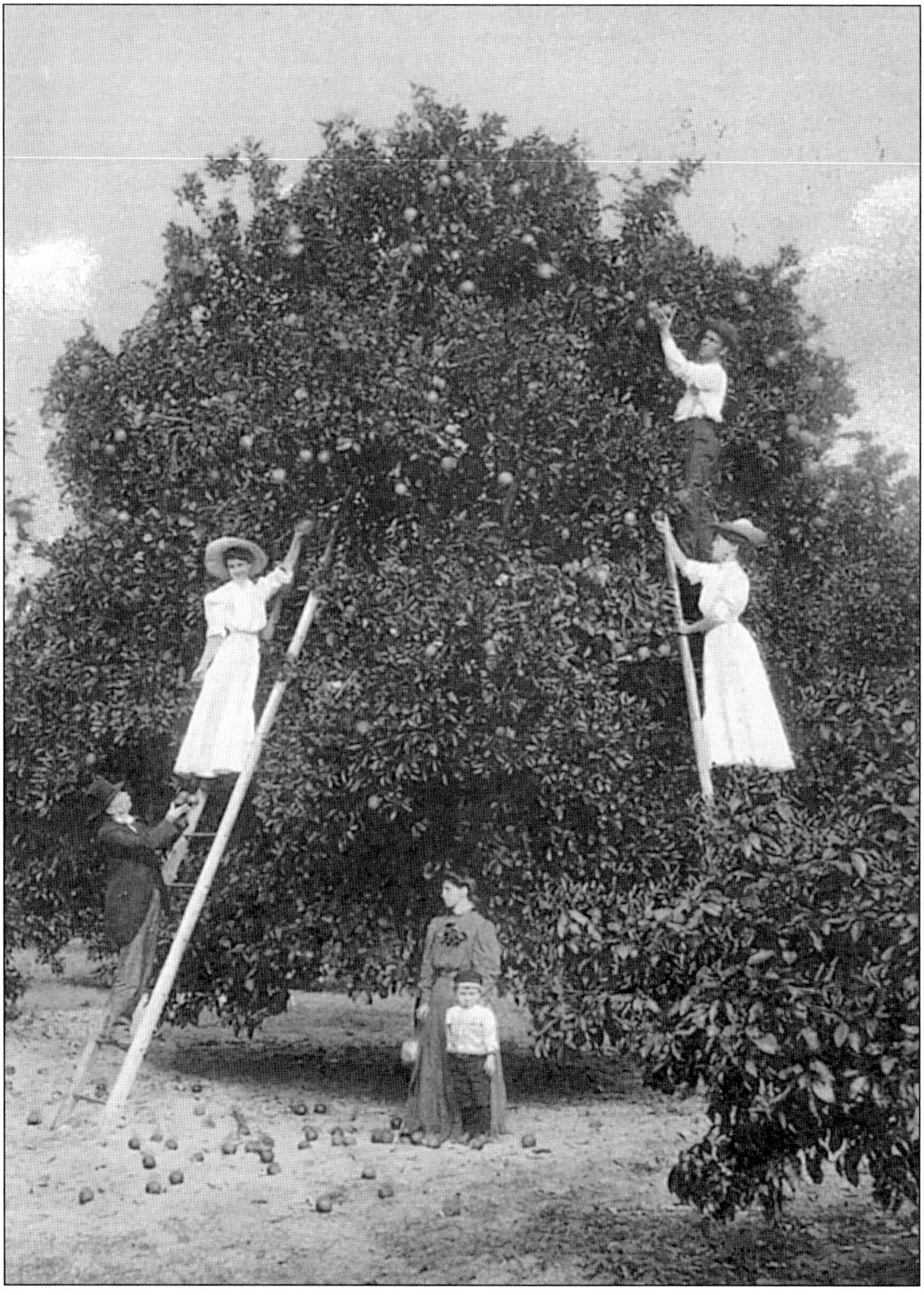

"Here's how you make it, and it's best if you get everything out and ready before you start. Well, first you cream together three quarters of a cup of Crisco and one and a half cups of plain white sugar." This card is postmarked Rockledge, January 26, 1907.

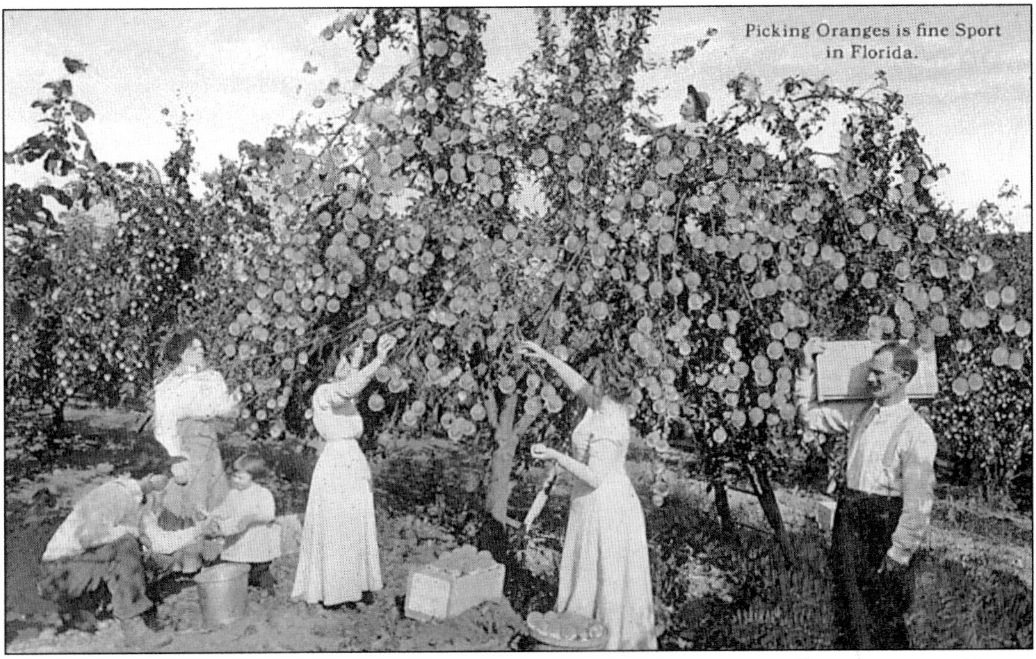

"Then you add three eggs, one at a time, continuing to mix it up well. Next you add two tablespoons of fresh orange juice. I usually use Navel oranges because they flavor it so good (and Papa has a whole grove of them at his farm). But you really can use any kind of orange."

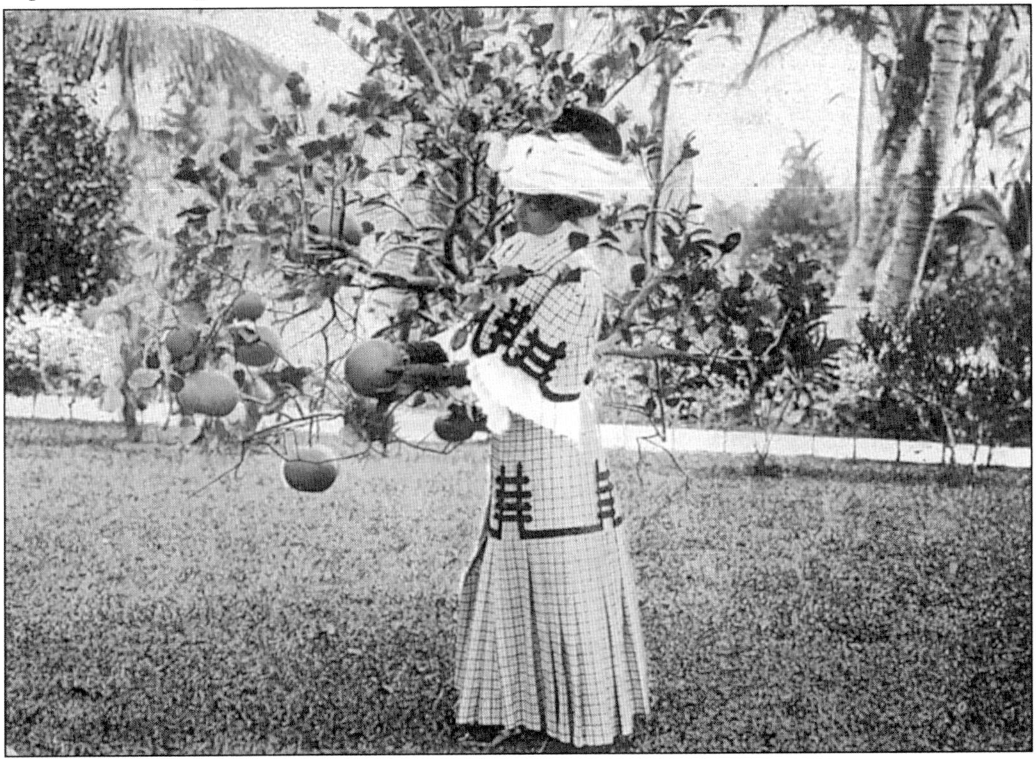

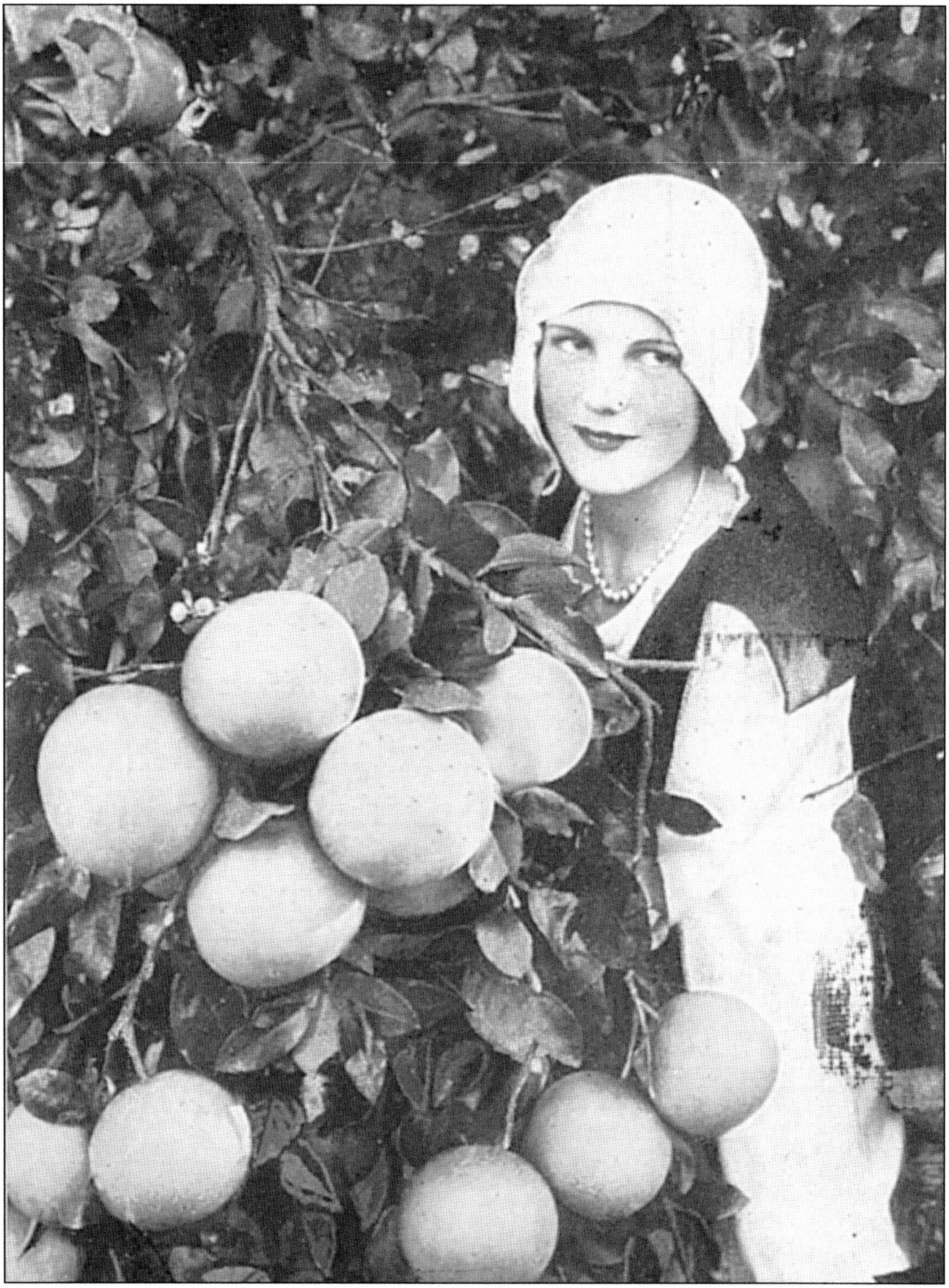

"Next grate the rind of one and a half oranges and mix this with everything else. Then you add one and a half cups of buttermilk, one and a half teaspoons of baking soda, and a half teaspoon of salt and mix it some more. Now you dump in one cup of chopped dates and one cup of chopped nuts. I like to use pecans, but you can use walnuts." This image is postmarked Saint Petersburg, January 12, 1938.

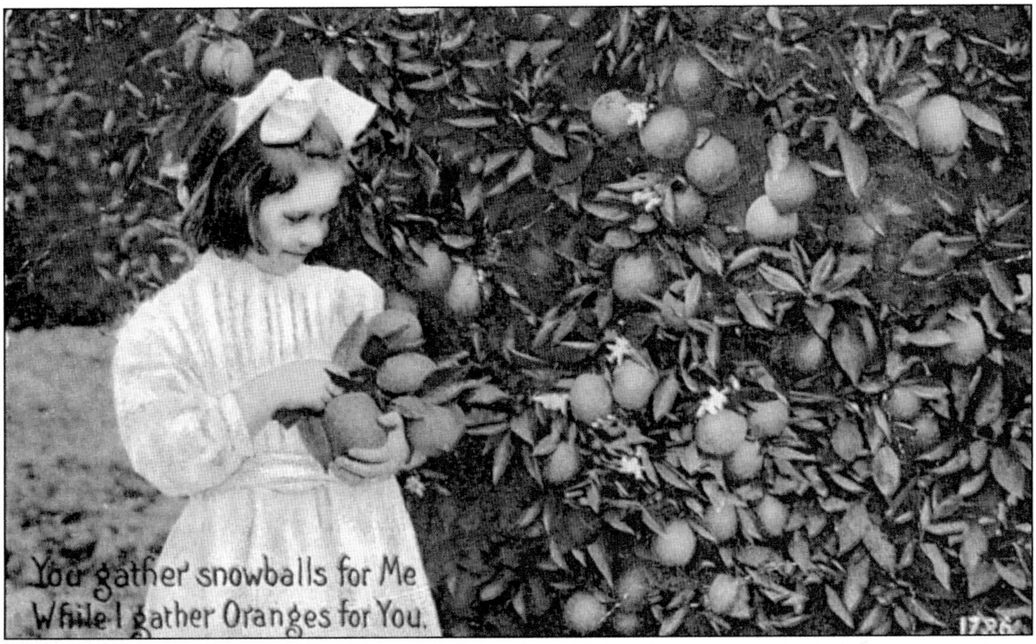

"Now in another bowl mix one cup of golden raisins with three cups of sifted all-purpose flour. Add this to you first mixture and beat it up well. Bake it in a tube pan at 325 degrees for an hour or a little more, it all depends on your own oven. (Or you can use 4 or 5 small loaf pans)." The above card is postmarked June 13, 1920.

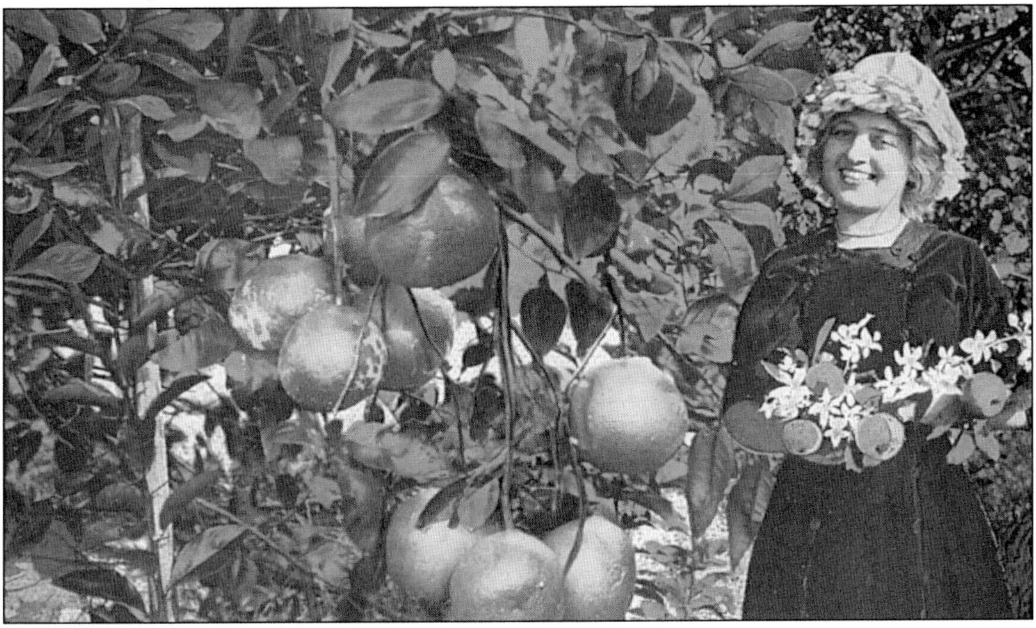

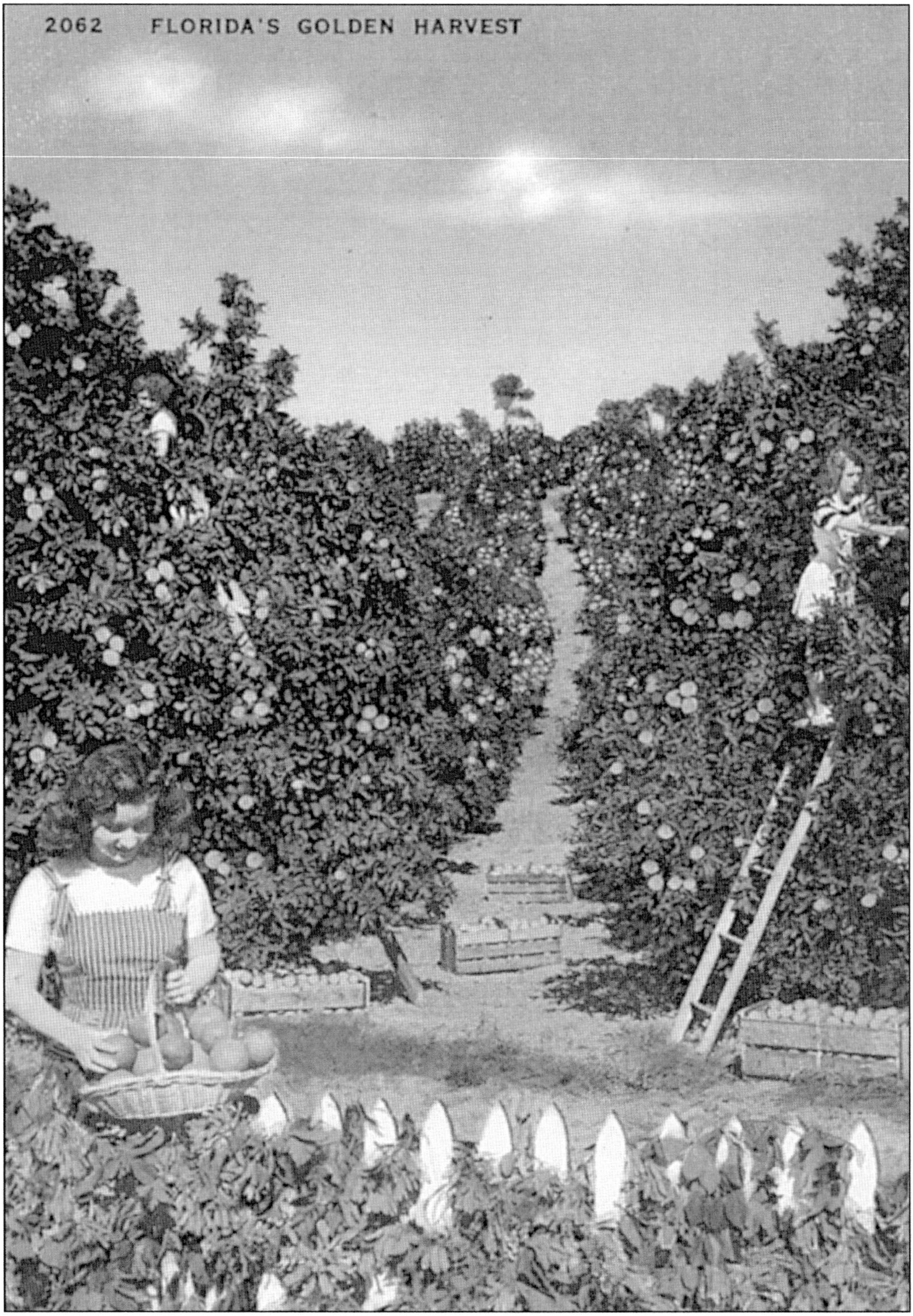

"Just before the cake is done, boil the following mixture for three minutes in a pot on your stove: one half cup fresh orange juice, one cup sugar, and the rind of one orange."

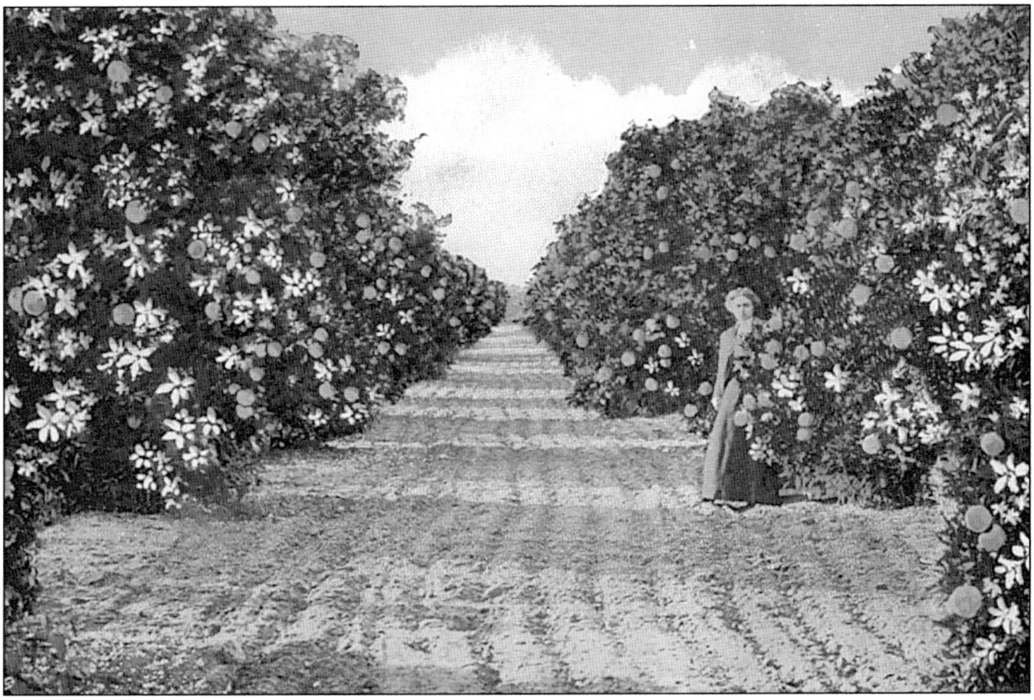

"Now when you take the cake out of the oven, while it is still very hot, pour the juice mixture over it. You leave the cake in the pan until it is almost cold so that the juice will soak up in the cake. And that's it. I hope you will like it as much as we do."

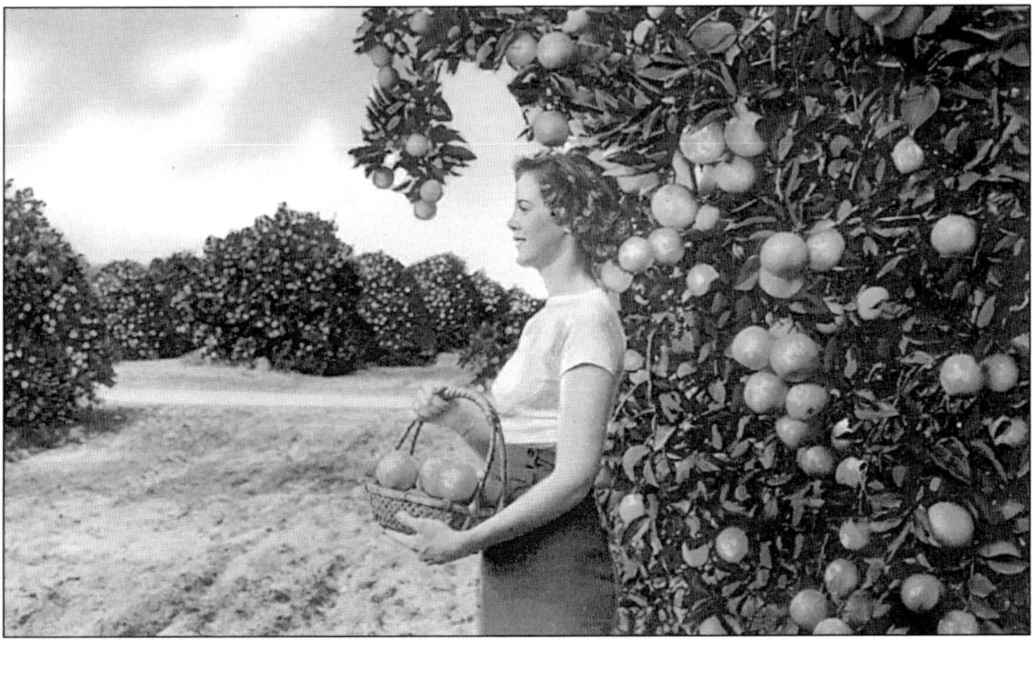

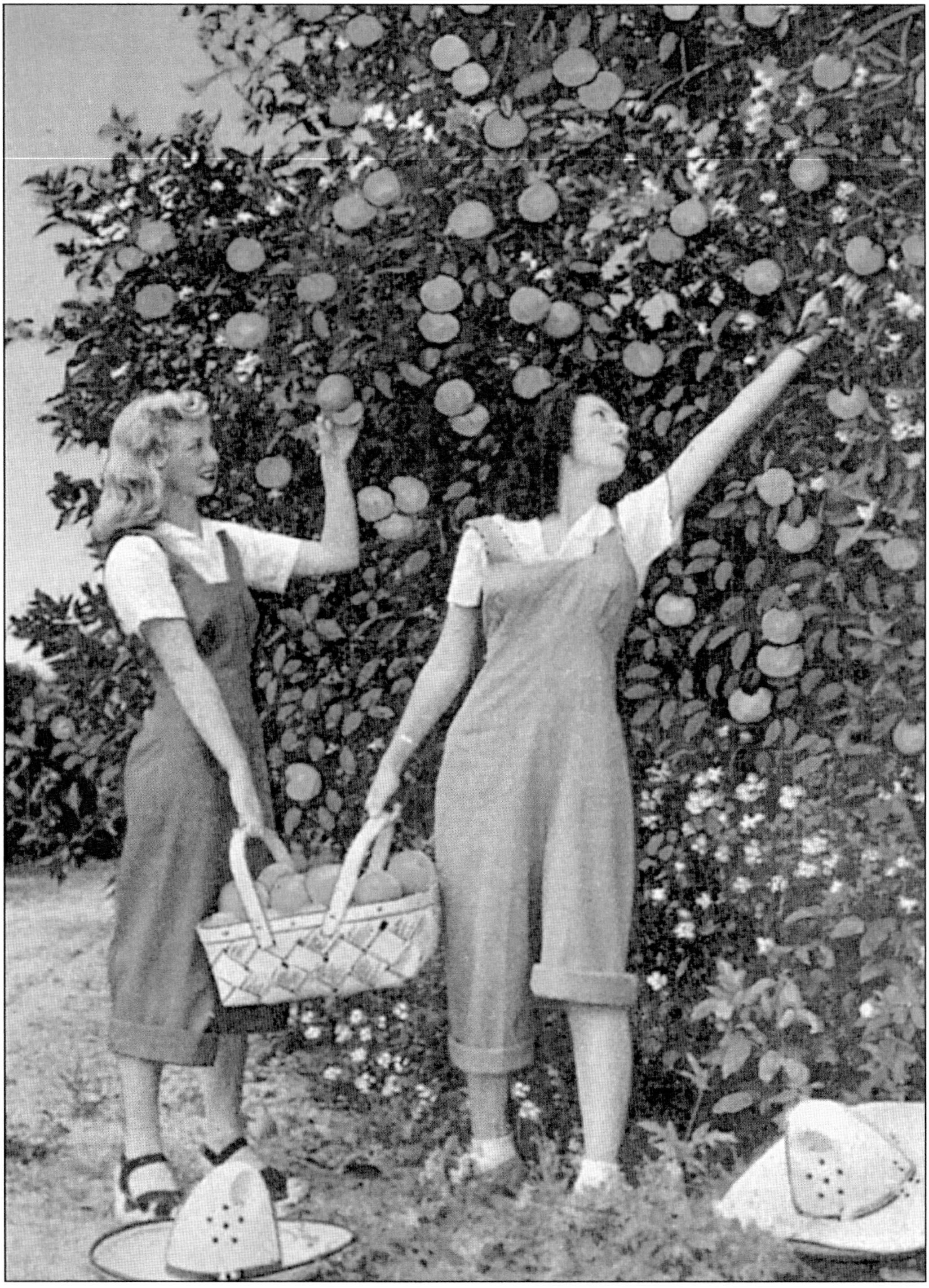

Nana's Orange Cake recipe is another citrus delight. "Brian used to request this cake all the time. You'll need a box of lemon or yellow cake mix, four eggs, three quarters of a cup of salad oil, three-quarters of a cup of water, a package of lemon Jello, and the grated rind of one lemon (I don't usually bother with this, but you can)."

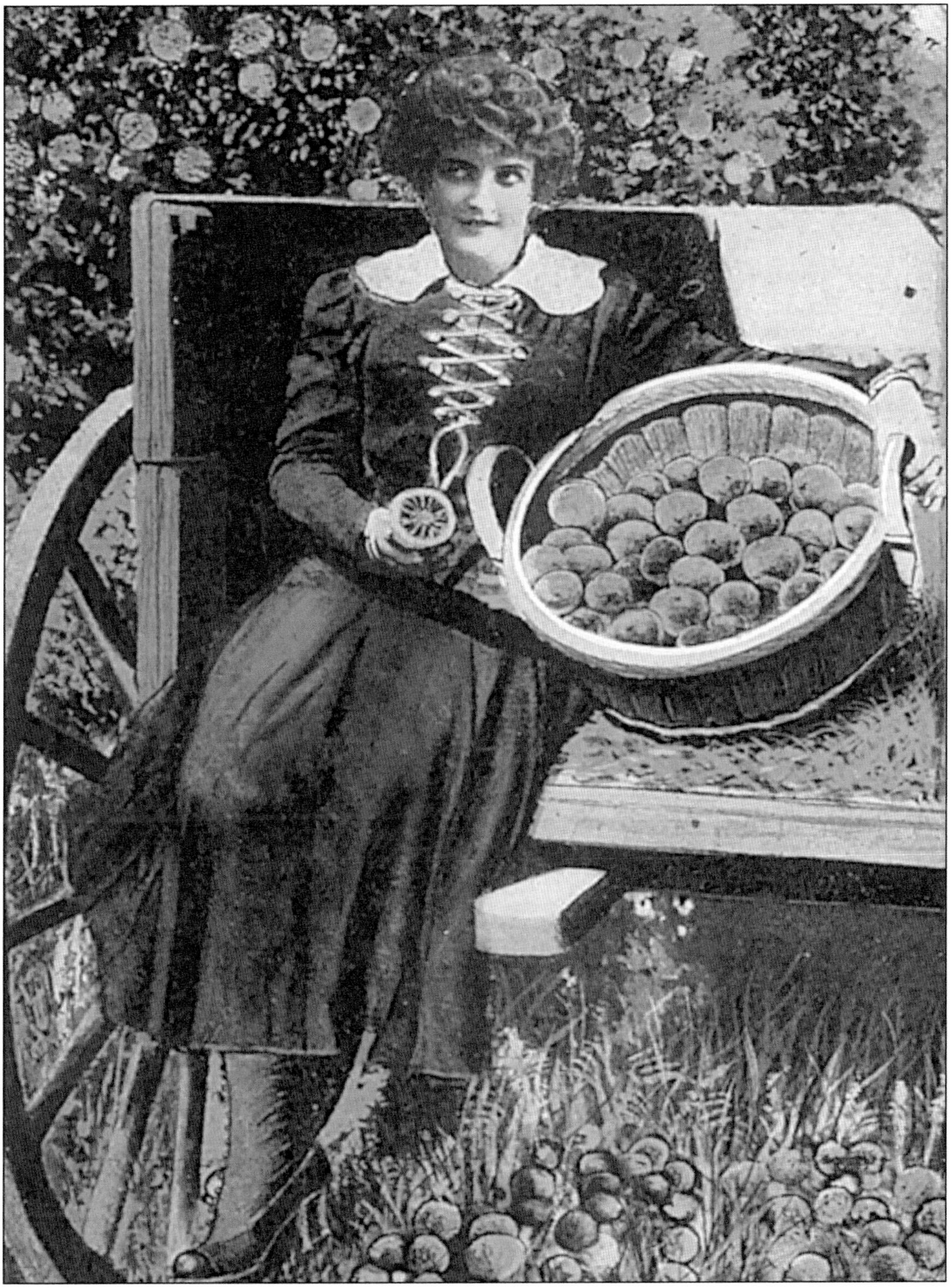

"Combine all of the ingredients and beat well. Bake in a tube pan, the kind that has the hole in the middle, for 40 to 45 minutes at 350 degrees. While the cake is in the oven, you can work on making your glaze. You will need one small can of orange concentrate, two tablespoons of lemon juice, and one pound of confectioners sugar. Mix those ingredients and let stand." This image is postmarked St. Petersburg, December 22, 1920.

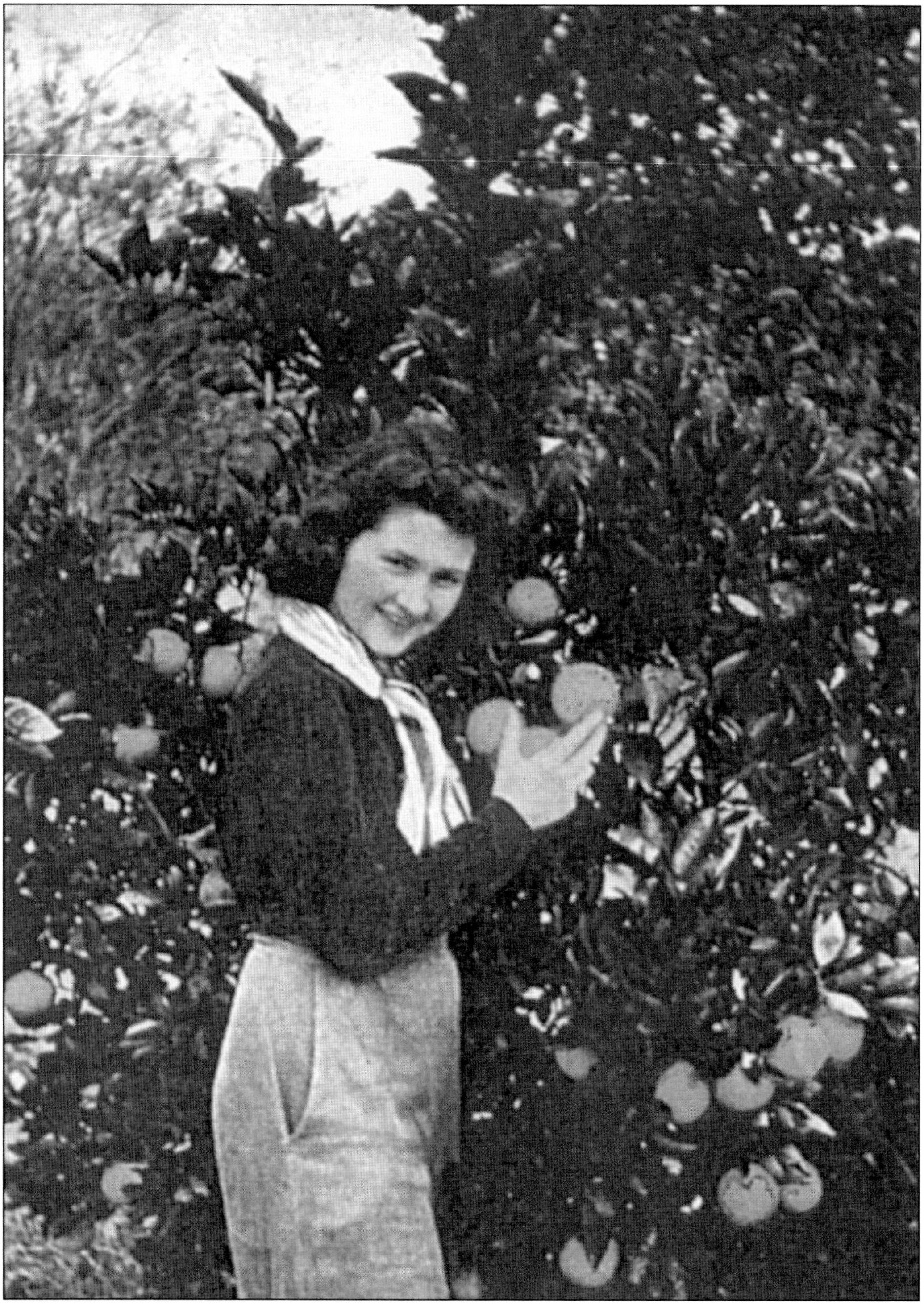

"After the cake has spent its time in the oven, let it cool for 15 minutes, then puncture the top with a fork. Pour the glaze on top. People seem to like the cake; it's moist, and it has a good sweetness and tartness." (Courtesy of Barbara Eggleson.)

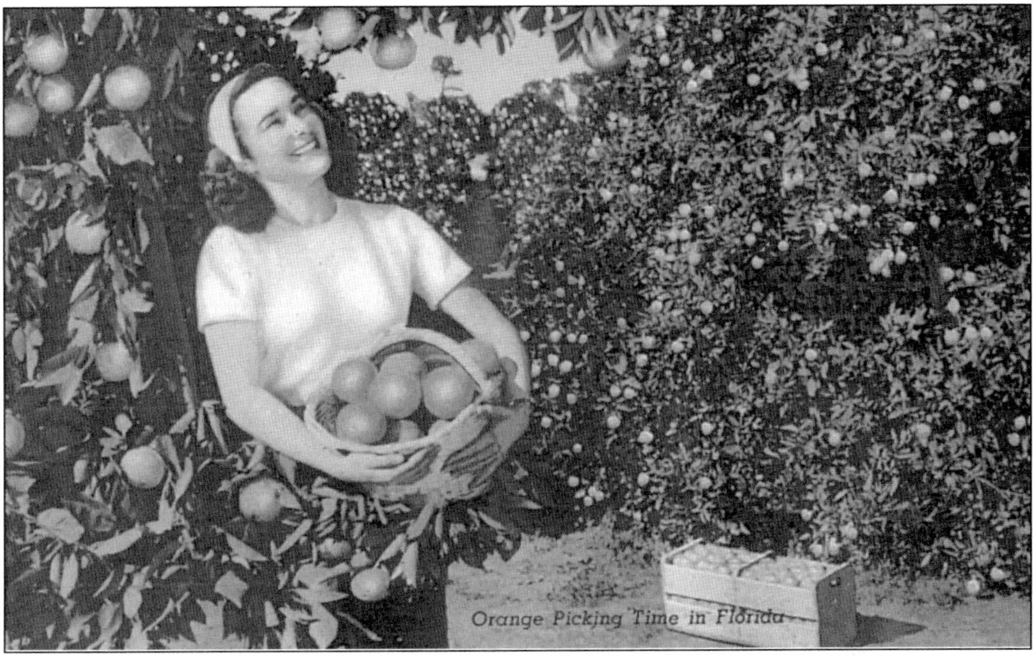

"Hi there! How's this for a peach among the oranges? Better come down and grab one. Having a delightful time. Play shuffle-board with the other old folks—weather lovely. Herb and Catherine." This card is postmarked St. Petersburg, March 22, 1953.

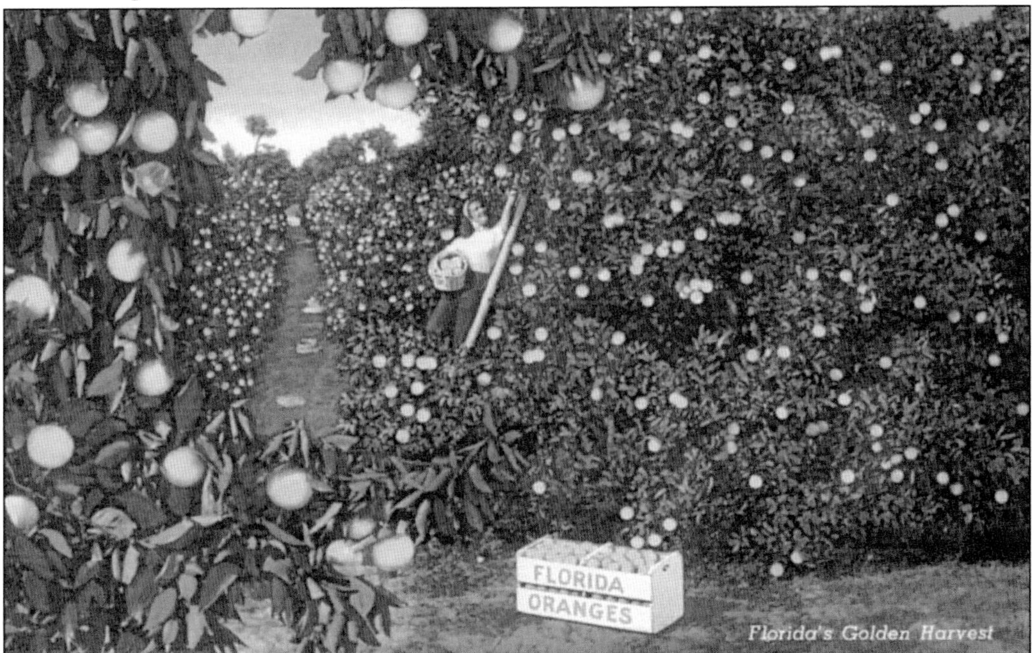

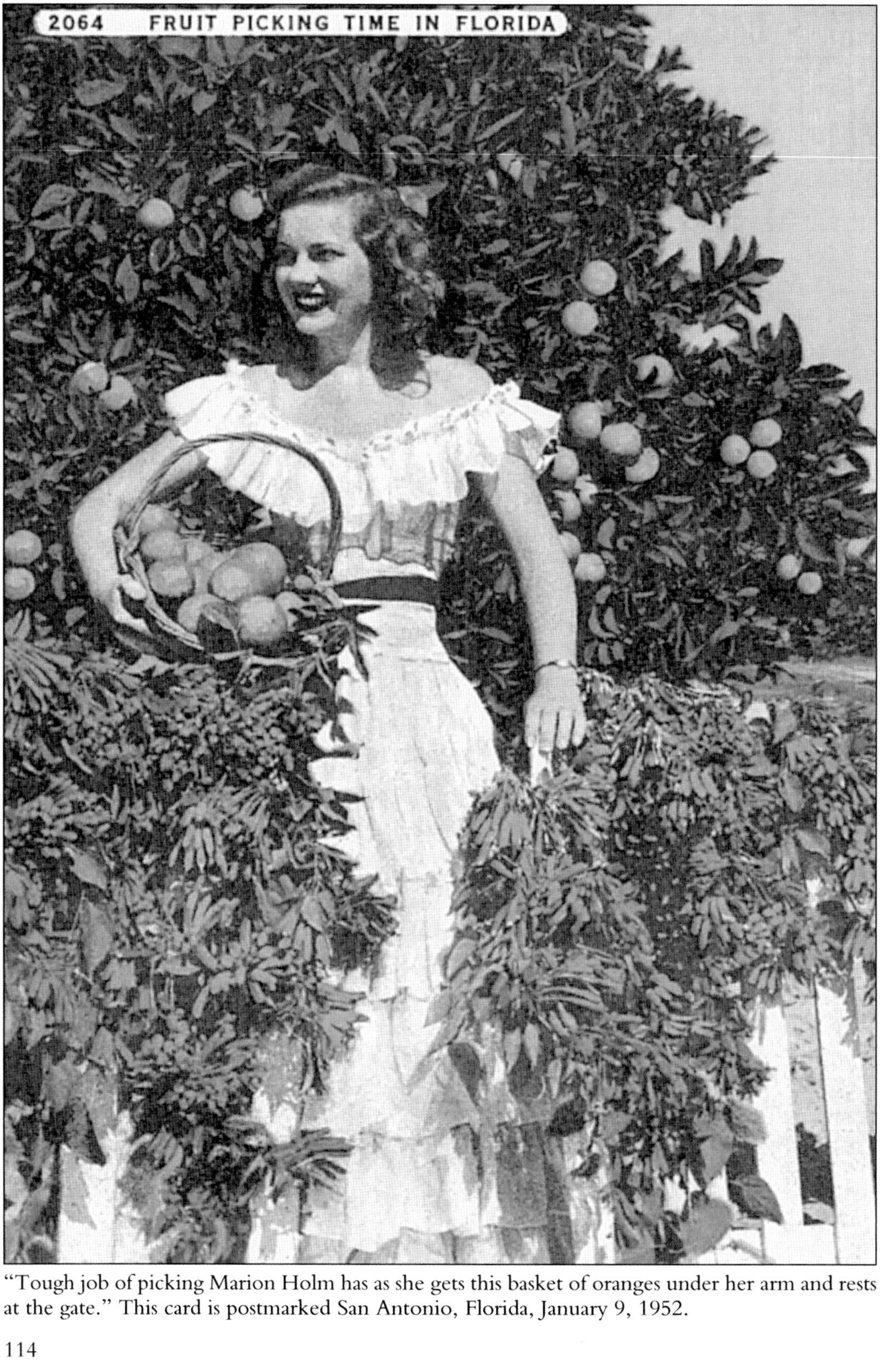

"Tough job of picking Marion Holm has as she gets this basket of oranges under her arm and rests at the gate." This card is postmarked San Antonio, Florida, January 9, 1952.

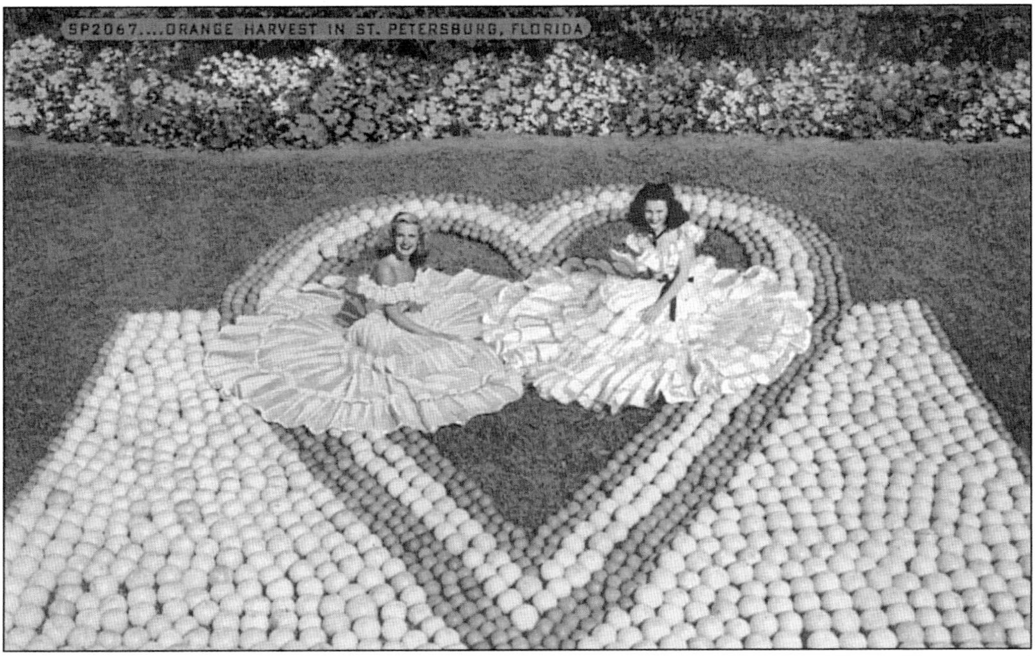

"It's Citrus Time in Florida and two lovely girls at Cypress Gardens pose with the oranges and grapefruit from which America's Fruit Salad is made." Entrepreneur Dick Pope Sr. dressed his beauties in Southern belle costumes; other businessmen thought bathing suits would do for their postcards. Many of those cards found their way out of Florida.

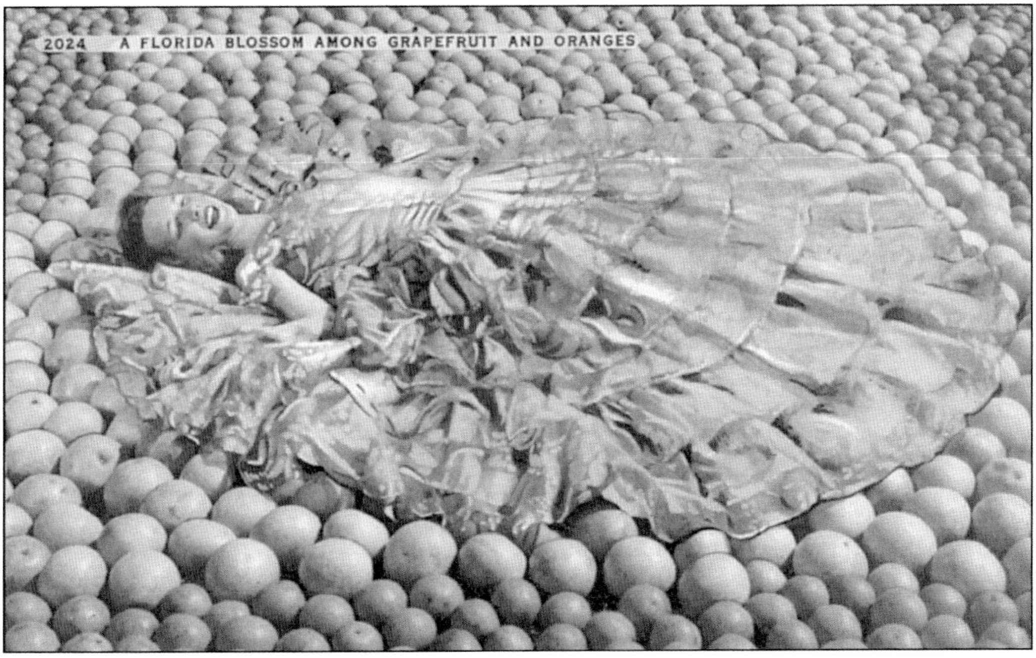

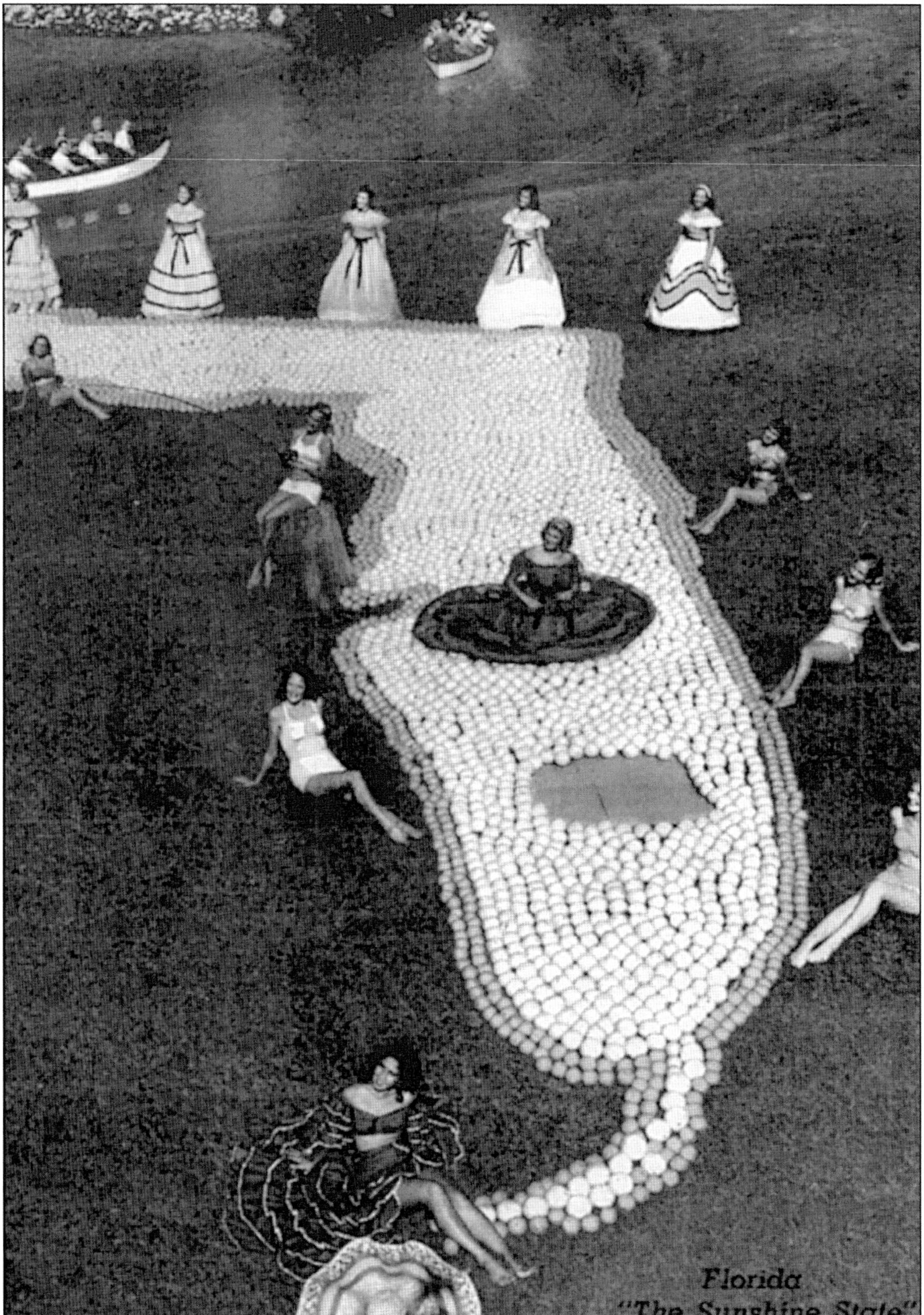

"Dear Bruce, Did the Easter Bunny bring you candy? Wish I were there to have some—we will see you soon, Love Granny." This image is postmarked Palm Beach, March 29, 1951.

Seven

"Down South We Roam"

Who could resist reminding Northern relations of the fun to be had by those lucky enough to visit or live in Florida? With slight variations, many postcards pointed out the abundance of two kinds of common spheres—oranges and snowballs.

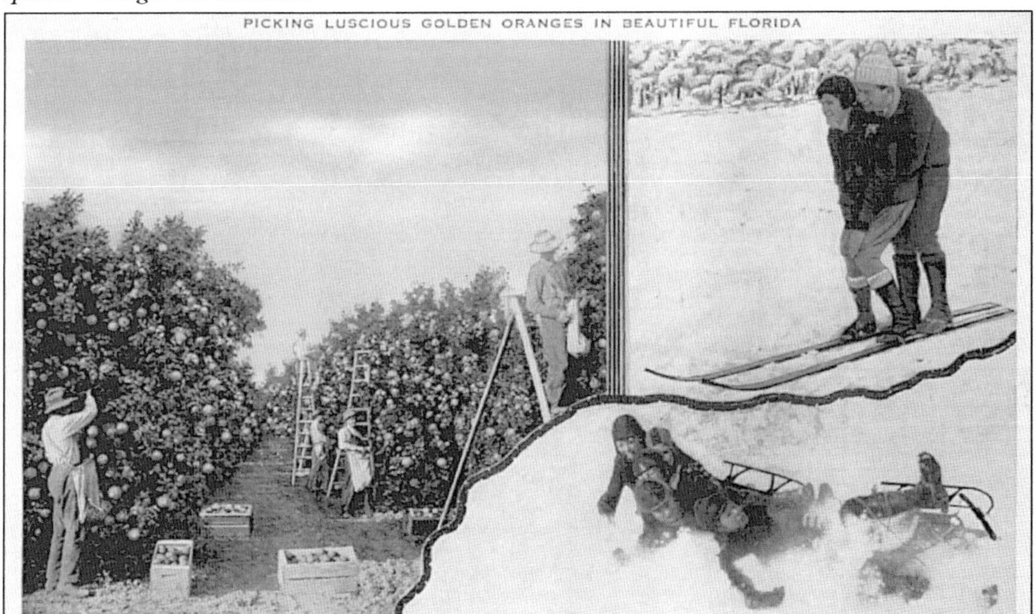

"When wintry winds begin to blow/ And northern lands are wrapped in snow/ Leave sleet and chilling winds behind/ And hie to Florida to find/ Bright sunny days and magic nights/ Where never any snowstorm blights/ Where birds pour out their roundelay/ And flowers blossom every day." This poetic card is postmarked West Palm Beach, December 20, 1935.

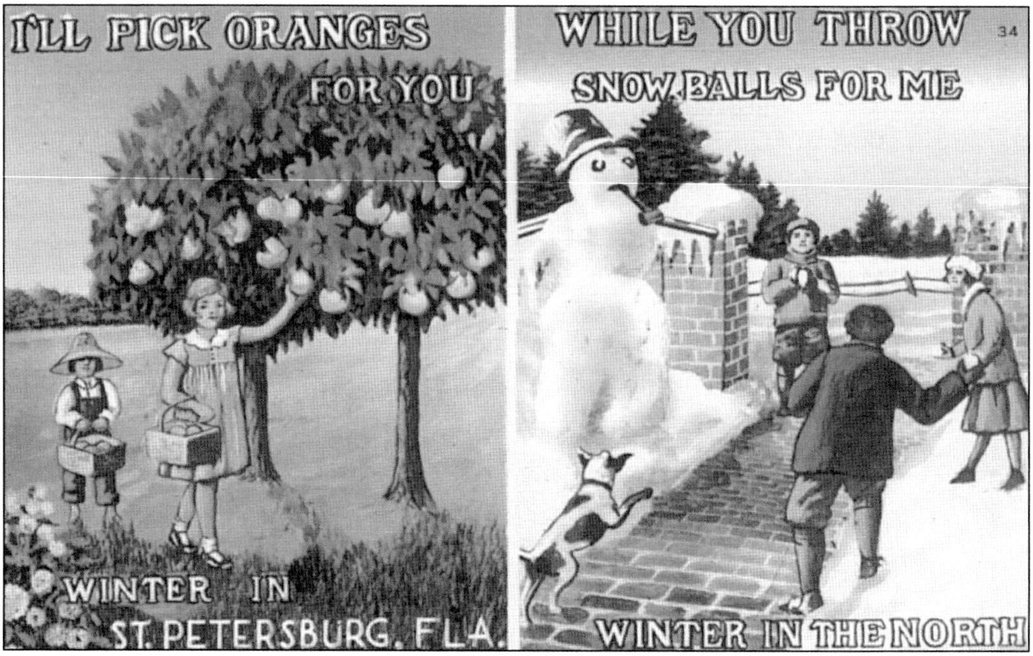

Many Floridians can drop by the beach on Christmas to get some sun. Usually only the Northern visitors brave the chilly water for a holiday swim. Snow is a rare occurrence in northern portions of the state; it never sticks and is usually gone before someone can run for their camera to document the oddity.

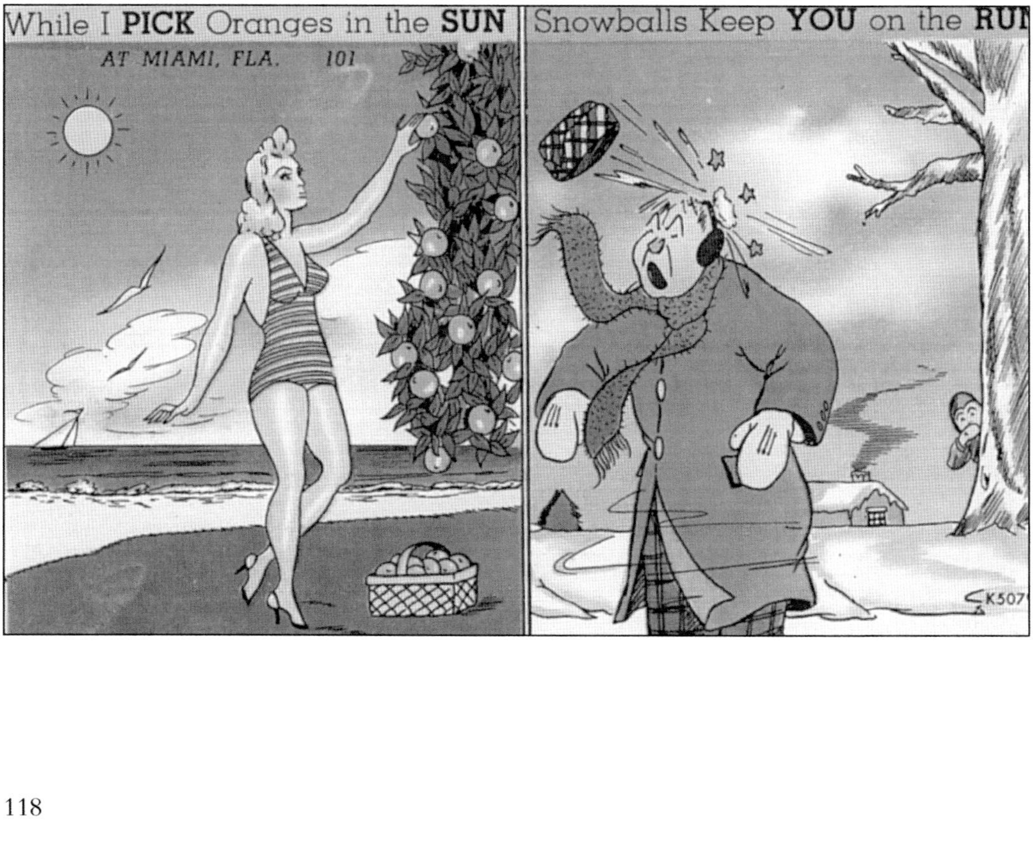

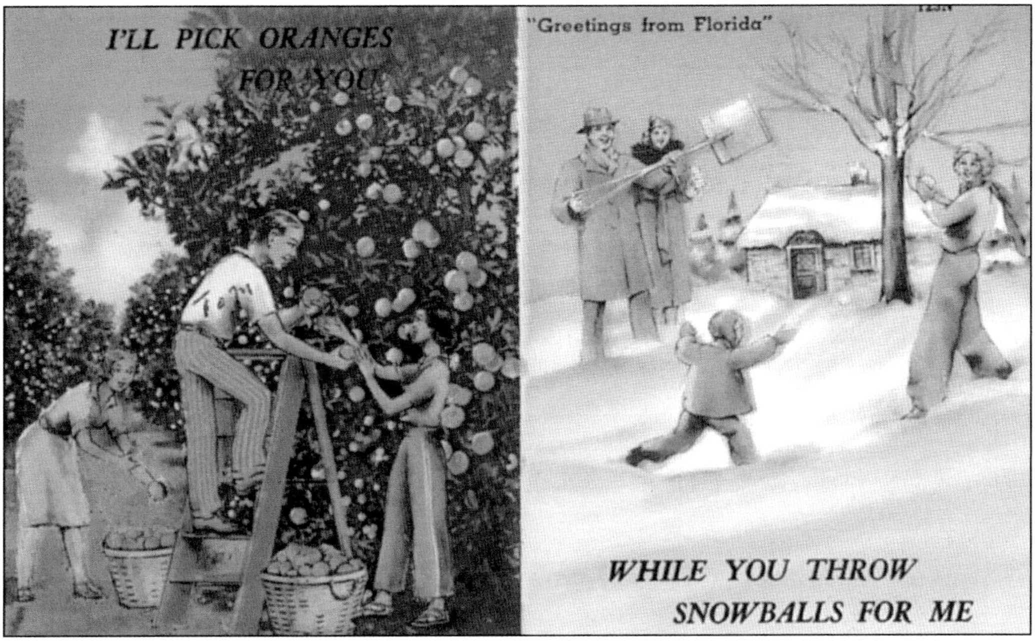

The postcard above, postmarked St. Petersburg, March 3, 1958, contains the following message: "Florida, land of sunshine, is the Winter Playground of the nation. Every known form of outdoor pleasuring is pursued without the necessity of considering winter conditions—for winter skies are always smiling and December breezes are as balmy as May." The card below is postmarked Jacksonville, October 5, 1946.

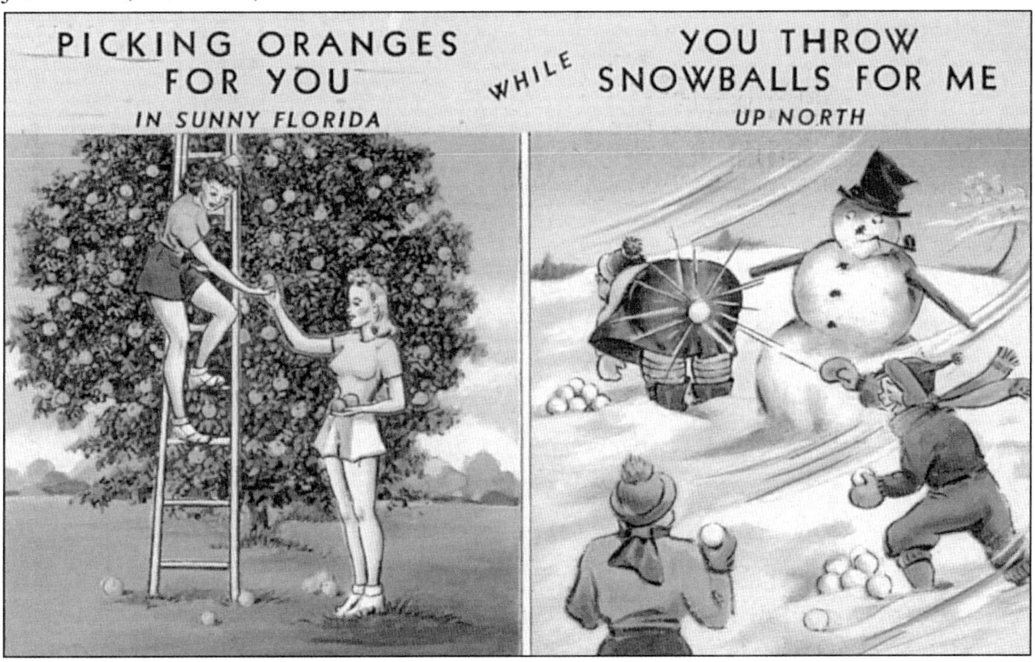

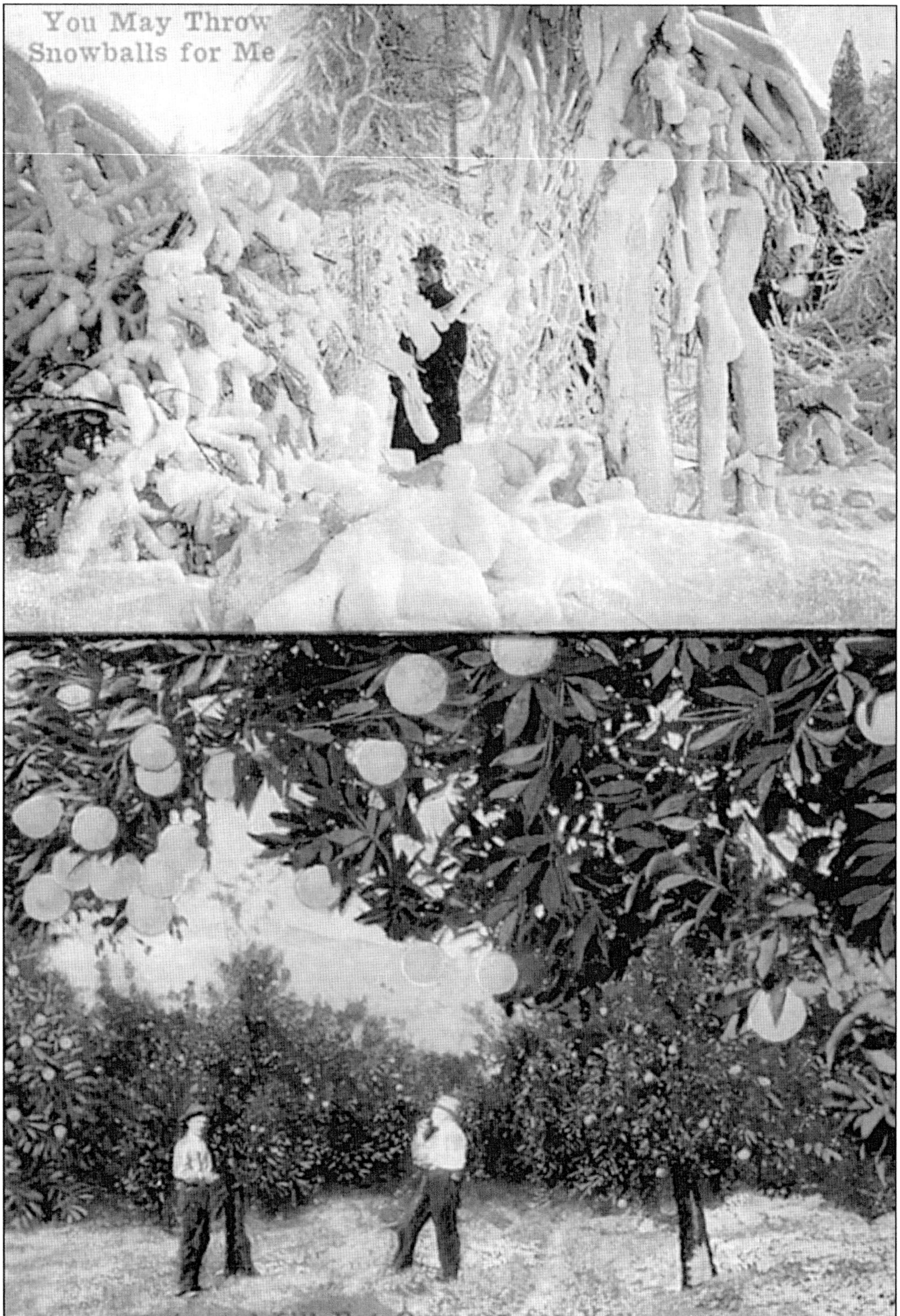
You May Throw
Snowballs for Me
and I'll Eat Oranges for You

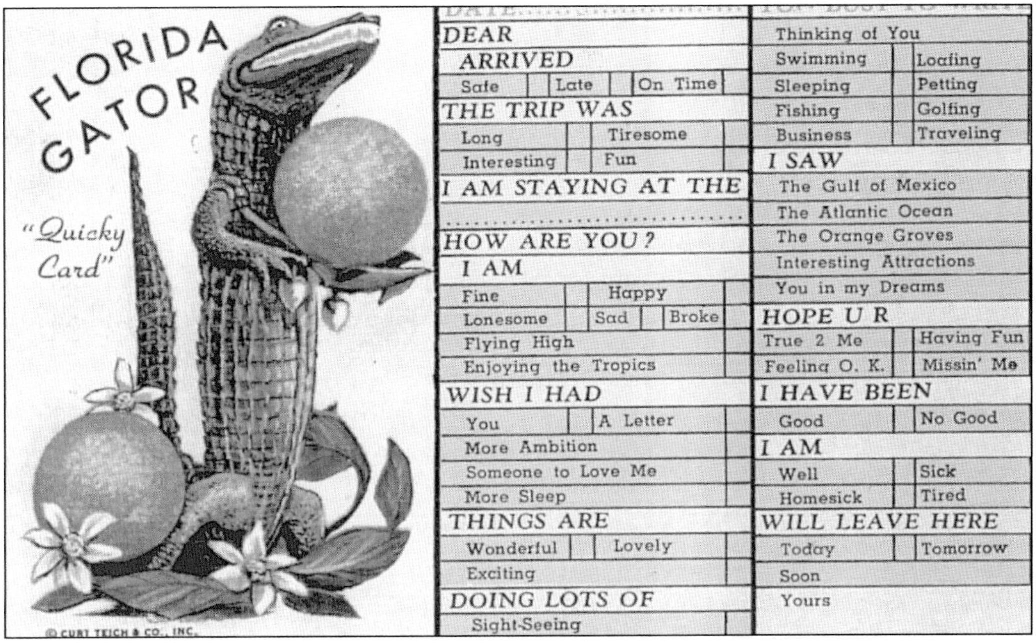

Florida visitors would have no excuse for not writing home with this "busy person's correspondence card." They could simply check off a full report about their activities with very little time and effort spent. (Top card courtesy of Barbara Eggleson.)

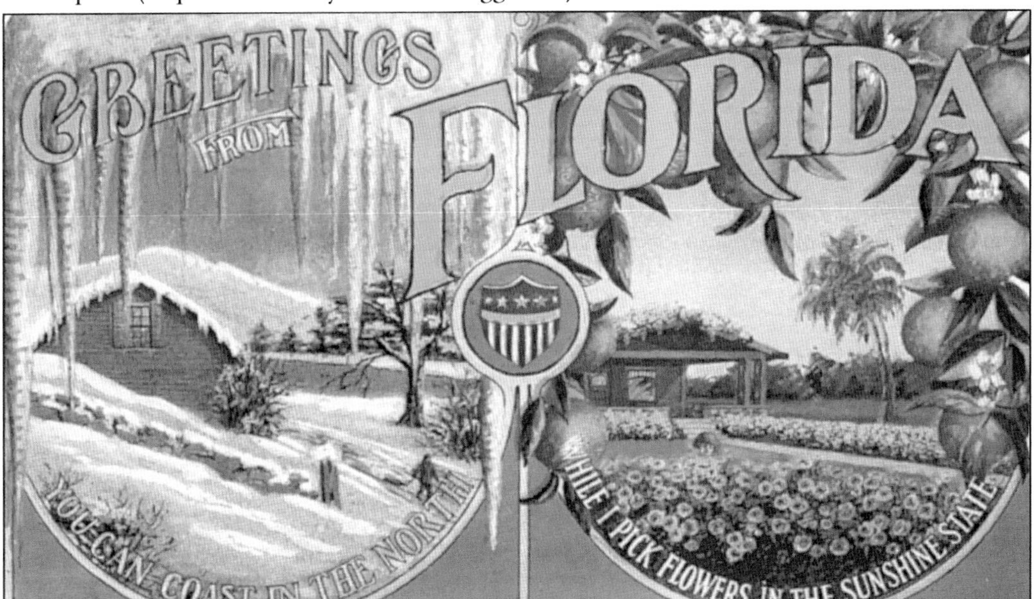

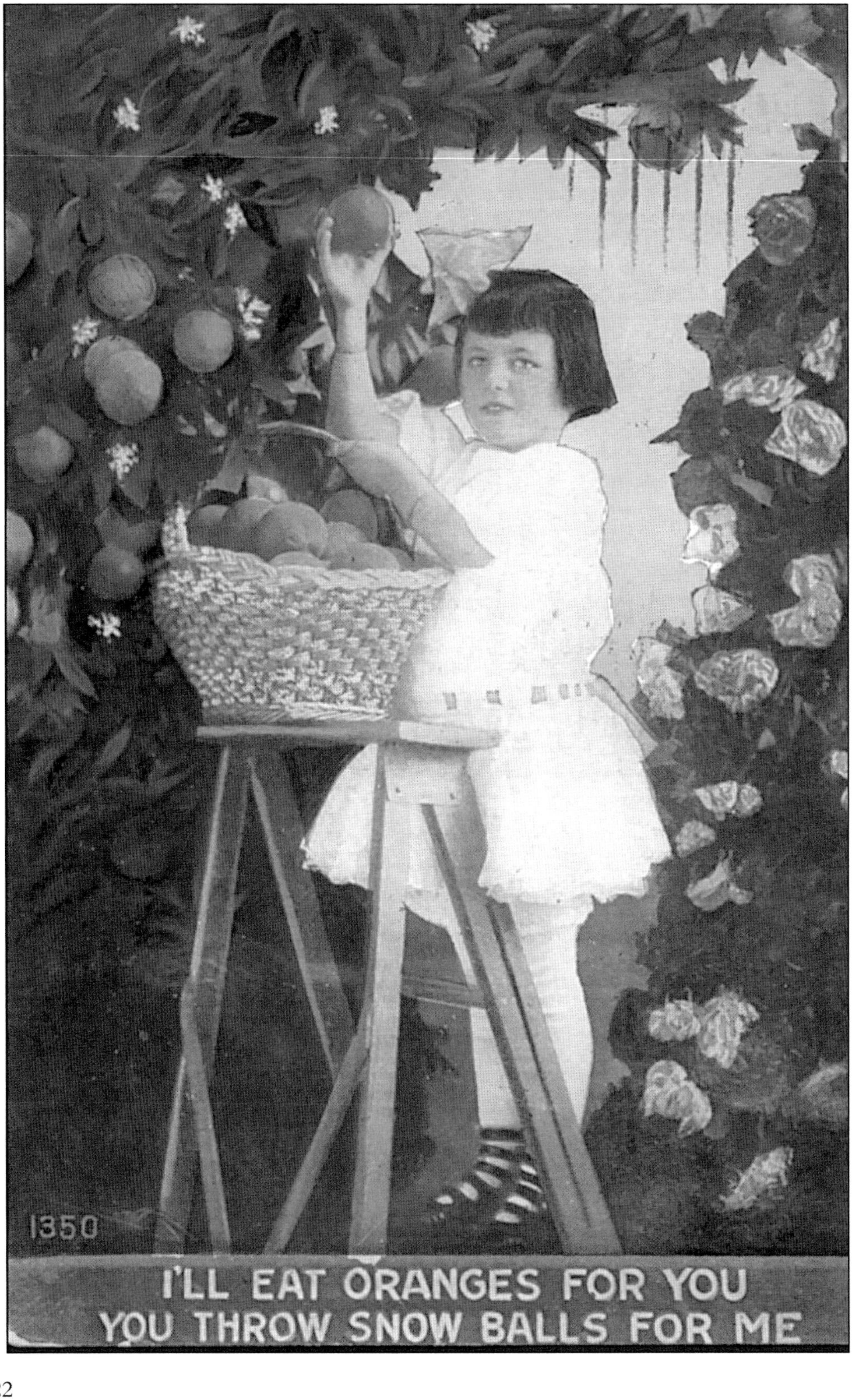
1350
I'LL EAT ORANGES FOR YOU
YOU THROW SNOW BALLS FOR ME

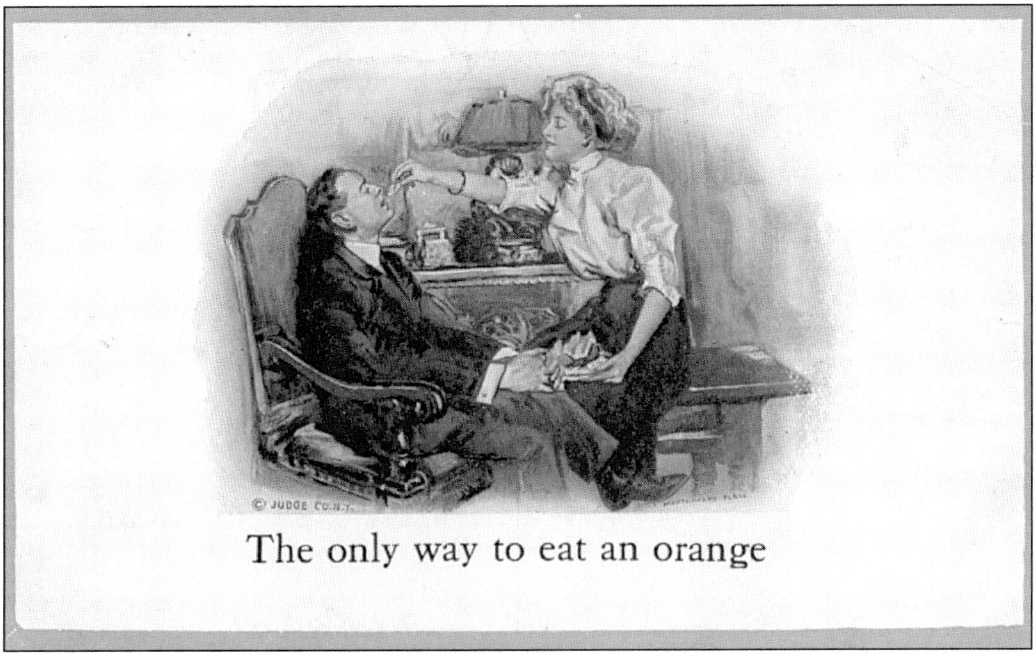

The following caption is from the postcard above: "I am going to school everyday . . . like it fine. I sold my pony for $60. Papa has rented a farm . . ." The card is postmarked Stratton, Nebraska, March 12, 1913, and the postcard below is Sebring, December 20, 1927.

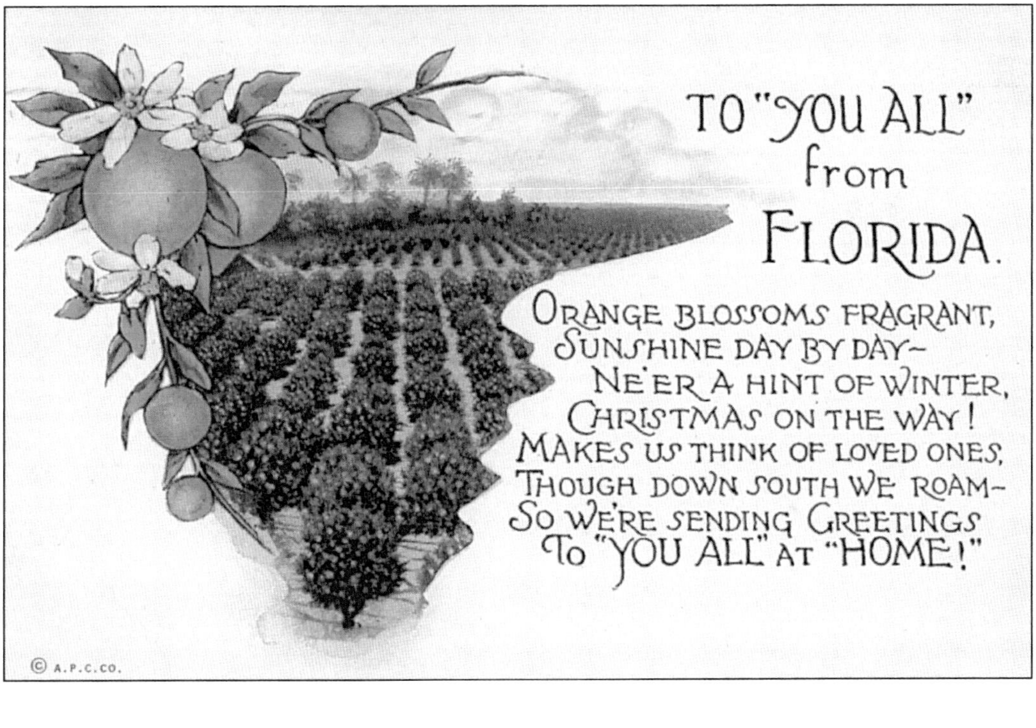

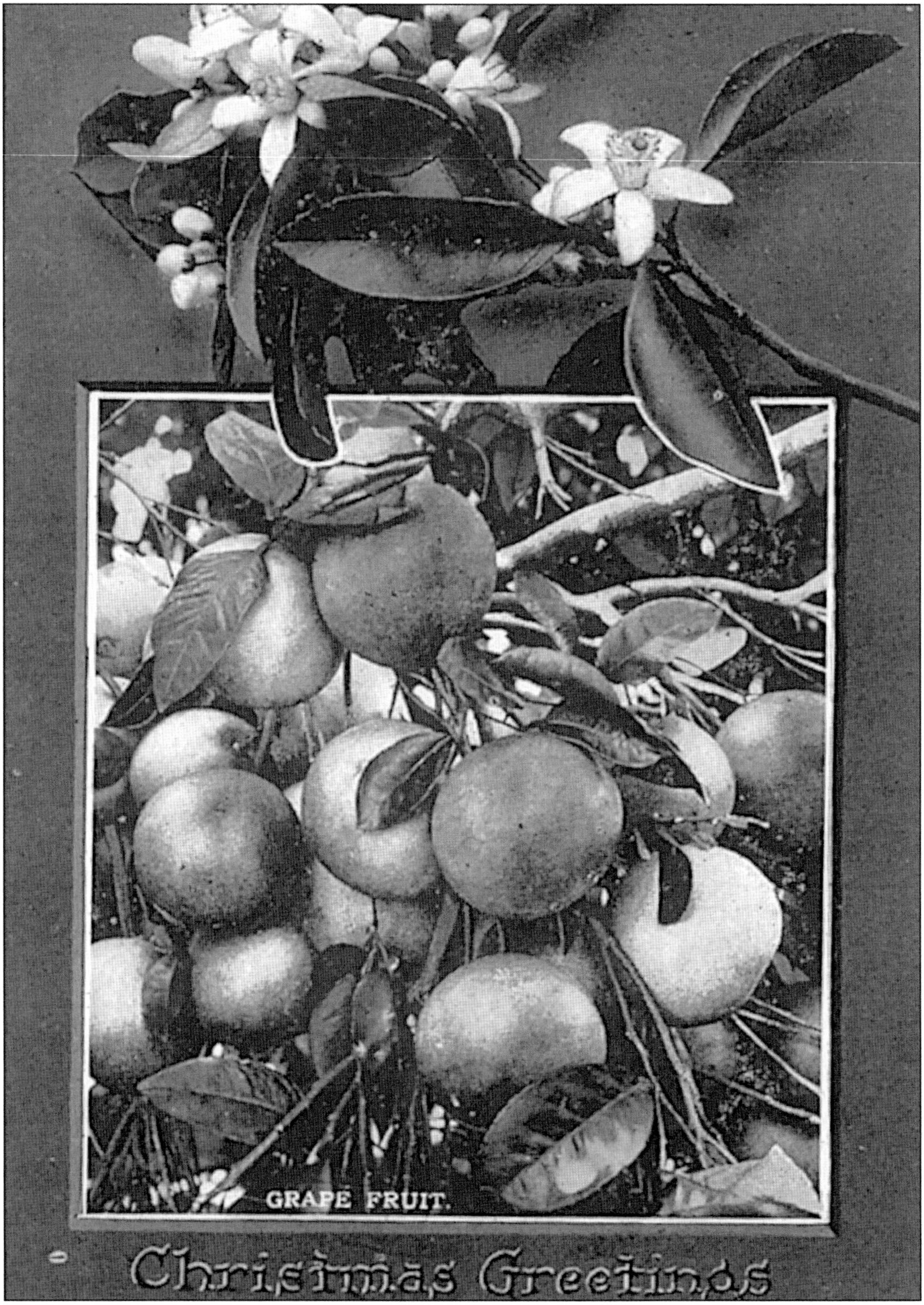

Many people send gift packages of citrus fruit at Christmas time, brightening the days of family and friends stuck in a cold Northern winter. Florida residents and visitors feel fortunate to have mild winters with an abundance of sunshine.

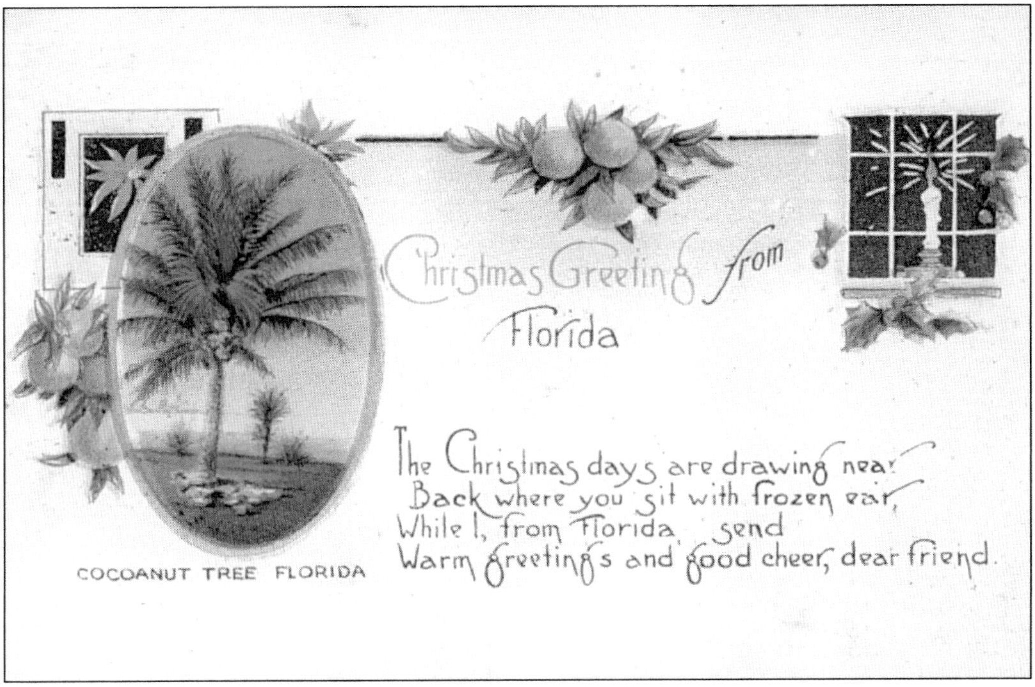

"Wishing you all a Merry Christmas and a Happy New Year. We are all well. Would be glad to get a long letter from you folks once. Love to all, Minnie Harrel." The above postcard is postmarked December 20, 1924.

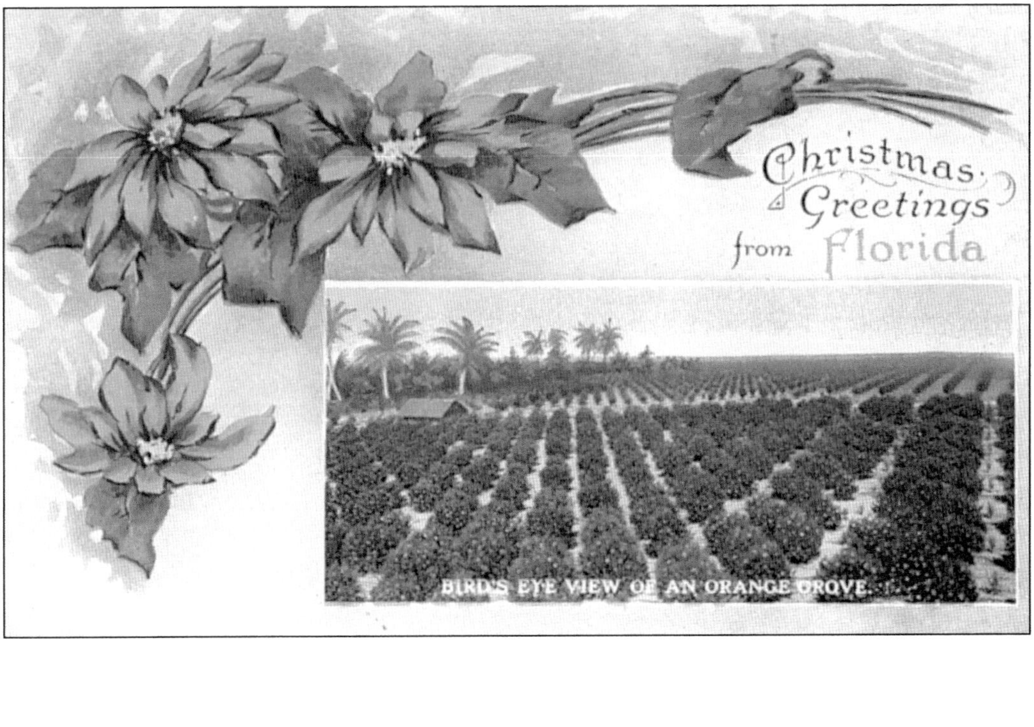

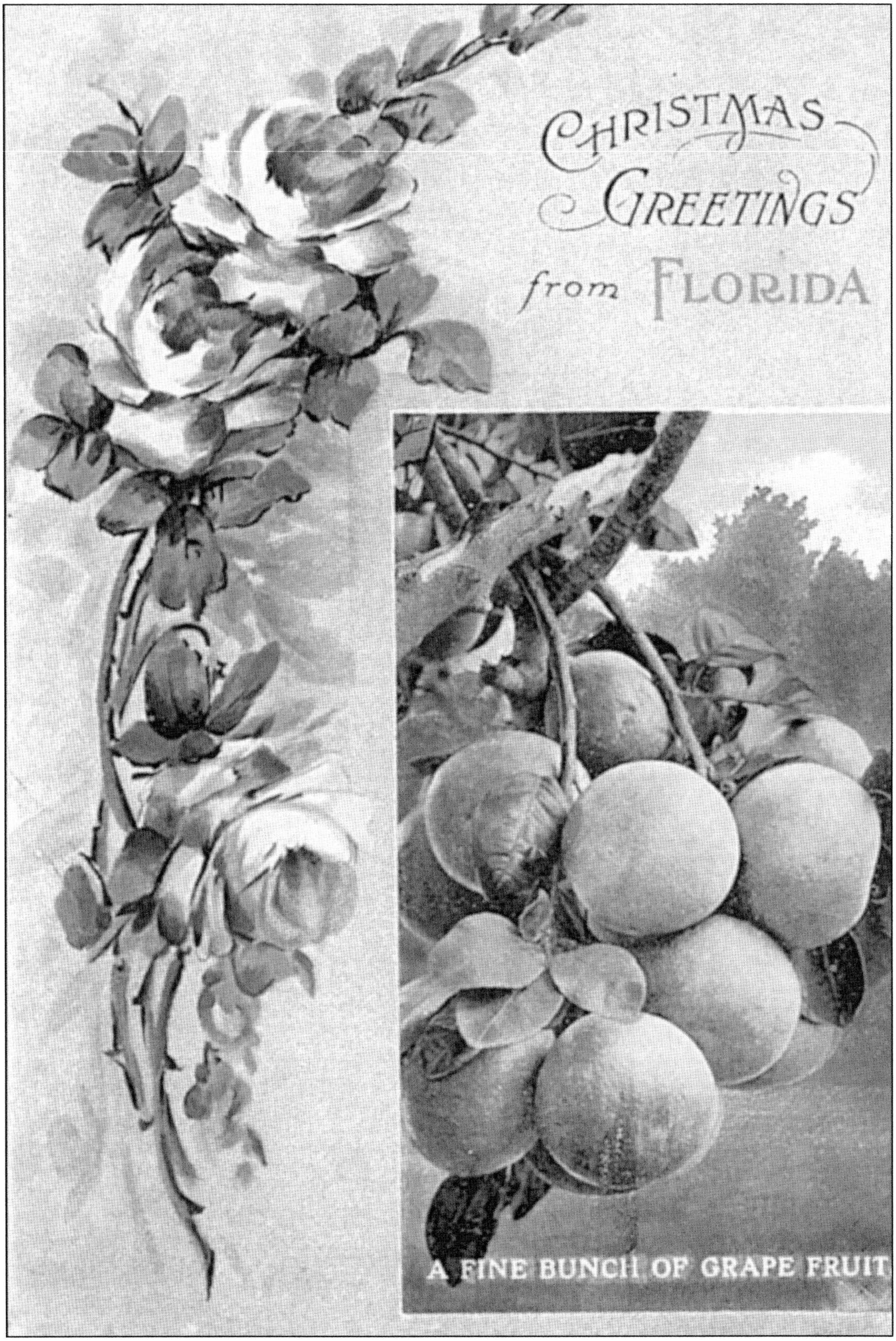
CHRISTMAS GREETINGS from FLORIDA
A FINE BUNCH OF GRAPE FRUIT

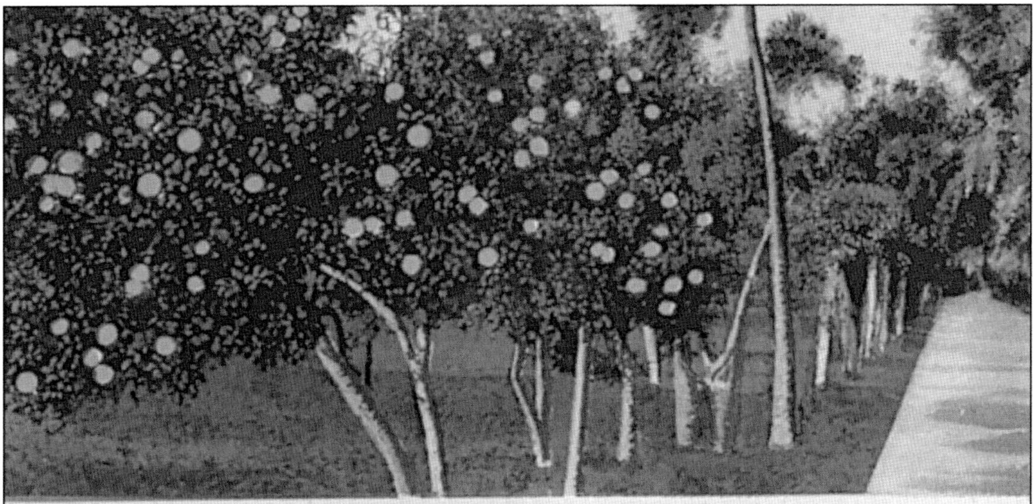

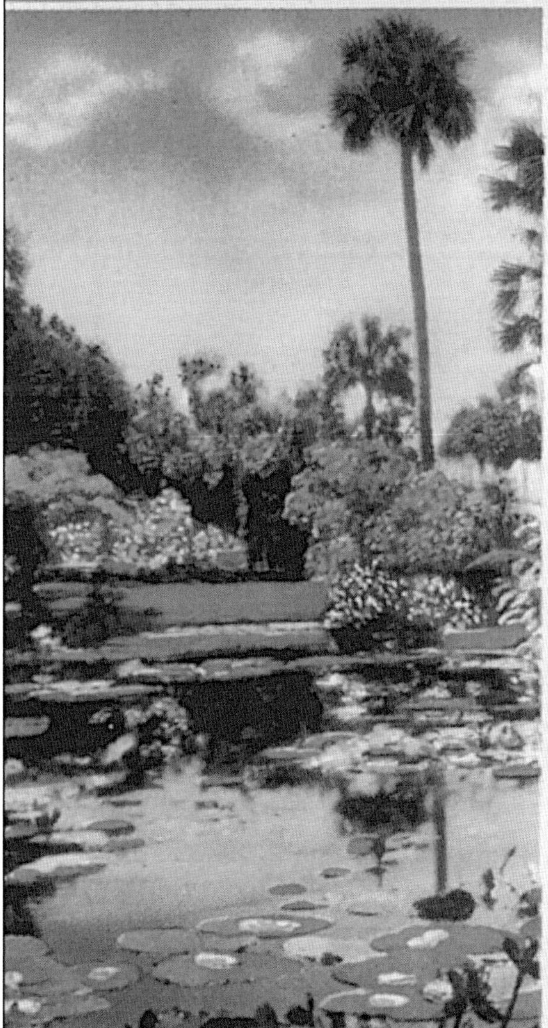

IN FLORIDA

The Sky is ever bluest
And friendship is the truest
And enemies the fewest—
In Florida

Sunshine is the brightest,
Merry hearts are the lightest,
And moonbeams are whitest—
In Florida

Blue lakes are the clearest,
Home-hearts are the dearest,
And heaven is the nearest—
In Florida

Maidens are the sweetest,
Sailboats are the fleetest,
And bungalows the neatest—
In Florida

Sea-bathing here is funny
The beach is fine and sunny
And it's worth your money—
In Florida

Evergreens are greenest,
Beach-Sand is the cleanest
And Realtors are the keenest
In Florida

Grass Widows are the tamest
Bachelors the lamest,
And tarpons the gamest—
In Florida

Lovers are the boldest,
Oranges are the goldest,
And people live the oldest—
In Florida

INDEX

Bean, Eban B. 64
Beekeeping 38
Blossoms 37, 92
Bulk trailers 79
Buds 24
Chimera 18
Citrus Canker 42
Columbus, Christopher 9
Cypress Gardens 115, 116
Degreening 88
Dummitt, Captain D.D. 19
Egan, Bernard and Company 96
Eggleson, Barbara 6
Evapotranspiration 25
Fertilizer 26
Florida Southern College 6, 36, 60
Fruit Cake 103-112
Fruit Flies 41
Ft. Pierce Growers Cooperative 96
Hamlins 10, 11
Hammocks 22
Hays and Malcolm 31
Holm, Marion 114
Honey 38
Hurricanes 28
Indian River Farms Company 43, 44
Irrigation 25, 30
Labels, Fruit Box 85, 86
Lightning Loaders 78
Mack, Thomas B. 6
Melanose 40
Meriwether, Helen 103
Merritt Island 19
Milne-O'Berry Packing Company 95
Minute-Maid Corporation 36
Mites, Rust 40
Navels 11, 105
Oxen 65
Phillips, Dr. 94
Pineapples 11
Pomelo 9, 14
Ponce de Leon 9
Pope, Dick 115
Rootstocks 24
Rubies 11
Second Seminole Indian War 19
Smudge pots 36
Temples 10, 57
Trains 100, 101, 102
Valencias 11
Walker, E.C. 44
Weaver, Montie 7, 67, 102
Weaver, Randy 60, 70
Weaver, Richard 70
Weaver, Roberta 103
Wever Groves 95
White Marsh 11